TOWARD SELF-UNDERSTANDING

Group Techniques in Self-confrontation

Publication Number 612
AMERICAN LECTURE SERIES®

A Monograph in
The BANNERSTONE DIVISION *of*
AMERICAN LECTURES IN PSYCHOLOGY

Edited by

MOLLY HARROWER, Ph.D.

Professor of Research in Clinical Psychology
Department of Psychiatry
Temple University School of Medicine
Philadelphia, Pennsylvania

Third Printing

TOWARD SELF-UNDERSTANDING

Group Techniques in Self-confrontation

By

DANIEL I. MALAMUD, Ph.D.

Adjunct Assistant Professor
Division of General Education, New York University
Formerly Director, Mental Health Education Project
Department of Psychiatry
State University of New York Downstate Medical Center
Formerly Staff Psychologist
Kings County Hospital
Brooklyn, New York

and

SOLOMON MACHOVER, Ph.D.

Professor, Department of Psychiatry
State University of New York Downstate Medical Center
Chief Psychologist
Kings County Hospital
Formerly Co-Director, Mental Health Education Project
Department of Psychiatry
State University of New York Downstate Medical Center
Brooklyn, New York

CHARLES C THOMAS PUBLISHER
Springfield • Illinois • U.S.A.

Published and Distributed Throughout the World by
CHARLES C THOMAS • PUBLISHER
BANNERSTONE HOUSE
301-327 East Lawrence Avenue, Springfield, Illinois, U.S.A.
NATCHEZ PLANTATION HOUSE
735 North Atlantic Boulevard, Fort Lauderdale, Florida, U.S.A.

© *1965, by* CHARLES C THOMAS • PUBLISHER
Library of Congress Catalog Card Number: 65-11311

First Printing, 1965
Second Printing, 1969
Third Printing, 1970

With THOMAS BOOKS *careful attention is given to all details of manufacturing and design. It is the Publisher's desire to present books that are satisfactory as to their physical qualities and artistic possibilities and appropriate for their particular use.* THOMAS BOOKS *will be true to those laws of quality that assure a good name and good will.*

Printed in the United States of America

DEDICATION

To
Annie May
and
Karen

ACKNOWLEDGMENTS

WE TAKE this opportunity to express our gratitude to Dean Paul A. McGhee and Associate Dean Russell F. W. Smith, of the Division of General Education of New York University, for the full measure of support and encouragement which they have given to the development of the Workshop, and for the freedom and latitude which they have provided for experimentation with new teaching methods.

It is a pleasure to acknowledge our indebtedness to Professor Howard W. Potter, formerly Dean of the Downstate Medical Center, to Professor I. Charles Kaufman, Chairman of the Department of Psychiatry, Downstate Medical Center, and to Professor David M. Engelhardt, who in various ways facilitated the exploratory conduct of the Workshop with patients of the Mental Health Clinic of the Kings County Hospital Center.

Mrs. Danica Deutsch, Executive Director of the Alfred Adler Consultation Center, generously extended the facilities of her agency enabling us to expand our experiences with the Workshop as a way of preparing patients for therapy.

Special appreciation is due Dr. Solomon Adelman and Dr. Nat Asherman, Psychiatric Consultant and Research Psychologist respectively on the staff of the project, for their dedication to the work and for a collaboration that was rewarding both personally and professionally.

The project described in this book was supported in part by a mental health project grant, No. OM-6 (C3R1) from the National Institute of Mental Health, U. S. Public Health Service. Dr. Harold M. Hildreth, Consultant, Community Service Branch, National Institute of Mental Health, contributed a generous personal interest in the aims of the project which we found invaluable. His vision of the potential role of the educator in the mental health field was particularly inspiring.

Thanks are due Karen Machover, Senior Psychologist, Kings County Hospital Center, and Clinical Assistant Professor, Downstate Medical Center, for her penetrating observations and her discussion of theoretical issues at post-session staff conferences.

The senior author feels a special gratitude to Dr. Harry Bone and Mrs. Asya L. Kadis. They contributed in no small measure to the development of his conceptions and feelings about the personal self.

We should like to express our admiration and profound appreciation to Ann Malamud and Frieda Herman for devoted contributions to the project in various secretarial, administrative, and executive roles. Their deftness, graciousness, and tact in mediating contacts with Workshop members and in resolving a plethora of petty complications were truly admirable.

Beatrice Wexler gave generously of her time and skill in helping with the preparation of the manuscript.

Finally, we wish to express our appreciation to all those Workshop members who ventured with us into the uncertain and unknown, and who taught us how to teach.

D. I. M.
S. M.

CONTENTS

Part Two: Leading a Workshop

TOWARD SELF-UNDERSTANDING

Group Techniques in Self-confrontation

INTRODUCTION

IN RECENT YEARS we have witnessed a rapidly grow-
ing interest in the promotion of mental health in the population
at large. This interest has been responsive to increasing recognition, expressed most cogently in the report of the Joint Commission on Mental Illness and Health,[13] of the widespread incidence
of severe maladaptation, emotional disturbance, and personality
disorder. In addition, there are great numbers of persons with
emotional problems who need help in understanding themselves
and others as a means of increasing authentic feelings of integration and mastery, as well as their capacity to enjoy life. Conventional mass methods of mental health education, as represented
in magazine articles, book-length popularizations, newspaper
columns, public lectures, television programs, and the like, may
make a certain contribution to the prevention and amelioration of
serious problems and to the promotion of constructive self-understanding. However, as the report of the recent National Assembly
on Mental Health Education[7] has pointed out, the usefulness of
these methods has never been satisfactorily investigated. Too
often, in the absence of professional supervision, they stir up excessive anxieties, inspire short-lived resolutions to reform, or
represent sterile, intellectual experiences in which new terms and
concepts are absorbed in an abstract way without the kind of
personalized impact which stimulates growth emotionally as well
as on a cerebral level.

The various techniques of individual and group psychotherapy,
on the other hand, have the advantage of working with the client's
personal-emotional involvement but suffer the drawback of
limited availability. There are too few therapists to meet the
needs of all who seek therapy. Besides, many people who need
psychotherapy are either unaware of their need or shrink from
the acknowledgment, the effort, or the expense. Most impor-

3

tant, many people who could profit from effective mental health education may not really require so intensive and extended an experience as is involved in psychotherapy.

Clearly, an approach is needed in mental health education which can reach large numbers of people at the same time that it makes use of some of the principles of dynamic psychotherapy indispensable to genuine learning about the self. It is in the context of this need that the approach described in this book has developed. The Workshop in Self-Understanding, as we have come to call this approach, is a large group course which employs methods that stimulate intense, personal-emotional involvement. With suitable adaptations of procedure and content, the Workshop is capable of application in a variety of contexts, including colleges, university extension courses, psychiatric hospitals, and mental health clinics. It can accommodate groups of up to sixty adults varying widely in age, education, and socio-economic background. In its applications so far, the Workshop has typically been structured as a fifteen-week course, meeting once weekly in two-hour sessions. The Workshop has been undergoing development since 1950 mainly at New York University's Division of General Education where it is offered as a noncredit course open to the public at large. Earlier versions of this course have been reported elsewhere.[3, 17, 18, 19]

Our purpose in this book is to describe the Workshop in Self-Understanding, largely through an empirical account of its application. In addition, we shall be concerned with such questions as: Can adults be "taught" in a planned course to understand themselves better in ways which make a difference in their lives? What planned group procedures are available for promoting such growth in self-understanding? What concepts and principles should make up the content of such a course? What are some possible roles of the leader in this course? What typical opportunities and anxiety-producing situations arise and how might the leader best deal with them?

The Workshop as it has developed, and continues to develop, owes much to Roger's views[26] on self-discovered learning in therapy and education, the focus in the fields of group therapy and group dynamics on the use of the group as a medium of change, and the growing emphasis in adult education[22, 32] on furthering the total self-development of the individual as well as his fund of knowledge and skills. Predicated on the assumption that self-understanding is an essential ingredient particularly of positive mental health, the Workship aims at helping students achieve a sharper awareness of much that is ordinarily implicit in their experience and behavior. Through a series of carefully planned and arranged classroom situations, students are provided with opportunities for personalized, first-hand experience with such psychodynamic concepts as the following: that all behavior is caused, that unconscious phenomena are real and meaningful, that childhood experiences have a crucial bearing on personality development, that the apparently trivial is often significant as self-revelation and as communication, that a coherent and understandable style may often be discerned threading its way through the core of one's life, and that the self is an active agent in its development.

The self-confrontation experiment is the chief vehicle of the course. Here we use the term "experiment" in the special sense of an open-ended, novel, planned situation, task, or procedure in which members are invited to engage as participant-observers with an exploratory attitude of relaxed alertness. The following summary of the Seat-Changing Experiment is an example:

The leader instructs the students to shift their seats to seating places as different as possible from their present ones. The leader too changes his seat. When the members have settled in their new seats, the leader asks what they observed and experienced as they went about the task. The discussion may touch on such aspects of the experience as the felt resistance to change, the wish to sit or not to sit next to a specific member, or the reactions to the leader's new seating position. The leader next raises questions such as the following: "How radically different is your new seat from your old one?" "Who thought of sitting in the leader's chair?" "On the arm of the chair, on the table, or on the floor?" "What early experiences did you have which might account for the assumption that you could not sit on the floor?" At one or another point the leader asks members to close their eyes and notice what images and recollections pop into mind. The leader requests the group to return to their old seats, and once they have done this, he asks them for their reactions to this new change. See page 228 for a detailed description of this experiment.

The Seat-Changing Experiment meets the criteria we have come to recognize as characteristic of most useful Workshop experiments. These criteria require that the experiment: (a) be simple enough so that all in the group can participate, (b) be sufficiently novel and disarming so that students' conventional stereotyped responses are circumvented, (c) possess a "surprise" effect similar to that experienced when one stands in front of a triple mirror and suddenly sees oneself from an unfamiliar perspective, (d) evoke a wide variety of individual differences, (e) provoke students to wonder whether their reactions were as inevitable or as objectively determined as they had assumed, and to seach out for themselves the personal significance of these reactions, and (f) stimulate emotional involvement, yet produce no more anxiety than is manageable.

To date, we have developed a repertoire of over sixty experiments designed to excite the students' curiosity about aspects of their behavior falling into one or another of the following interrelated areas: Formative Influences in Childhood, Personal Characteristics and Processes, and Interpersonal Relations. By observing themselves in a series of experiments, the students have an opportunity to compare their reactions with those of others, to note regularities in their own responses, and explore possible origins of such observed trends. In going through these operations, the student is not unlike the scientific naturalist, except that he himself is the object under study.

The leader encourages frank and open communication in various ways. Particularly helpful is the example he sets in sharing with the class his own thoughts and feelings, including reactions of puzzlement, anxiety, or irritation. Also, after every session, members write one-page letters to him reporting their reactions to the events of the session. From time to time, he reads to the class, without identifying the writers, excerpts from these letters which refer to students' reactions to him and to each other, thus enabling the group to explore interpersonal currents which might otherwise never be brought into the open.

The attack on established defenses, which effective learning about the self entails, inevitably generates anxiety. Although welcome as an indicator of potentially catalytic involvement, reactions of anxiety, if uncontrolled, may induce confusion and flight. Consequently, various safeguards and supports, to be described later, have become a built-in part of the Workshop process.

It seems likely that future social necessities will lead to an increasing shift in activity in the mental health field from the function of psychotherapy to that of mental health education. The kind of education that is needed would provide large numbers of relatively normal persons with opportunities for confronting themselves in ways which can sharpen their sense of identity, heighten their feelings of self-acceptance, and make a real difference in how they relate to other people. We think of this course as possessing possible merit in providing this kind of education to people in a wide variety of contexts. For example, we see it as potentially useful for adolescents groping for a sharper sense of their own identity, for married couples who seek to understand better their roles in a crucial interpersonal area, or for students of clinical psychology, social work, and related fields who need to sharpen their powers of observation and become more aware of their personal biases.

Although the Workshop in Self-Understanding had its origin as a university adult course, it seemed to us that the Workshop approach might be a useful adjunct to the treatment resources of the overtaxed mental health clinic. Indeed, it is through a detailed description and discussion of two Workshops with groups mainly of mental health clinic outpatients awaiting psychotherapy that we attempt here to convey the nature of the Workshop approach, its values, and its limitations.

In offering this account, we have in mind the possibility that others may be stimulated to try out the Workshop method and that the material here presented can serve as a useful guide. In Part I we include an account of how the clinic Workshops were set up, narrative summaries of all the Workshop sessions, critical commentaries on each session, and an evaluation of the impact of the two Workshops on the members. Part II deals with matters of principle and technique in Workshop methodology based on our accumulated experience to date. This section also includes a repertoire of recommended experiments, a comparison of the Workshop and psychotherapy, and a brief review of related approaches.

It is with no sense of finality, insofar as the development of the Workshop approach is concerned, that we present this report of our concrete experiences. We hope that the reader will look at the Workshop from the point of view of its potentialities and as an exploratory penetration into a relatively new area, and that he will be stimulated to think creatively about the Workshop approach as a method in mental health education.

Part One

THE CLINICAL APPLICATION
OF THE WORKSHOP METHOD

~~~~~~~~~~~~~~~~~~~~~~~~~~~~~~~~~~~~~~

CHAPTER 1

THE WORKSHOP IN THE SETTING
OF THE MENTAL HEALTH CLINIC

W E HAD several aims in introducing the Workshop approach into the clinic. In the first place, we wished to test the applicability of Workshop methods to prospective patients, to see whether applicants awaiting psychotherapy could enter into the Workshop experience and use it productively in the enhancement of personal growth. We were also interested to explore the Workshop's potentialities as a kind of clinical adjunct in the case of outpatients left too long to languish on waiting lists which, in so many clinics, overtax the supply of available therapists. Could the Workshop experience serve as a stopgap form of help in appeasing the acute distress which brings the patient to the clinic but which would otherwise go unattended? Would participation in the Workshop help to sustain the initial incentive for therapy which, when neglected, withers into an unproductive and wasteful attrition of waiting lists? Would the group experience in the Workshop lead to a voluntary acceptance of group therapy, thus alleviating some of the pressure occasioned by limited resources for individual therapy? Would the Workshop be useful in correcting misapprehensions and illusions concerning the nature of psychotherapy? Finally, we were interested in the possibility that the Workshop experience might facilitate the actual process of later therapy.

In an effort to explore the above questions, a Workshop was started in October, 1955 with eighteen patients at the Mental

Health Clinic of the Kings County Hospital.* A second Workshop was conducted a year later with twenty-five patients. Our experience with these pilot studies was sufficiently encouraging to warrant formulation of a project which would allow further development of Workshop methods. Support by the National Institute of Mental Health from 1957 to 1962 under its Mental Health Project Grants program made possible the conduct of two additional Workshops at the Mental Health Clinic of the Kings County Hospital under conditions permitting their careful recording and study, and their description and discussion in this report.**

Most of the participants in the two grant Workshops were drawn from the waiting lists. The clinic charts were scrutinized as a first step in the selection process. We excluded from consideration persons with severe pathology as defined by diagnoses of schizophrenia, mental deficiency, organic deficit, or sociopathic personality disorder. In other words, we attempted to exclude people whose structuring of the Workshop experience would be too unreliable and unpredictable, who would not understand what was going on, or whose behavior might arouse uncontrollable anxiety in the group, or otherwise disrupt it.

Based on an initial screening of clinic charts, a selection of patients was made and letters were sent inviting them to come in for an interview with one of the staff members. These interviews were brief, scarcely lasting more than fifteen minutes on the average. Prior to the interview, each patient was asked to read over a brief statement describing the Workshop. When the patient came in, the interviewer introduced himself and said something along the following lines:

We understand that you have applied for psychotherapy. We

---

*The Kings County Hospital Mental Health Clinic is an outpatient unit of the Psychiatric Division of the Kings County Hospital Center, an agency of the Department of Hospitals of the City of New York. As such, it accepts for diagnostic study, treatment, and referral to other agencies, residents of Brooklyn who cannot afford private psychiatric or psychological consultation or treatment. Patients may be self-referred or referred by courts or other social agencies.

**During the period of the grant, but independent of it, two Workshops were also conducted at the Alfred Adler Consultation Center with patients prior to their entrance into psychotherapy.

are sorry to say, however, that at the present time, psychotherapy is not immediately available. There may be a waiting
period anywhere from three to six months. In the meantime
the clinic has developed the Workshop for people who might
be interested in participating in an educational experience
relating to mental health while they are awaiting their turn in
therapy. We have reviewed your record, and we feel that this
might be something that would be useful to you. We are having this interview with you in order to give you a chance to
explore the possibilities of coming to the Workshop and to
clarify any questions that you might have. We do not expect to
be able to take in everybody who will be interested in joining,
but we would like to know from you whether you would be
interested in being considered. If you are not selected, it would
have no personal meaning, for we will be selecting people with
an eye on balancing the group according to sex, age, type of
problem, and so forth. Have you read this sheet describing the
Workshop? Are there some questions you would like to ask
about it? (At this point the interviewer takes up any questions
that the applicant may have.) You understand that this course
will be different from the usual kind of course. There won't be
anybody lecturing or giving answers. It's the kind of course in
which the leader will encourage you to arrive at your own
answers and at your own self-understanding. How do you
think you might feel about that? (The patient's answer to this
question was often useful in making a decision on his suitabil-
ity.) You understand that your position on the waiting list will
not be affected in any way whether you join this group or not.

All selected patients were informed that they had the option
of bringing a relative or a friend with them who would be free to
join the class as a guest. This invitation was motivated by our
recognition that some potentially effective participants might be
dissuaded from joining the Workshop by their own anxieties, and
it was our thought that if they had the opportunity to bring a
friend or a relative, then the feeling of threat might be diminished to a tolerable level.

A group of five patients, in group therapy for over a year at
the Kings County Hospital Mental Health Clinic, accepted an
invitation to join the second Workshop, providing us with the
opportunity of studying the extent to which "experienced" ther-

apy patients can serve as catalysts for other Workshop members, as well as the extent to which the Workshop can serve as a catalytic experience for a group concurrently in therapy.

For each Workshop we canvassed over a hundred charts, interviewed over fifty people, and selected thirty-five to forty persons for inclusion. Of those selected, twenty-eight in the first Workshop and twenty-nine in the second became regularly attending members. The majority of participants in both Workshops were diagnosed by the intake psychiatrist as suffering from character neuroses with acute symptomatology, including phobia, anxiety and depression, and hysterical conversion. Much the same was true of those guest participants who entered therapy at the Mental Health Clinic following the Workshop. The people finally selected covered a wide range of personalities, defenses, and behaviors. There were some who communicated readily, some who were quite silent, some who were relatively domineering, a great many who were dependent, some very introspective, and others quite externalizing.

The composition of the two Workshops is summarized in Table I. In general, it will be noted that the participants in the two Workshops rather closely resemble each other in sex, age, education, and the like. The two Workshops differed in distribution of referral sources in that the second Workshop accepted referrals from a more diversified range of sources.

TABLE I

BACKGROUND CHARACTERISTICS OF REGULARLY ATTENDING WORKSHOP PARTICIPANTS

	Workshop I	Workshop II
Sex:		
Male	6	3
Female	22	26
Age:		
Range	24-47	19-49
Median	34	35
Education:		
Elementary School Graduate	3	2
Some High School	2	8
High School Graduate	15	10
Some College	1	8
College Graduate	6	0
Nursing School Graduate	1	1

Marital Status:

Married	22	24
Single	4	5
Separated	2	0

Referral Source:

KCH Mental Health Clinic	21	19
Guest of Patient	7	2
Jewish Family Service	0	6
Coordinated Clinics	0	2

Attendance:

Median sessions per participant	14	13

The two Workshops were conducted by two different leaders so that we could appraise the adaptability of the Workshop approach and its methodology to different leadership approaches. Each Workshop ran for fifteen consecutive weeks. Each session began at 9:30 in the morning and ended at approximately 11:30. Workshop sessions were held in a comfortably appointed, sound-treated lounge whose size was sufficient to accommodate the people involved in each group. There were couches and chairs arranged around a large conference table.

There were a number of nonparticipant observers who for the most part were members of the professional staff of the project, including, at various times, the director, co-director, psychiatric consultant, and the research psychologist. In addition, there was a senior member of the psychology staff of Kings County Hospital. The leader made it a point to introduce all the observers at the very beginning of each Workshop, explaining their presence in factual terms, namely, that they were members of the project, interested in the procedures and would participate not in the Workshops themselves but in later staff discussion oriented toward the most effective development of the course.

In addition to being taken down in stenographic notes, all the sessions were tape-recorded. Both procedures were used so each could supplement the other in order to get an accurate, continuous, and comprehensive verbatim record of session events. It was obvious to the Workshop members that the sessions were being observed and recorded. Nevertheless, there was no doubt that whatever self-consciousness these procedures may have generated was very rapidly dispelled.

~~~~~~

CHAPTER 2

THE FIRST WORKSHOP

IN THIS chapter and in the one that follows, we present summaries and interpretive commentaries for each of the fifteen sessions in the two Workshops. The summaries have been extremely condensed so as to portray as sharply as possible the main trends of the two groups' experiences. In order to summarize a Workshop session we read through its typescript repeatedly in an effort to single out salient events, those which appear to have had enduring significance relative to the progress of the group as a whole, and those which appear to have been of central importance to particular members. For each highlight event we cite only the most significant and representative communications. Thus, many statements are not reported because they are essentially repetitive or would add little to the reader's grasp of the interchange among the members.

In our commentaries we attempt to assess the significance of what occurred in each session. We place under critical scrutiny the aims entertained for the particular session, the behavior and implicit orientation of the leader, and the value, sequence, and pacing of his class experiments. Insofar as possible, we try to trace the main cause-and-effect trends underlying the various Workshop developments. Further, we indicate where we felt situations were well handled and where we felt dissatisfied, though we are well aware that there is no one cut-and-dried way of conducting Workshops.

Our judgments in the commentaries are necessarily tentative.

The reader may think them ill-directed, unjustified, overdrawn, too severe, or insufficiently severe. We offer them simply as expressions of our own thinking, leaving it to the reader to make the final judgment in relation to his own beliefs, principles, and anticipated applications. At this stage, it is our hope that our necessarily condensed report and our analysis of concrete Workshop experiences, viewed against the background of the leader's intentions and of the methods introduced to implement them, will serve to communicate a faithful picture of what transpires in a Workshop.

It should be useful to the reader to compare the first and second Workshops. He will notice differences in the two group experiences in content, sequence, and leadership approach. A comparison of the two Workshops should be useful to prospective Workshop leaders in alerting them to the wide range of situations that can arise in such a course and to a variety of theoretical issues that a leader must be aware of and think through for himself.

Session One

Summary. Twenty-nine members attended the first session. As they trooped in, they handed in photographs of themselves (requested by the leader so that he could more rapidly memorize names and faces), and pinned on previously prepared first-name badges. After they were seated, the leader stepped forward, introduced himself, and gave a brief orientation talk, the gist of which was as follows: "The goal of the Workshop is to help you to better understand yourself and others, and to prepare you for more effective collaboration with your therapist. This course is not intended to be a form of psychotherapy. Nor shall I be lecturing to you. Instead I shall try to help you to discuss and think through situations for yourselves. We shall try to develop an atmosphere here where you will feel free to share your thoughts and feelings, even those you have about each other or about me. This sharing may be difficult at first, but I expect that gradually this will become easier to do. It is not necessary to participate verbally in the class in order to profit from it. At the end of every session I will ask you to write a letter to me in which you can include any of your unexpressed reactions to what occurred in the session. I will annotate these letters in the margin with comments and questions that occur to me. In this first meeting you will get a sample taste of some of the things we will be doing here." The observers were then introduced, and their functions explained.

As a means of breaking the ice and encouraging maximum group participation, the leader then presented a series of cartoon slides:* Joe Doakes, bawled out by his boss, comes home and shouts at his wife for some trivial oversight on her part; his wife then bawls out Junior, who, in turn, kicks his dog. As each slide in this story was projected on the screen, the leader invited the group to report what it saw and to speculate about what was going on and why. In the next-to-last slide in this series, the dog is seen licking the boy's face affectionately. At this point the leader asked the group to predict how the child would react. Most members, having anticipated some positive response, were very surprised to see the boy kick the dog in the next slide. Prompted by the leader, the members then discussed those factors in themselves, for example, wishful thinking, which might have determined the majority prediction. The slides stimulated much relaxed laughter and animated commentary.

The leader then presented the first scene from the film, "This Charming Couple,"** in which an engaged couple is shown out on a picnic. The leader stopped the film at the end of the scene and asked for the group's observations and reactions. The actor's scar was brought up. Some members had been very much aware of the scar, while other participants had either failed to notice it at all or had soon forgotten it. The leader expressed puzzled interest in these differences in perception. DINAH*** stated that various ailments have bothered her so much in the past that she

---

*See Bettis[3] for pictures of these cartoons.

**Descriptions of the films referred to in these pages, as well as information concerning their rental and purchase, will be found in various sources such as the *New York University Film Library Catalogue, Mental Health Motion Pictures, A Selective Guide,* 1960, U. S. Department of Health, Education, and Welfare, Public Health Service, National Institutes of Health, Washington, D. C., the *Psychological Cinema Register Catalog,* 1963, 1964, 1965, Pennsylvania State University, University Park, Pa.

***All names of Workshop members are pseudonyms.

now would immediately notice a scar. ROSA speculated that some members might not have seen the scar because of poor eyesight. MOLLY stated that people hope others won't notice their afflictions and so they avoid noticing those of others. BESS stated that she was brought up to notice a person's looks. IAN suggested that some people may simply not want to see certain things. This prompted SALLY to recall that she never really saw her mother's facial birthmark, but she hurriedly added that this didn't mean she was hiding from the fact.

Toward the end of the session the leader asked the members what they had been noticing about the group. DINAH was struck by how differently people could think about things. BETTY believed this was so because each of them was reacting in personal terms. With much feeling DAWN declared, "I was always brought up with the idea that my mother was right and that there was only one answer . . . her answer . . . Now I can see there are different answers, and no one answer is right or wrong, but it's just how you see it."

MOLLY expected the other members to be inhibited, but she was pleasantly surprised to find them so willing to participate. DAWN expressed amazement at her freedom to talk in the group. ROSA was surprised to find such a nice looking, intelligent group. DINAH stated, "I expected to find people that didn't know what's doing . . ." DENISE believed that most people were good actors and hid their feelings.

At the end of the session the leader asked the group to write one-page letters to him. As paper was being passed out, ROSA asked if one could prevent presenting a false face to the world and if there was happiness to be found in that. The leader replied, "Let's see what you decide after the fifteen weeks. I want to encourage you to try to work on your own questions. . ." ROSA responded with an accepting nod.

Commentary. The group terminated the first session with optimism and a burst of enthusiasm which probably resulted, in part, from sheer relief of their anticipatory anxiety. They had all come to this novel situation undoubtedly aware, however vaguely, of the presence of conflicts, feelings, and wishes in themselves which they had been keeping well hidden, and they did not know how far it was going to be necessary to make these public in a course of this kind. Although they were told that this was a course, they knew that they and their personalities were somehow to be the subject matter. However, they discovered that other members presented very acceptable masks, even though, like themselves, they were patients with presumably similar problems. This may have given them some feeling of reassurance that they, too, must be doing the same. In addition, the relaxed way in which they were received, and the nonthreatening character of the procedures must have been reassuring. It was quickly evident that they were not going to be criticized, ridiculed, or humiliated.

The relative painlessness of this first session, while it may have been reassuring, may have at the same time aroused illusory expectations which became the seeds of a later disappointment and frustration expressed in Session Four. Nothing was openly said to suggest that dependency needs were going to be gratified, that their questions were going to be answered, or that their problems were going to be solved. In fact, the leader made a special point of stating that just the opposite would be the case. Nonetheless, we can speculate that the structured situation, the confident leadership, and the friendly interest of the observers all served to nourish their hopes for some miraculous help, or at least the authoritative guidance and affection for which they had been longing.

It is possible, thus, that contrary to the realistic structuring which the leader attempted, there may have actually been communications from the leader which could be interpreted too easily as a promise: "I will help you much more in accord with your wishes than my words intimate." These considerations suggest the following: Overoptimistic expectations, doubts, and resistances exist in every first session, and it would be useful to bring these into the open for discussion as early as possible, and to forewarn the group about the stresses, strains, and frustrations likely to occur in the Workshop.

Certain characteristics of the leader's approach were already prominent: He listened to all the responses in an interested, welcoming manner, refrained from criticisms, and expressed appreciation for the contributions of each participant. Despite his inner tension, he displayed a sense of humor and an informality that was easygoing and relaxing. He shared his own feelings with the group on occasion. He sidestepped questions which were directed to him and yet, when not pressed by anyone to do so, he occasionally volunteered brief didactic comments. Toward the end of the session, he shifted the group's attention away from the film and slides onto themselves and their own observations and private feeling-reactions.

The first session was so full of participation, personal references, and positive response that the leader conferred on the members a kind of radiant glow. He saw them as unusual people who could confront themselves more honestly and more rapidly than most other groups that he had worked with before. This misperception of the group (as well as his eagerness to use this group as a demonstration of how much could be accomplished by the Workshop method) led him in subsequent sessions to move more quickly in his presentation of provocative and potentially threatening procedures than he normally would.

Session Two

Summary. The second meeting focused on the themes of over-compliance and self-suppression. The film, "The Feeling of Rejection," portraying the case history of Margaret, an overly-submissive personality, was stopped at various points to allow discussion of the role of early experiences within the family in fostering Margaret's compliance.

At one point, as the group was criticizing Margaret's mother, KEVIN said that he felt sorry for the mother, for she may have had a rough life that had turned her into the kind of woman she was. The leader asked KEVIN whether he felt that the group was picking on the mother. KEVIN answered, "Yes. Well, no. Why?" The leader replied, "Because you came in with such defensiveness in your voice . . ." KEVIN replied, "Well, no, I did that just because it's just a natural feeling for the underdog . . . is it a natural thing for her to be that way, or are there other things?" The leader conceded: "Well, I think you're right. There must have been experiences that she had that led to this kind of very drab, nagging. . ." ROSALIE interrupted, "In other words, it all goes back to Adam and Eve. There's nobody normal in this world." The group burst out laughing, and the leader joined in but made no further comment on the issue. Instead, he invited them to resume watching the next scene of the film.

After a discussion of Margaret's headaches and how headaches frequently relate to bottled-up feelings, the leader asked whether anybody had noticed a headache developing in himself during the session. Some members reported that their palms were moist. MABEL announced that she was indeed developing a headache because, like Margaret, she always put herself in the other person's position. JEAN told the group that she had developed a headache the previous night when she lacked the courage to express some things she had on her mind. Here JULIA protested: "We can't always let out our emotions. It's sometimes better to discipline ourselves." The leader agreed that sometimes it is appropriate to keep our feelings to ourselves, but that many people have difficulty letting out feelings even when it is appropriate or necessary to do so. ROSA pressed the leader to say when it was appropriate to let out anger. To this the leader simply replied that this was often difficult to decide and that there was no ready-made answer. He then resumed showing the film.

At the end of the film, members expressed some uneasiness about how well they were rearing their own children. With the aim of having the members focus upon themselves and what they were feeling in the immediate moment, the leader inquired, "What did you notice in this session that was either the same or different from last week's session?" ROSALIE complained that the same people always did the talking. She would like to hear from the silent members in order to know what they were like. DINAH and JUNE felt they could get more ideas and opinions if more people talked. At this point the leader declared protectively that those who did not feel like talking did not have to. He wondered why silent members might make some talkers uneasy. ROSALIE admitted that sometimes she regretted talking too much, lest others think she didn't know anything. KEVIN also feared exposing himself lest he make an ass of himself.

At this point the leader suddenly changed the subject and asked the group for its reactions to the new arrangement of chairs. (The chairs were now arranged in a circle instead of in rows.) In response, several members reported feeling more comfortable. As the leader was about to close the session KEVIN asked how a timid person could become an aggressive one. The leader suggested that consideration of the question be postponed to future sessions when films dealing with therapy would be presented. The session ended with many members appearing frustrated and somewhat depressed.

Commentary. This session was effective in confronting the group with its habitual pattern of self-sacrificing compliance. Most members, however, apparently took this discussion to mean that they were expected to behave assertively whenever they felt like it. This could not but be conceived as an expectation beyond their capacity to fulfill. It is little wonder that an anxious discussion developed around the theme, "We can't always let out our emotions." By acknowledging that there were situations where it would not be politic to do this, and that it was often difficult to determine when it was appropriate, the leader may have lightened the burden of those who were all too painfully aware that they lacked the courage to express their hostility. But at the very end of the session, KEVIN appeared to reflect the group's persistent anxiety when he asked how a timid person could become an aggressive one. In a sense, KEVIN's question may have summed up the group's feeling of impotence in being confronted so sharply with a central life problem that they saw no way of overcoming. The leader's sidestepping of KEVIN'S query left the group tense and up in the air.

The leader needs to be very clear on the issue of letting out angry feelings since it is bound to come up in every Workshop. The following points, consistent with this Workshop's emphasis on autonomy, would be useful for the leader to keep in mind:

1) Anger is a natural reaction which is in itself devoid of value implications.

2) There are no universal "rules" governing the right and wrong of experiencing, or reacting with, or expressing anger.

3) The meaning of anger, its acceptability, its destructiveness

or constructiveness, the dynamics which generate it and affect its expression, and its integration within the whole personality vary from person to person.

4) People vary in the degree to which they are motivated to become aware of the meaning of anger to them and to clarify its dynamics.

5) The Workshop provides an opportunity for members who wish to do so to clarify for themselves the role and dynamics of anger in their lives.

In the light of the foregoing, it seems to us that the present leader might more usefully have handled the issue of letting out feelings had he been better prepared with a sharply articulated position. Instead of telling JULIA that many people have difficulty in letting out feelings even when it is appropriate to do so, the leader would have put the focus in the right place had he stated that many persons have difficulty in letting out feelings even when they themselves believe it appropriate to do so. Also, in response to ROSA's question as to when it is appropriate to let out anger, the leader's reply that this was a very difficult question, one without a ready-made answer, was fine as far as it went. However, a sharper response might have been, "This is a very difficult question, one with which each of us struggles, including me, and one about which each of us has to make up his own mind. But one thing I can say. This question is very much bound up with why we're angry, and the why of our anger is often not fully clear to us."

At the end of the film the members focused on their relationships with their children, although the leader had hoped that the film would stimulate them to examine their own past formative experiences, particularly in relation to their own mothers and fathers. Most Workshop members, however, were themselves young mothers, and the film's emphasis on the role of parents in shaping children's personalities aroused the members' guilt and anxiety concerning their own role as parents. This immediate concern sharply limited their freedom to think of themselves as products of their own developmental experiences, and to regain contact with the children they themselves once were.

The very general reluctance to explore relationships with one's own parents is understandably often encountered in Workshop

groups. Yet, one Workshop aim is to help members achieve sufficient detachment from this interlocking involvement so that they
can begin to think of their parents as fallible human beings who,
like themselves, are partially the products of past influences. At
one point, KEVIN's reference to the movie mother's own problems gave the leader an opportunity to help the group to see the
mother in an individualized and understanding rather than in a
condemning way. Unfortunately, however, because he was intent on getting the members to face themselves, he at first focused
on KEVIN's defensiveness.

Given the leader's intention to get the members to focus on
themselves and the course of their own development, how might
he have responded to their preoccupation with their own adequacy in the parental role? Many possibilities occur to us. For
example, he might simply have focused the members' attention
on their difficulty in reacting to the movie in terms of themselves apart from their parental role. This would be consistent
with a major aim in the Workshop, that is, to help the group
achieve a measure of detachment from habitual modes of doing,
thinking, and feeling in the expectation that the resulting ob-
jectivity might permit participation in the learning process in
new ways.

Toward the end of the session the leader attempted to focus
the members' attention onto their own immediate feelings.
ROSALIE's response to this touched off some scapegoating
against the "non-talkers." The leader defended the silent members by pointing out that they did not need to talk, but he failed
to carry this discussion through to some meaningful conclusion.
Instead of coming to grips with the group's anxiety, he himself
sought reassurance by turning the discussion to a consideration
of the group's reactions to the new chair arrangement. The
leader probably could have handled this part of the session much
more effectively if he had simply said what was on his mind directly and frankly, somewhat as follows: "I have the feeling that
the atmosphere in our group right now is just thick with tension.
How do you feel about that?" Or, "You know, I feel that a lot of
people in the group are tense about something. In fact, I am too.
Let's talk about it."

At the end of the session, the leader evaded KEVIN's question about how a timid person could become aggressive. Such questions frequently occur in Workshops. Members often look to the leader to tell them how to change this or that habit or behavior with which they are discontented. In postponing an answer to KEVIN's question, the leader may have unwittingly implied that this question was a legitimate one which could usefully be taken at face value, and that the resolution of this problem of timidity did indeed involve some fixed rules that authorities could dispense at will. The leader might have been more helpful to KEVIN by replying somewhat as follows: "That's a very difficult question to answer, Kevin, because it assumes that I or some other authority have the answer in our hip pocket, but this is something that each person needs to work out in his own way and to his own satisfaction. If this question personally concerns you, then it might be useful for you to ask yourself such questions as the following: What do timidity and aggressiveness mean to you? What past experiences have made it necessary for you to be timid? Are you timid under certain circumstances but not under others? What bothers you about being timid? Some such reply would have given both KEVIN and the group much to mull over.

Session Three

Summary. In this session, the leader introduced the First Names Experiment with the aims of: (a) relaxing some of the tension generated in the previous week's meeting, (b) helping members to become acquainted on a more informal first-name basis, and (c) stimulating them to begin thinking about their reactions to each other as possible clues to self-understanding.

First the leader invited the members to take turns in reporting their first names (name badges had been dispensed with) and telling the group about a "favorite something" from childhood, be it a person, an activity, a book, or whatever. He started off the go-around by giving his first name and confiding that his favorite activity, reading, was in part an escape from tensions at home. Many members followed the leader's example and added some comments about the significance of their favorite choices. For example, LARRY recalled that his parents wouldn't let him participate in any activity because he had asthma, and so he had always played in the back yard and became an ardent nature lover. Members listened to each other with high interest and frequently broke out into laughter in response to one or another humorous revelation.

Following this go-around, the leader asked the members what they had observed as they listened to each other. The group was, at first, reluctant to give observations. Instead of easing the situation by making some comments of his own, the leader chose to wait it out. After a few moments of silence, JUNE noted that many members felt that they had done nothing outstanding. This was followed by ETTA's observation on how alone members were in childhood. ROSALIE felt there were no "great successes" in the group because most members had been frustrated. SALLY objected, declaring that there were no more frustrations in this group than in any other group. BELLE expressed resentment at hearing these sweeping generalizations. The leader refrained from sharing his own observations. He simply listened attentively, and when the group was through, introduced the next task.

He asked the members to write down as many of the first names in the group as they could recall. A discussion followed on individual differences in techniques of recall. Some had written names down as they spontaneously came to mind, while some had been more orderly, listing names according to seating order. The group became intensely involved in the question as to why some members remembered many names and some few. IAN felt it was simply a matter of concentration. DAWN reported that she was so often told as a child that she had a poor memory that she finally stopped trying. JEAN noted that she remembered mostly men's names. The leader asked members to read off the first three names that had come to mind, and to consider whether these names might have had some special significance for them. IAN noticed that the first two names he recalled began with the same letter as his own name. PEGGY stated that she recalled GRETA first because she was quiet and retiring as herself, and MOLLY second because this was her mother's name.

The leader noticed that some people included him among the first three names and others did not. He wondered what might be involved in this difference. IAN included the leader's name because he saw him as being human like the others in the group. ETTA stated that she accepted the leader's not giving answers, and that, therefore, she did not see him as part of the group. DINAH saw him as an outside person who is here to help the group by pointing out ". . . where we are wrong and where we are right."

Without commenting on the foregoing, the leader asked each member to repeat his own name over and over to himself with eyes closed, until some image, feeling, or thought popped into mind. These name-associations were then reported, with the leader being the first to do so. DAWN stated that her name reminded her of "a fat little tub running around of no use to anyone." ETTA associated her name with someone "dumpy, illogical, and untalented." LARRY "heard" his mother calling him by name to ask if he had forgotten his scarf. JEAN connected her name with Napoleon and thought of herself as floating on a white cloud. The leader suggested that our associations to our names might reflect feelings about ourselves.

The leader invited the members to point out whom in the group they still could not remember and to ask for their names. IAN went around the group asking for the name of almost each person, much to the amusement of the others. JEAN remarked that he must be afraid of women. (Most of the members were women.)

The leader asked the group what observations they had made about themselves or about him or about other members in the group. MOLLY said she was puzzled by the experiment because she had never attached any significance to her name before. BETTY was impressed with the fact that the leader had had an unhappy childhood and yet was able to rise so far above it. To this the leader replied that he was still not entirely free from a number of problems which had begun in childhood. A number of members reacted with obvious surprise to this confession but made no comment. ROSA noted that the group was like a "Saturday night social gathering" except that it was far more courteous.

Commentary. This session was a good deal less threatening than the previous one. The spontaneous recollection and sharing of childhood experiences, the many good-natured exchanges among the members, and the frequent explosions of group laughter were evidence of the degree to which a relaxed group intimacy had developed. In contrast to the procedures of the previous session, the personally dynamic implications of the First Names Experiment which were brought up were substantially freer of judgmental implications. In a simple, nonthreatening way, this experiment encouraged members to share little, but nonetheless significant, intimacies which are ordinarily kept hidden, thus helping the group to widen its range of communication on a personal level.

A significant aspect of these go-around experiences was the leader's active participation as though he were a fellow Workshop member. For example, he took the initiative in reporting a "favorite something" from childhood and offering a simple, dynamic explanation for his preferred activity. Similarly, he took the initiative in offering his spontaneous, unguarded, free associations to his own name. Clearly, it was the leader's intention to help Workshop members overcome their resistance to sharing personal reactions by setting an example. If the authority figure could reveal intimacies about himself, if he could publicly acknowledge limitations and personal feelings, why, indeed, should the rank-and-file Workshop member not be able to do likewise? Also, by deliberately taking these steps, he was challenging the group's idealized conception of authority, their tendency to put him on a pedestal or in a class apart from the human race. The leader's self-revelations did indeed appear to have the effect of relaxing the atmosphere and of narrowing the gap between him and the members.

The session, however, was not without its anxious moments. The first go-around was followed by a period of silence. The leader deliberately refrained from offering some catalytic observation which might ease the tension. Rather, he saw the situation as offering an opportunity for the group to profit from the experience of coping with its own resistance. He operated on the assumptions: (a) that when a person experiences a difficulty within himself and then himself surmounts that difficulty, the gain in the sense of personal power is very much greater, and

(b) that the attitude of expecting to be given, which is the one that members usually start out with in a Workshop, needs gradually to be replaced by a readiness to accept the challenges which the Workshop offers.

While the leader was active in throwing out questions to the group, in participating in his own experiments, and in making occasional humorous remarks, he frequently abstained from giving brief summarizing statements or specific interpretive comments which might have usefully crystallized some significant developments or issues which arose. To a large extent, the group was left on its own insofar as making sense of the session was concerned. The leader was simply content with promoting an inquiring attitude along what he conceived to be productive lines. He regarded the Workshop as an experience for training the member in how to inquire into himself and what to look for, but he held that it was up to the individual to take as many or as few steps as he wished in exploring this or that aspect of himself. The leader's implicit attitude seemed to be, "Is it not interesting that so many of the things we take for granted are handled in such different ways by different people? There are no uniform ways of reacting, then, are there? There must be some reasons for the different ways in which people react. If you are interested in pursuing this further, go ahead."

Another leader in this session might well have preferred to have been a more active commentator, presenting his comments in a somewhat open-ended manner or at a high enough level of abstraction so that Workshop members might have been left to do further thinking on their own. But what generalizations might the leader have offered? Below are some suggestions:

1) In relation to the "favorite something" go-around: "Isn't it interesting that many of these casual, ordinary, little experiences that you mentioned, when we dig a little deeper, reflect some pretty important experiences or feelings or needs? Isn't it possible that a lot of other things that we take for granted in our lives, ordinary, conventional things, were we to examine them more closely, would also reveal much about us as human beings that we had not been aware of?"

2) In relation to remembering names: "Memory is a tricky

thing. How well we remember, and what and whom we remember, seem to be very much affected by our feelings and our needs and, as one or two of you have indicated, by the picture of ourselves that we have accepted from others."

3) In relation to including or excluding the leader's name among the list of those recalled: "Apparently, people in the group differ in their readiness to see me as a member of the group. Perhaps the way in which you see me, whether as a member of the group or as someone who is outside of it, depends on your attitude toward people of authority in general, and it may be that such habitual attitudes influence very much the ways in which we interrelate to each other."

4) In relation to associating to one's name: "The way we experience things, including even our names, is very much influenced by how we feel about ourselves, our values, and our general outlook. The thoughts and feelings that came to us in relation to our names are worth some attention and reflection, for they might help to clarify what we think of ourselves."

5) In relation to the group's surprise at the leader's having had an unhappy childhood and to his not being free of current problems: "I noticed that a number of you were surprised at my saying that I still am not free of some problems which have persisted from childhood. Would it not be worth while to consider how we think of our parents, our teachers, our bosses, maybe even the butcher, the baker, the candlestick maker? Do we fail to see them as individual people and only as figures occupying particular roles? Have you ever thought of your father as a person who was once a child and had, and still has, conflicts, problems, difficulties in relationships, things he himself likes and dislikes about himself? Would it make any difference to you to see yourself in this way, and your teachers, your husbands and wives, your bosses, me? How about it?"

6) At one point, DINAH stated, "You are here to help us and to tell us where we are wrong and where we are right." The leader did not contradict this, even though it diverged so sharply from his own conception of his role. He preferred to ignore it and to proceed with his syllabus, resting content with the idea that this would come up again at a more opportune time which would

fit in better with the syllabus that he had prepared. Another
leader, having more confidence in not losing track of his ultimate
goal by apparent digressions, might have flexibly adjusted to
this, sacked the rest of what he had in mind for the session, recognized the importance of the issue and dealt with it right then
and there by simply saying, "Well, it's interesting that you expect this. How do the others feel?"

Session Four

Summary. The group's evident relaxation in the previous meeting suggested they might be ready to confront one of its most
deeply rooted problems, that of dependency. Hence, the fourth
session centered on excessive dependency needs and their origin
in early childhood experience. The main text for this session was
the film, "Overdependency," a dramatized portrayal of the case
history of Jimmy. At the film's conclusion, the group was invited
to share what thoughts and feelings had been stirred up by it.
Some members recalled examples from their own experience
similar to Jimmy's life events. BELLE, somewhat cynically,
wondered how Jimmy would have turned out if he had been
neglected rather than overprotected. A few moments later she
asked the leader if her mother should not have let her stay home
the day when children were being weighed in school, so that
she could have been spared embarrassment about being over-
weight. The leader asked what others in the group thought about
this question. Some members commented sympathetically, but
BELLE tended to brush these comments aside, and ended up
still wondering how much protection it was right to give a child.

DINAH questioned whiningly why everything had to go back
to childhood. She declared that her own childhood was a happy
one, and it was only her very real problems in the present that
made a misery of her life. The leader recognized that many people found it difficult to connect their current problems with their
childhood experiences. He hoped that such connections would
become clearer as they moved along.

Noting growing currents of unrest and depression in the group,
the leader asked the members to compare their mood with that
of the preceding session. Dinah felt that the previous meeting

was more jolly and sociable, and that now the members were a bit depressed. SHIRLEY and MABEL agreed. The leader asked what might be going on in this session that made for the difference. MABEL thought that the discussion was touching them much more deeply. According to JEAN the topic was a depressing one that they ordinarily avoided. ROSA felt that the discussion was touching immature, helpless feelings that they all had. In contrast to these views, ETTA felt exuberant at the final outcome of the film, for it showed that one can overcome childhood influences. Somewhat dryly, the leader commented that he saw no exuberance in the group.

The leader returned to the group's depression and wondered what it might be about. JEAN wondered whether the course was really helping, for she became confused in thinking about the things that were being discussed. DINAH declared that the course was not helping at all. She felt just as badly as when she first came. TRUDE wondered whether the members were depressed because the movie made them see themselves as they really were. She added that she understood that the leader wouldn't give answers and that anything she would get she would derive from the group, but she didn't know what they were looking for. When the leader asked her whether she felt discouraged about getting answers to her questions without more help from him, she replied that she didn't know. ROSA asserted that it was lack of self-confidence which made them doubt whether they could do this for themselves.

DAWN thought she must be getting worse, for while she has never been angry in her life, she has been like a volcano lately. ETTA wondered why DAWN believed that she should suppress her anger. Perhaps she could be honest now and not sacrifice herself for someone else's good opinion. DAWN retorted that her family's opinions of her were important to her. BESS declared that before coming to the Workshop she had never spoken back to mother, but now she got things off her chest: "If she's hurt, she will just have to be hurt . . . I want to be allowed to grow up, so I felt that that film two weeks ago did me more good than anything I've done here in the past few weeks. . ."

The leader expressed his sympathetic acceptance of the group's frustration, disappointment, and depression, as well as of their fear that in the absence of some guiding formulas from him, they might not be capable of the talent, patience, and effort that progress would require. He reassured them that their reactions were understandable, indeed, inevitable. SALLY asked the leader to tell them exactly what they could expect from the group. He replied that they could anticipate plenty of stimulation, but that it remained to be seen how they were going to respond to this stimulation.

BETTY denied feeling discouraged. REGINA was happy to attend even though she felt depressed, but she wondered what she could do about her depression. The leader suggested trying to understand where the depression came from. Some members continued to protest Workshop methods that only lead to confusion and depression. ROSA declared, "Why come and see films that are going to depress you?" ETTA angrily retorted, "Well, what would you want us to do, sugar-coat it?"

The leader again recognized how uncomfortable they were feeling but suggested that something constructive could come out of these feelings if they tried to find out what was behind them: "What is it in your needs? What is it in the situation?" ROSA noted soberly that everyone was showing tremendous courage, ". . . coming here knowing that they are going to be hurt." The leader nodded in simple agreement and brought the session to a close. By this time there had been much release of feeling, and the air appeared to have cleared considerably.

Commentary. In this session the leader picked up where he had left off in the second session, confronting the members with their problems. Having faced their self-effacing tendencies in the second session, they were now challenged to examine their over-dependent trends. This focusing on shortcomings and difficulties in living must have been emphasized by the fact that the two films thus far presented were dramatized case histories dealing with "sick" persons.

Thus, while members felt a need for help and support, so far all they were receiving, as they probably saw it, were repeated invitations to engage in procedures which painfully underscored that they had this or that problem. At the same time the leader made it increasingly clear that they could not turn to him for relieving or soothing answers. Neither BELLE nor DINAH received responses to their queries which satisfied them. When SALLY asked the leader point-blank exactly what the group could expect, he replied, in effect, that he would merely bring in stimulating opportunities for them to react to, but that it was up to the group to make what it would of these opportunities. Little wonder, then, that various members seemed to be protesting that the Workshop was expecting too much of them. The charm of belonging to a specially selected group, and the hope of receiving relief from immediate pressing problems began to wear thin, and currents of unrest, stirred by a minority of articulate and hostile members, threatened to deluge the group.

At such a juncture, the leader needs to be crystal clear concerning his purposes and his methods and the risks they entail. If his aim is, at the very least, to chart paths to self-knowledge through the evocation of intense experiences, and if he believes that such effective charting cannot take place without pain, uncertainty, intensity, and honesty of commitment, then he cannot shirk his responsibility to challenge, to confront, to invite into involvement, and to induce a degree of anxiety and frustration. He needs to be concerned, to be sure, that he does not move so fast and in such roughshod manner as to induce flight from the group or marked intensification of defenses. At the same time, he must keep in mind that the emergence of disappointment and depression is almost inevitable if he, with a measure of unswerving relentlessness, refrains from "giving" and emphasizes instead the values of autonomous self-discovery, confrontation, and decision. From this point of view, the complaining, demanding, and despairing reactions of the group may be viewed as a potentially progressive development, particularly since the overwhelming majority of the group continued to attend the Workshop with high interest and emotional commitment.

This is not to deny, however, that the leader may well have been pressing the group too hard, confronting members with their limitations before they had had an opportunity to build up a self-accepting point of view about their difficulties, one in which these could be seen as inevitable consequences of past experiences and as problems which could be worked through. A more gradualistic approach on the part of the leader might well have been preferable. In such an approach, the first item on the agenda would have been to help the members to accept themselves as persons whose development, given the circumstances under which they lived, took certain relatively inevitable directions, who are still in a process of change, and who can participate actively in it. Underlying this orientation is the assumption that the group can move in a realistically self-critical direction only to the extent that self-accepting feelings have first been generated.

Could the leader have better met the group's challenge in this session? He brought out into the open (and this was a crucial turning point) the group's depression and disappointment, declaring that these feelings were understandable to the point of having been predictable. He sympathized with the group's fear and reluctance to work hard at their problems in the absence of pat answers. He urged patience and avoidance of discouragement. This was a very necessary intervention, but he might have added some sympathetic recognition of their underlying magical expectations of him, of their assumption that he had all the answers. And he might have also stated that learning to understand oneself involves a considerable degree of discomfort. It was left to a member of the group, ETTA, to emphasize the inevitable harshness of the process of learning. Should the leader not have underscored her comment by taking this opportunity to structure again the nature of the Workshop and its purposes as well as something of his conviction concerning the nature of the processes by means of which learning takes place? Among other things, he might have said something like this: "You look to me for answers, but the answers to the fundamental questions of life are not answers that anybody can give us. Each person has to determine his own answers for himself, those which best suit him depending upon his needs and outlook and background. Most people in our culture grow up having been conditioned to look outside of themselves for the answers to their lives and so I can understand your doing this here, and I realize that what I am saying must be disappointing to you."

Some readers may regard such a comment as placing Workshop members too sharply on their own responsibility. We confess we have mixed feelings about it. After all, a certain degree of dependency on the leader is realistic. He does provide structuring and guidance, and members need the leader to lead. This suggests that the leader, in coping with his own need to abjure the level of responsibility for giving which the group wishes to place on him, will still recognize the members' needs for some degree of "feeding" and will be able to give to the group with some moderation, gradually tapering off as the group's independence grows. However, in meeting the group's dependency needs to some extent, the leader needs to guard against doing so in a manner which confirms their transference reactions.

BELLE's question about mother's forcing her to go to school could have been better handled by the leader. He turned this question over to the members, who were hardly in a position to deal with it, and who, in fact, became embroiled in some fruitless interactions with BELLE. Would it not have been better for the leader to have made some comment such as the following: "Belle, that must be a very meaningful question to you. I don't know whether we can do justice to it right now, but we are going to have some sessions later devoted to early childhood experiences, and maybe at that time something meaningful will occur to you in relation to it. In particular, you may be able then to see more clearly past and present attitudes and feelings toward your parents which exert a persistent influence in your life to this very day."

DINAH's protest that she had had a happy childhood, and her feeling that the Workshop's focus on childhood was wholly irrelevant to her current problems, represent a typical reaction occurring in almost every Workshop. The leader needs to be prepared to deal with the kind of issue that she raises in a more adequate way than was the case in this session. To a member who can see no relationship between past and present, the leader might simply state that while such relationships are often difficult to see in the beginning of this kind of self-exploratory process, it has been the repeated experience of people actively seeking to understand themselves that they come to recognize that such relationships not only exist, but are highly significant. The member who wants and demands immediate help with current problems might need to be told by the leader that the group cannot do justice to any one individual's personal problems within the limited framework of the Workshop, but that what the member learns in the Workshop, particularly insofar as a better understanding of childhood experiences is achieved, will probably sooner or later be found to have a bearing on current problems. To the member who challengingly insists that he had a happy childhood, the leader might reply in any of the following ways: "Yes, it is possible that your childhood was happy in some ways, but perhaps it was also frustrating in other ways," "Perhaps the kind of devices that you used as a child to achieve happiness are inappropriate now," or "Maybe a happy childhood involved being pampered and having everything done for you, and maybe this is what you miss today."

At one point BESS stated that for the first time she was getting things off her chest in relation to mother, even when this meant hurting mother. This kind of acting out of one's anger occurs with some members at one point or another in most Workshops. It would seem important for the leader not to discourage the beginnings of behavior which formerly was severely inhibited and yet, at the same time, to emphasize the importance of understanding the origins of the members' anger rather than simply to act it out.

Session Five

Summary. The leader felt that the crisis in the previous session, far from setting the group back, might actually have cleared the way for a resumption of the work of self-exploration. At the same time he recognized the group's needs to be rescued from the self-blaming attitudes which the stimulus material had thus far stirred up, and to be given something more structured to hold onto. With these considerations in mind he introduced the Birth Order Experiment as a vehicle for examining childhood experiences relating to early sibling patterns, and of current attitudes, values, and coping mechanisms traceable to these experiences.

The film, "Sibling Relationships and Personality," was shown first to set the stage. After a brief discussion of the film, the group was subdivided into six birth-order groups consisting of eight members who were the oldest children in their own sibling group, four who were youngest, six females who were youngest with only male siblings, four who were only children, five who were middles with small families, and six who were middles in large families.* The members within each subgroup were asked to explore similarities in their experiences and in their personalities which might be the result of their common sibling positon. Each subgroup located itself in a different part of the lounge.

After a half-hour's discussion, the subgroups were brought together and reports were solicited from each subgroup in turn. At the conclusion of each subgroup's report, the leader invited general discussion. From time to time he introduced some research findings pertinent to the particular birth-order group. In this manner the group shared a variety of recollections and speculations.

KEVIN, an oldest, noticed that several members of his group wanted to shed responsibility in marriage. IAN, an oldest, recalled that his mother's requirement that he set an example "put a monkey" on his back. BELLE, a youngest, reported that everyone in her group expressed a strong resentment against authority. ETTA, a youngest, noted that most members in her group competed with their brothers. JEAN, a youngest, observed that too many things were done for the members in her group so that they were unable to cope with crises later in life. DAWN, an only, stated that the parents of her group did not get along with each other. She added that she always felt that her father had stayed with mother for her sake and that he had sacrificed his life for her. MABEL, also an only, agreed, "I think we all felt the responsibility of our parents, that we either were the cause, or we should have been able to do something about it." DAWN chimed in that she always had to behave as an adult. DINAH, a middle, recalled that her siblings resented her for being loved more by her parents, and she wondered whether she had been loved more because she had always been sick. ROSALIE, a middle, announced that her group discovered that their parents had not had enough time for them and that they had felt "left out completely."

---

*The leader had obtained the relevant birth-order data from the members in an earlier meeting.

DINAH suddenly complained that the group was not getting the answers that it needed for its individual problems. The leader reflected her desperate feelings sympathetically and suggested that the Workshop might still be useful to her even though it fell short of fulfilling her immediate needs. DAWN asserted dramatically that she would have cracked completely were it not for the Workshop. ROSA felt that the group was not lost but was trying to find its way. KEVIN cried out, "Fahblondget!"* provoking much laughter. LARRY connected his own "do-something-for-me" feeling with the fact that he had never been given responsibility as a child. He recognized, however, that the Workshop involved a kind of self-growth rather than getting answers to questions. ROXANNE pointed out that there was no quick cure, that therapy was such an involved, lengthy process that the best they could hope for was an opening so that a little light might peek in somewhere. The leader assured the group that nobody could be blamed for wanting "a quick cure," that it was not easy to take responsibility for self-searching, particularly in view of their lack of experience in this regard, that we grew by coming to our own insights, and that he had faith in their having more capacity to learn about themselves in this kind of situation than they might now feel. ETTA wondered whether those members who wished for answers wouldn't resent getting them.

At this point, IDA, a youngest, returned to the birth-order discussion. She expressed the belief that some of the people in her youngest group married as a way of leaving home. ROSALIE reported that members in her group felt that their parents had not wanted so many children but hadn't known enough about precautions. PEGGY, a middle, stated that like the youngest, she felt coddled too much, but that like an oldest, she treated her younger brother as if he were her child.

The leader asked the group whether they could see any connections between their birth-order experiences and the roles they played in the Workshop. ETTA wondered whether in the Workshop, as when she was the youngest child, she did too much talking in order to get attention. KEVIN stated skeptically that

---

*A Yiddish word meaning bewildered and lost.

he could not find any marked differentiation among the birth-order groups. DAWN mused sadly that she had ended up in the Workshop because she had been an only child, for otherwise, she wouldn't have been so alone. The leader noted that the onlies were the only subgroup still sitting together. He recalled that they had said earlier that they always looked for companionship.

IDA thought each person was in the Workshop because they wanted to take stock of themselves and that this didn't have too much to do with birth order. ROSALIE observed that she had the same protective feelings toward the group as she had toward her family. SHERMAN noted that, like ROSALIE, he too wanted to take care of others and yet he was a youngest. KEVIN wondered whether this birth-order discussion was justifying his actions or explaining them. The leader replied that it was up to him to decide how to use whatever understanding he derived. JEAN doubted that it was fair to assume that the birth-order position was one's primary problem. The leader again asserted that birth order was only one of many factors that influenced development.

Commentary. There was more person-to-person contact and sense of group belonging in this session than in any previous one. The leader's sympathetic understanding of the group's plight in the fourth session, and the fact that in this session there was far more leader management and giving of information than had been previously the case, apparently effectively reunited the group and elevated its morale.

Although the tenor of this session indicated that the crisis of the fourth meeting had been safely passed, the hard core of resistance that remained was dramatically expressed by DINAH who shifted the entire group's attention from the birth-order discussion and in effect expostulated, "Sibling schmibling, what am I getting out of this?" Here was a crucial moment, indeed. Would she be able to recruit other members to her banner, or would the group pass her by? As the reader knows, the group allied itself staunchly with the leader. LARRY especially made a telling point when he said that in getting answers the group would be confirming the very attitudes of overdependence that they needed to overcome. The group seemed to be accepting the Workshop situation with its limitations more realistically. Perhaps in this session, in which they were getting something in the way of didactic answers, they were beginning to feel that some tangible benefit might be in store for them were they to cooperate with the leader, and so they would have no part of DINAH's upsetting the apple cart.

Incidentally, it was after this session that the leader discussed with the observers some of his reactions to being observed. Up until now, it had been the custom, immediately after each session, for him to confer with the observers. At these conferences, the observers criticized or raised questions about this or that action by the leader. Intellectually, the leader welcomed these evaluative discussions, but at the same time, he found that the observers' comments added to an already existing anxiety about doing well. Instead of being able to lead the group with a sense of freedom and spontaneity, he felt from time to time like a self-conscious centipede watching its own legs. When the leader shared these feelings with the other staff members, a significant clearing of the air resulted. In the sessions which followed, the leader's tension was sharply reduced, and he was much more his old self, though perhaps never quite as free as he felt in Workships where he had not been observed.

Session Six

Summary. In this session the leader, without any conscious rationale other than a feeling that the group was now ready for it, aimed at centering the members' attention on their tendency to externalize blame onto other for difficulties to which they themselves contributed. He opened the session with various anecdotes illustrating this tendency, some from his own life. Several members responded with experiences in which their own venality allowed them to be victimized by others with equally venal intent. BELLE then declared that she used to blame mother for many of her feelings but, realizing in the previous session that her childhood experiences were better than those of others in the group, she has come to believe that "... some of these things that I feel may be just coming from me. ..."

The leader next showed the last scene of the film, "Learning to Understand Children: Part I." The teacher of Ada Adams, a self-conscious adolescent, is seen visiting Ada's home and listening sympathetically to Ada's mother's recital of her troubles. The leader stopped the film at the end of this scene and stimulated the group to explore what they had noticed about their own listening to each other in the Workshop. At one point in this discussion, KEVIN made the impersonal generalization that how members listened to each other depended on how preoccupied they were with their own problems. With the intent of involving KEVIN in a more personalized way, the leader, with provocative suddenness, said, "Let's talk about Kevin. What about Kevin?" KEVIN replied, ". . . Where I feel that the comments might run parallel, or have a particular interest to me, my ears perk up, and the radar goes out. . . ."

At this point, ROSALIE took the opportunity to express her resentment at KEVIN's previous week's remark that the group was "fahblondget." She thought he was trying to prove to himself that the Workshop was "all for naught." The leader asked if others had a feeling like this. DINAH declared, "We all feel that KEVIN feels he is too much above everyone of us here whenever he talks." ROXANNE defended KEVIN. His terminology might not appeal to the others, but anyone who came for help could hardly have a feeling of superiority. JEAN saw KEVIN as a challenge. BELLE, KEVIN's wife, observed how very carefully everyone seemed to be listening to KEVIN. The leader pointed out how differently members reacted to KEVIN, and wondered what might make for these differences. MABEL admitted that she was reacting to her own feelings of inferiority.

The leader asked KEVIN if he had been aware of these different feelings toward him. He replied that he had not been, but that he didn't mean to sound superior, and he couldn't help his language. The leader suggested that KEVIN's way of speaking may have developed as a means of getting acceptance from his family. PEGGY confided that her first reaction to KEVIN was that he talked "like a man," but later, she realized that this was just his way of talking. ETTA stated that in her youth she used her vocabulary to display superiority, but people's antagonism

brought her vocabulary level down. This touched off a denial on
ROSALIE's part that she resented KEVIN. On the contrary, she
envied his guts to speak out against people. The leader told the
group that he was very glad they had talked this out.

SALLY wondered whether it was fair to discuss KEVIN without having asked him for permission. Furthermore, this discussion might make other people extremely self-conscious. KEVIN
declared firmly, "It didn't bother me a bit. I'm going to keep
talking." ROXANNE suggested that people who felt resentful
against KEVIN might examine why they reacted this way. She
thought MABEL's reference to a feeling of inferiority shed a
little light. The leader endorsed ROXANNE's statement strongly.
KEVIN wondered jokingly how the group got along without him
for the two weeks he was away. There was an outburst of laughter from the group, but SHERMAN retorted sarcastically, "We
did absolutely nothing, Kevin," and the leader chimed in "It was
hard, Kevin."

Following this KEVIN incident, the film, "Learning to Understand Children: Part II," was resumed. The leader stopped the
film at the point where Ada Adams is encouraged by her class-
mate to put up her hair in a more attractive style, and she decides
to show this new hair-do to her mother. The leader then asked
the group to predict the mother's reaction. Most members, having
perceived the mother on the basis of an earlier scene in a negative
way, predicted that she would be critical, envious, or resentful.
In the following scene, contrary to the group's expectations, Ada's
mother actually, even warmly, did accept Ada's new hair-do.

The leader asked the group how it would account for its predictions being so far off the mark. Discussion centered on members' sympathetic identification with Ada and how, out of this
feeling, there emerged a wish to blame the mother and to condemn her as altogether rejecting. Some members, albeit somewhat intellectually, took this incident as an example of a general
tendency to blame others for our own failures and unhappiness.
ROXANNE felt that it was hard to be self-critical, especially
when one feels that others do an adequate job of tearing one
down. DAWN recognized her need to hold on to her feeling of
self-pity and to blame someone else. This made her feel like a

stinker. The leader suggested that maybe neither she nor the people she had been blaming were stinkers.

In the last scene of the movie, Ada Adams and her fellow students put on a class play. Parents have been invited to attend. Her mother told Ada that she had so much housework to do that she was not sure that she could come. Ada stares expectantly at the entrance to the auditorium, obviously hoping that mother would show up. At this point, the leader stopped the film and asked the group to predict whether Ada's mother would come or not. With intense feeling, the group predicted that she would, but again the movie failed to support the members' expectations. The leader wondered what might have led to the group's incorrect prediction this time. Some members recognized that their wishes for a happy ending influenced their judgments. REBECCA guessed that her wish for mother to come to see Ada was related to the fact that her own parents never came to hear her sing.

The leader asked the group what ideas they had about the vehemence with which they had shouted, "Yes. She'll come!" SALLY saw the group as a bunch of kids saying what was expected of them. DINAH thought it had to do with the way the leader asked the question. "It's my fault?" the leader challenged. The group burst out laughing. ETTA thought this showed how we act and think according to what is expected of us. PEGGY admitted that she did not think mother would come, but feared that the group would look down on her if she had said so.

The leader suggested that the group's vehemence might have reflected some annoyance on the members' part for his having trapped them. Some nervous laughter swept through the group. LARRY thought the group was being manipulated to give the wrong answers. Again the leader challenged, "It's all my fault that you gave the wrong answers?" LARRY laughingly retreated, "Well, not necessarily your fault, the picture's fault." JEAN stated that she could tell from the leader's expression that the mother was not going to come, but PEGGY recalled that the leader looked like the answer should have been "Yes."

The leader again pressed the group as to whether it was aware of feeling annoyed toward him. DINAH blurted out, "No! I mean, yes." DAWN recalled such feelings, but couldn't put them into words. SALLY denied feeling resentful. The leader then suggested that some members could not let themselves feel annoyed with him. ROSALIE and LARRY immediately stated that they could see absolutely nothing wrong with the leader. This prompted the leader to wonder whether some members protected themselves against feeling annoyed with him by putting him on a pedestal. ROXANNE stated that she distrusted him at first, but did not now see him as someone who could do no wrong.

When the leader then suggested that everyone in the group had felt annoyed with him at one time or another and that such feelings were inevitable, ROSA exploded, "That in itself is an annoying statement. . . . Why should you want to shake our trust in you?" ETTA recalled that she had been annoyed with the leader once momentarily. The leader inquired if the group could conceive of the importance of its paying attention to its feelings of annoyance. LARRY recalled that he could not say anything when his therapist repeatedly changed his fee. The leader suggested that perhaps he needed his therapist too much to let himself feel anger. SALLY said that she saw the leader simply as a human being who happened to have training for his job. The leader said that he was glad that the group had been able to come out with a lot of feelings in relation to him and to KEVIN. SALLY stated that the KEVIN situation made her fear that people might criticize her. The leader suggested that it might be useful for her to explore this fear. SALLY nodded in agreement.

Commentary. This was a wild and woolly, emotionally-stirring session with active hopping from one critical event to another, diffuse on the surface, yet with an inherent unity between the initial anecdotes illustrating the tendency to cast blame on others for our own difficulties, and the group's externalizing rationalizations for their erroneous predictions of the behavior of Ada's mother.

The KEVIN incident was an extremely critical one. For the first time, one member's personal characteristics became the focus of criticism on the part of other members. In boldly centering attention on KEVIN, the leader hoped to increase the tempo and intensity of interaction within the group and to stimulate more immediately concrete and emotional cross-communication. On the whole, we would judge that the leader's efforts misfired because they were premature and inopportune. Having been pressed to face their inadequacies and shortcomings for most of the sessions up to this point, the group had been more or less on the defensive. KEVIN, with his surface air of superiority, became an easy scapegoat for those in the group who needed someone on whom to displace their own self-dissatisfaction. Furthermore, this incident developed before there was a sufficient growth of group cohesion and mutual supportiveness. Finally, the leader, in his own anxiety to move on to the remaining agenda for the session, did not allow sufficient time to himself and to the group for making something more productive out of this event.

Granted that under certain circumstances it might be desirable to focus on a group member to this extent, one question may still be asked: Why pick on KEVIN? Was this a manifestation of countertransference on the leader's part, a way of turning the wolves onto an enemy who threatened him and whom he wanted to destroy without himself taking the responsibility for the attack? After all, it was the leader who first challenged KEVIN's intellectualized style of commenting when he suddenly said, "Let's talk about Kevin. What about Kevin?" And once ROSALIE's criticism was touched off, it was the leader who inquired whether others in the group had similar feelings.

There is no doubt that KEVIN was a dramatic figure in the group and that he had stimulated a diversity of fairly deeply felt attitudes which remained covert in the group. It may even be acknowledged that the elicitation of these attitudes was a good thing as an example of the importance of becoming aware of, and attempting to understand the reasons for, covert feelings in which significant transference attitudes are imbedded. But would it not have been better to await some action of the group which might justify this kind of focusing? And once this situation had developed, should not the leader have taken a clear-cut protective stand in relation to KEVIN, one in which he pointed out that each person in the group is obviously entitled to his own way of talking, and that members' reactions to each other's characteristics were important chiefly as further material for self-exploration?

It seems to us that the leader, in his anxiety to achieve particular effects, was too demanding and confronting. In opening the session with anecdotes illustrating the tendency to externalize, he was, in effect, telling the group, "See how you yourselves contribute to your difficulties and yet you blame others." By manipulating the members into making wrong predictions, he probably sharpened their sense of inadequacy. It must have added insult to injury for him then to ask members to explore what factors in themselves led to their incorrect predictions. This was, in effect, a request for them to again face and acknowledge openly their limitations and difficulties.

Especially toward the end of the session the leader seemed to be pressing much too hard in getting the members to acknowledge that the vehemence of their second prediction reflected their annoyance with him. After all, they had hardly gotten used to the idea of expressing their annoyance with each other, let alone towards an authority upon whom they depended so much. From the leader's point of view, this was an effort to make capital of the last prediction situation as an example of externalization expressed mainly in a shifting of blame onto him. The group, on the other hand, may have by this time experienced the whole session as one in which they were being called to task: first, for externalizing; second, for seeing others in all black or all white terms; third, for allowing themselves to be manipulated by the leader; and finally, for not acknowledging their annoyance with him out of a need to keep him perfect in conformity with their idealized authority image.

While he may have overplayed his focusing on the group's annoyance with him, this emphasis was probably not without some benefit. It broke ground in getting the group to realize that it was permissible to talk about the leader in negative terms. They would not be slapped down for doing so, and, in fact, any attitudes or feelings toward the leader were acceptable grist for the Workshop mill.

Still, it would seem worthwhile to examine the leader's own motivation in this session. For one thing, he was sensitive to the existence of a pervasive underlying conflict in aims and in orientation between himself and the group, and he evidently felt obstructed by it. He was also anxious to do well in the eyes of his observing colleagues. His reaction to the group's insistent dependency included some dimly felt irritation. In the interests partly of discharging this irritation and partly to rid himself of the irritant, he exposed the group's gullibility in the implicit hope that they would be inspired to move toward greater autonomy. Further, he had come to feel that his pressure on the group for self-confrontation had generated considerable hostility toward him which, however, had remained almost wholly unexpressed. It was his belief that further progress would be blocked until this undercover hostility was brought to the surface and in some measure resolved. His effort to do so foundered against the group's inability to experience or to acknowledge such hostility in the first place. The group's denial was so impressive that one is inclined to wonder whether the leader had not erred in projecting into the group an intensity of hostility which did not exist at *any* level, and whether such projection might not have resulted partly from the leader's own anger at himself for not being a more perfect leader.

Session Seven

Summary. Because he felt that too much had remained unresolved in the previous session, the leader set aside any preconceived notions of syllabus, and opened the session by inviting the group to give its reactions to the previous meeting, particularly its feelings about the KEVIN incident. The group divided itself sharply between those who favored members expressing openly their feelings toward each other and those who viewed such exchanges as alarming and of dubious value. JEAN thought that tearing KEVIN apart had been unfair to him. ROSALIE denied that she meant to attack him. MOLLY believed it might be helpful for others to point out things in us that we ourselves could not see. SHERMAN agreed, but added that a line should be drawn somewhere. MABEL suggested that the members explore why they were so angry at KEVIN, but the group did not seem interested in pursuing this.

The leader noted that members were uneasy about giving their personal reactions to each other, and he wondered what this uneasiness might be about. ROXANNE, JEAN, and others referred to fears of tongue-lashings, and of being exposed and torn apart. The leader recognized the existence of such fears and then half-jokingly proposed that, if they wished, they could stop this discussion, put out the lights, and find safety in watching a movie. But the group laughingly rejected this proposal and continued exploring their uneasy feelings. BETTY reflected that if one member were to be criticized she would feel that she might be next, and being criticized would make her cry. BELLE added that she would be ashamed and frightened to reveal herself, particularly her jealous feelings.

The leader asked the members if they could see any chance of the group's developing an "understanding" rather than a "tearing down" atmosphere. DAWN sensed a common bond in the group already and felt unafraid of being criticized. ROXANNE, however, could never see herself revealing her secret thoughts in a group. She received so much criticism as a child that she started to feel that everyone was out to destroy her. Furthermore, the other members were poorly qualified to give criticisms. MOLLY viewed the group's criticism as constructive rather than destructive in intent. PEGGY pointed out that people saw each other differently and would therefore give different criticisms. The leader said that some criticisms might reflect the other person's problems more than one's own. Then, feeling that the discussion had moved forward as far as it could, he suggested that the group move on to the film and that members simply note what happens henceforth in the group without prejudging what should happen.

The remainder of the session focused attention on possible relationships among early intrafamilial experiences, early school attitudes, and finally, attitudes toward fellow Workshop members and the Workshop leader in the present situation. As an initial stimulus, the leader presented the film, "Feeling of Hostility," up to the point where the central character, Claire, discouraged about winning love, resolves to gain admiration through school achievements. After stopping the film, the leader reported his own childhood feelings toward school and teachers. With much emotional involvement the members shared a wide range of satisfactions, fears, and disappointments which they had experienced in school.

The leader then asked if the members could see any relationship between the reactions they had developed toward teachers and experiences with their parents. In response the group reported a variety of ways in which school attitudes either literally reproduced attitudes toward parents and siblings, or else served as compensations or reaction-formations. For example, SHERMAN stated that he had been discouraged about competing scholastically because his brothers were so brilliant. DAWN had been as petrified of teachers as she had been of mother. MABEL recognized that her antagonistic feeling toward father carried over to all male teachers. ETTA stated that, convinced that she couldn't compete with her brothers, she became afraid of all learning situations. It suddenly occurred to JUNE that she must have become a teacher as a means of gaining approval from her family.

The leader surprised the group with his next question: Could members recognize any similarities between their past attitudes toward teachers and classmates and their present attitudes toward him and toward each other? ETTA speculated that she would probably have dropped out of the Workshop if she had felt the slightest reprimand from the leader. IDA recalled that her mother used to bring her problems to the teacher, and that would somehow make it easier for her to reveal her problems in the Workshop. For DAWN the Workshop seemed to be picking up where she left off with a high school teacher who counseled her and took a great interest in her. JUNE recalled knotting up in the first Workshop session, wondering whether the leader would approve of her. The leader stated that their feelings toward other members in the Workshop, toward the leader, and ultimately toward any therapist with whom they might be working in the future were very rich raw data whose exploration could deepen their understanding of themselves.

By the end of the session the group was quite relaxed. ETTA confided that she has been laughing more since coming to the

Workshop than she had in years. SHERMAN said that he experienced good feelings after each Workshop session though they lasted for only a few days.

Before closing the session the leader passed out paper and asked each member to write out his very earliest childhood memory. These memories were then collected by the leader so that he could review them in preparation for the following session.

Commentary. The leader, aware that the KEVIN incident had stirred up the group considerably, decided to plunge into the matter at the very outset of the session, and to bring into the open feelings which, if left unexamined, might hinder future progress. While it would have been preferable to examine the group's reactions to the incident in the very session in which it occurred, waiting a week proved to be no fatal mistake, for the group's feelings came out with apparently undiminished intensity.

The discussion of this incident brought into the open a strong, articulate subgroup which vehemently opposed any frank exchange of members' feelings toward each other. Apparently the Workshop had failed to encourage sufficiently the kind of accepting atmosphere which would have enabled more members in the group to feel not only safe about expressing their frank feelings toward each other, but even eager to do so, with a sense that the risks involved would not be too great and that unprecedented but productive experiences might develop. It seems clear that the Workshop leader needs to plan for ways of encouraging from the outset a perspective in which an interest in cause and effect, in which an accepting curiosity about one's reactions to others, and the reactions of others to oneself, prevail over the usual evaluative, moralistic, condemnatory orientation.

Certain features of the leader's approach in this situation are noteworthy. For one thing, he consistently encouraged the group to express its resistance to emotional interchange. He did not try to persuade them to overcome their resistance. Instead, he sympathetically appreciated how one's past experiences might well lead to the very kinds of fears expressed. Apart from mildly raising the question as to whether the group could conceive of moving in a more free and open direction, he seemed content to drop the discussion once opposing views had been sufficiently aired.

That this discussion, though in a sense unresolved, was nonetheless beneficial, seems indicated by what followed. There was more frank and open talking about themselves and their past experiences than had occurred heretofore. It is true that the revelations centered on self rather than on feelings about other members, and for the most part they seemed to have a sympathy-seeking quality. Nonetheless, these self-revelations seemed to reflect a relatively new move in the group, a greater willingness to confide in each other and to trust each other.

The question remains: What could the leader have done in this situation to have made it even more productive? Clearly, he missed a crucial opportunity to emphasize the projective nature of the opposing viewpoints which emerged. The emergence of two opposing factions could have become a focal point for exploration. However, instead of analyzing their own positions, members tended to fortify them. We are suggesting that the leader could have helped the group to see that the central point was not simply whether it was a good thing or a bad thing for members to express their feelings toward each other, but that different members reacted very differently to this question. The participants needed to be led, in some way, to become curious about their own reactions and to be stimulated to question themselves along such lines as the following: "What does the situation mean to me which leads me to react in my particular way?" "In what ways do my past experiences tend to point me in one direction so that it becomes difficult for me to see the possibility of another orientation?" By means of such questions the Workshop member would have still another opportunity to explore the implicitly assumed inevitability of his feelings and ways of coping with particular situations, and to appraise the productivity, in terms of personal values, of these reactions.

It needs to be noted, however, that the second half of the session did bring the group around to this main point, for example, that we have developed very individual orientations toward life which we inject into our approaches to current situations. The discussion of their attitudes toward school, how these attitudes may have related to relationships with parents on the one hand, and to their immediate relationship with the Workshop situation on the other, appeared to be a very personally involving and meaningful one. We would only suggest that the leader might have tried to link the two halves of this session by raising some such questions as, "What do you feel has happened in this session as a whole?" Or, more directly, "Do you think that what we talked about in the first part of this session might be related in some way to what we are talking about now?"

Session Eight

Summary. The preceding session emphasized that there was much to learn about oneself through exploration of childhood experiences. The present session continued the examination of this area with the First Memory Experiment. The leader returned the group's previously submitted first memories. He then gave a lecturette in which he presented some sample childhood memories and discussed with the group various clues contained in them and possible inferences to which they might point. Following this orientation, he read his own first memory to the group and only after the group gave its reactions did he reveal, much to its surprise, that the memory was his own. He confirmed the relevance and accuracy of most of the members' comments. He then asked that each member write out his interpretation of his own first memory on the reverse side of the paper on which he had previously written it.

After collecting the papers, the leader invited the group to analyze and discuss in turn a number of memories selected from among those submitted by them. In each instance the leader read to the group a member's memory without revealing the identity of the author. He then asked for the group's reactions. After the members had given their interpretations, the person's own interpretation was read, and he was given an opportunity to react further to the group's comments. Some highlights of these memory discussions follow:

JUNE's memory: "The first thing I can recall has to do with a cat. I recall having taken my mother's pair of scissors and snipping off his whiskers because they seemed too long and bristly and didn't match the rest of his fur. I remember a feeling of the family being amused about it (Age 4)." JEAN called the author of this memory "a perfectionist." REGINA speculated that the author believed people would like her if she conformed. PEGGY thought the writer wished to get rid of failings in herself. REGINA guessed that this person would be likely to trim people down to her own size. ETTA saw her as somewhat opinionated. In her written self-interpretation JUNE referred to a desire to set things right and to her tendency to turn to animals for affection.

When the leader asked JUNE for her reactions to the group's comments, she stated with some excitement that for the first time she could admit to herself that she was a perfectionist and that she did set up very high standards for herself and others. REGINA felt that June was very critical of herself. SALLY advised JUNE that, being an adult, she didn't have to accept her parents' high ideals for herself. The leader pointed out that it was not easy to reshape a whole lifetime of conditioning. ROSA said that she suddenly saw herself as a "fixer" like JUNE, and seeing this about herself "terrified" her. JUNE recalled once how she resented her child's request for help because it upset a busy, well-planned day. ETTA suggested that people stick to a rigid schedule out of a need for security. SALLY advised JUNE to become less preoccupied with herself so that she could think of her child as a human being entitled to some time from her. The leader observed that it must be difficult to focus on another person's needs when one's own have not been sufficiently met.

ROSALIE's memory: "In Europe just before we were going to the consulate for a visa or something, I remember my mother counting her children and missing one. After a little panic and search she discovered that she was holding the missing child in her arms. I also remember one of us being stung by a bee and an aunt administering first aid (Age 5½)." LARRY and REGINA noted that the author recalled the memory as if she were an outsider looking in. IAN thought she may have been ashamed of her family. SALLY suggested that the child must have been in terror about leaving for a strange country. REGINA emphasized that the child might have been more afraid that mother would lose her. LARRY wondered why it wasn't mother who gave first aid, and whether the author was the kind of person who now went around looking for help.

In her written self-interpretation ROSALIE referred to her fear of losing something close to her and of being lost herself. She told the group that its comments were very true. She never had anybody to go to for help because mother had too many people to take care of. REGINA chided ROSALIE for feeling sorry for herself, but BELLE declared that ROSALIE failed to express enough self-pity. ROSA could see how ROSALIE might have lost her identity in a very large family. ETTA sympathized with ROSALIE. It was terrible to feel that one could never get mother's attention.

ROXANNE's memory: "I remember being in my crib and receiving a bottle of orange juice. I remember clearly that it was orange juice, from someone—probably my mother. The details I remember are quite clear of the room, etc., but I don't know whether it's because of my acquaintance with the room as I grew older. At the time of the orange juice, however, I must have been around two, no more than three years old." REGINA stated that this person was saying. in effect, that her mother had never given her anything nice and soothing like milk. ETTA saw in this memory a rejection of the mother and a withdrawal from people. BELLE noticed an absence of any reference to emotion. JUNE was struck by the person's passivity and the emphasis on somebody doing something for her. ROSALIE speculated that the child might be in doubt as to whether mother cared for her or not. MABEL wondered whether the member spent a lot of time in bed as a child.

In ROXANNE's written self-interpretation she referred to having to push herself in tasks requiring self-assertion, having been restricted in her activity because of a supposed bad heart, a possible desire to escape from unpleasant aspects of life, and a mixture of fondness and feelings of contempt for mother "who is Milquetoast personified." When invited to give her reactions to the group's comments, she confirmed that she had in fact been confined to bed quite a bit for various illnesses and that mother irritated her because she was too easygoing and sweet and could not stand up for her rights. LARRY suggested that ROXANNE's irritation with mother might really reflect irritation with herself. ETTA wondered whether ROXANNE regarded her mother's passivity as a cover-up for an unwillingness to constantly be waiting on her.

MABEL's memory: "Approximate age: two or three years. Costumed and dancing on Boardwalk at South Beach Carnival and winning the Loving Cup!" JEWELL saw a wish to return to a happy period of life. ETTA inferred a need to be the center of attention. ROSA thought that physical beauty was important to the author. PEGGY speculated that this was somebody who masqueraded as somebody else. In her self-interpretation MABEL wrote: "Putting on a false face for people . . . displaying only joyful and attractive facets of myself so that they find me always amusing . . . being at the top of the heap must be more important to me than I thought." When invited to respond to the group's reactions, MABEL said she felt "too sick" to do so.

Toward the end of the meeting the leader asked the group what thoughts they had about the session. ROXANNE defensively questioned whether there were any healthy memories. Could one not take the memory of any well-adjusted person and say, "Look at this poor unhealthy girl?" MOLLY wondered whether the members needed therapy since they seemed to understand and grasp things so readily. She was struck by the strength of people's needs for recognition. ROSALIE speculated that they wanted to get affection more than they wanted to give. PEGGY suggested that perhaps one gave affection hoping to get it in return. ETTA wondered how genuine was her "great love" for father. TRUDE mused aloud as to why some people must possess someone or something. SHERMAN now questioned whether his mother really loved his father as much as he had thought. ROSALIE was concerned about the Workshop's coming to an end, and SALLY asked how many more sessions remained.

Commentary. This session was quite compact and unified. The group worked hard and soberly with much emotional involvement. It was clear that the memory procedure stimulated a great amount of curiosity, reverie, and introspection.

In many ways, this session constitutes a near-perfect paradigm of the Workshop approach. The focus on first memories emerged as a natural development out of the group's work to date. Personal involvement was encouraged through the use of pertinent personal data. The leader participated in the experiment himself by submitting his own memory for group analysis. The give-and-take involved in interpreting each other's memories fostered group interaction. Observation of dynamic forces underlying other members' experiences led in some instances to an awareness, at times with dramatic emotional impact, of similar dynamic forces underlying one's own past experience. In exploring the significance of each other's memories, members had opportunities to recognize the role of their own biasing needs and attitudes as they projected selective, sometimes arbitrary, interpretations of other participants' experiences.

Mutual acceptance and sympathetic support among the members rose to a peak in this session. This is consistent with our observation of the reactions of most previous groups in this experiment. There is something about confronting past experiences, in which, necessarily, the central character is a child, which seems to elicit greater tenderness and understanding than the members can vouchsafe each other as adults.

The leader could have capitalized more on the opportunities which this experiment provided for furthering sympathetic self-acceptance by asking such questions as the following: "What needs seem to be central here?" "What kinds of difficulties might this child have had at home in relation to his parents?" "How do you think he tried to cope with these difficulties?" "What might the child have been learning about himself and other people in this experience?" By means of such questions, the leader might more actively use this experiment as a basis for emphasizing universal needs and how natural it is for people to develop various self-protective devices when these needs are frustrated. Such an emphasis might have overcome the tendency of some members to respond to memories as simply pointing to a variety of traits, usually shortcomings and deficiencies, rather than in terms of the dynamic meaning of these traits as they emerged from a child's early efforts at adaptation. Thus, for example, when MABEL referred to putting on a false face for people and needing to be at the top, it might have been helpful for the leader to suggest that these may have been techniques MABEL had to develop to cope with family pressures.

It should not be too difficult to effect a transition from the early situation to the present by asking the appropriate questions. The person offering the memory can be invited to consider ways in which the needs and coping mechanisms implicit in the first memory may be characteristic of his current experiences.

Despite the generally warm, supportive atmosphere in the group, ROXANNE reacted to the session as if it were some massive attack upon her (note her question as to whether there were any healthy memories). Instead of sidestepping ROXANNE, it might have been better if the leader had met the challenge by bringing out into the open her feelings about the session. She was obviously experiencing the attempts at clarification of early developmental influences as a finger-pointing condemnation of unhealthy processes, and hence of unhealthy people. The leader might have been justified to take the opportunity for a discussion of the concepts of normality and abnormality and of his purposes in encouraging exploration of the way people are, what needs and motives activate them, and what experiences might have led them to their present situation.

Out of such a discussion there should emerge such concepts as the following: All behavior, both self-defeating and self-realizing, is motivated; implicit in all behavior are motives, purposes, values, fears; these are often in conflict with each other; none of us is as aware of these implicit elements in our behavior as we might be; it is potentially useful to clarify them as much as possible so that each individual may be free to assume responsibility for his own fate in life, and to make those choices in his behavior which offer promise of optimal self-realization. There is no question here of value judgment, of condemnatory, or even of approving attitudes on the part of the leader. His function is simply, with all sympathy for the difficulty of the process and the pain involved, to help the Workshop members achieve as high as possible a level of clarification of their implicit motives and values and purposes and fears, and of the nature and consequences of the coping mechanisms they have adopted. The leader need not wait for such incidents as ROXANNE's challenge to provide him with an opportunity for communicating such content. It would be most desirable if these notions were clearly in mind from the very first session and communicated in his behavior, in his incidental comments, as well as in the experiments.

Toward the end of the session, the members were quite clearly preoccupied with their own first memories and with applying to themselves interpretations made of other people's first memories. This was not simply an interesting experience to them. It was also an unsettling one. They began to talk about their intense needs from people and how difficult it was to get them satisfied. They expressed their concern about their relationships with people more openly and self-questioningly than ever before. Their closing comments revolved around needs for love, attention, and giving and receiving. Clearly, the first-memory technique, besides drawing attention to dynamic relationships between past and present and to enduring life-style consistencies, had the effect of making manifest the group's intense dependency needs.

It is significant that this was only the eighth session, and already a number of members began to express anxieties over the all-too-imminent termination of the Workshop. This was of particular interest since only a few sessions earlier there had been a general expression of frustration and depression. Apparently, some dependence on the Workshop was developing. In the last two sessions, important personal problems had been touched upon. Communication had opened up. They had gotten a fleeting view of new perspectives, and they were beginning to fear that the Workshop experience might end before they had gotten all that they needed.

Session Nine

Summary. The central topic for this session was childhood hostility, its repression, and the corrosive guilt it generates. The leader felt that the group was prepared for this significant area by the previous session with its emphasis on the importance of childhood experience, by the hostility experienced in conjunction with the KEVIN incident, and by the earlier depression and hostility in reaction to the Workshop's failure to gratify dependency needs. Furthermore, by this time, the group had become considerably consolidated, with the members more ready to trust each other with personal revelations.

The film, "Fears of Children," dramatizing what develops when parents fail to accept a child's anger as a natural part of his growing up, was presented. The leader first set the stage in the following way: He asked two members to volunteer to play in turn the part of a parent who tries to get a five-year-old son to stop watching television and to come in to dinner. With each of the volunteers separately (PEGGY and LARRY), the leader played the part of the son who after a minute or two of irritable resistance to his "parent's" pressure burst out (quite to each "parent's" real surprise), "Oh, you rat! Why don't you drop dead and never bother me anymore!" Each "parent" reacted differently to this outburst.* PEGGY, taken aback, said, "That would make you very happy, wouldn't it?" LARRY was momentarily confused, and then, stepping out of role, said, "The book says this is the way a healthy child reacts, so I guess it is."

After the two enactments of this psychodrama, the leader asked the group for its reactions to the "child's" having said, "Drop dead." Some felt that this was a healthy reaction, some were horrified, others were embarrassed, and still others amused. PEGGY suddenly realized that she tried to make the "child" feel guilty as her father had tried to make her feel guilty. Upon the leader's inquiry, only two or three members could recall having such "drop dead" thoughts toward their own parents. In fact, most members found it difficult to believe that a five-year-old could really mean it when he said, "Drop dead."

The leader now presented the film. He stopped it following the scene in which the child, Paul, in a fit of anger at father, drowns his toy bear. The group easily recognized that he was drowning father symbolically. The leader at this point gave a five-minute lecturette on the natural development of angry, hating feelings toward one's parents, and some of the outcomes which could occur in the history of these feelings. The leader then asked the members what thoughts occurred to them as they had listened to him. ROSALIE immediately asked whether one should always

---

*One volunteer waited outside the room while the other role-played the situation.

express one's feelings right away, as they arise. The leader
promptly replied, "No, definitely not." Then ROSALIE, apparently trying to trap the leader in a contradiction, went on to ask,
"Are you saying that we should bury it anyway?" The leader
replied, "I'm not saying that either."

ROSA now could recall at age seven having strong death
wishes toward her parents. She used to hate herself for these
feelings, yet today she could see some justification. DAWN remembered sometimes wishing herself dead. The leader noted
that suicidal wishes in a child were sometimes indirect expressions
of anger against one's parents. BETTY, suddenly caught up in
an apparent wave of insight, declared: "I told my father at age
thirteen I didn't want to see him again, and a few months later
he died, and I feel as though I'm responsible." PEGGY confided
that she used to dream father was dead, though she felt very protective toward him. SHIRLEY said that when she had bad
dreams about her parents, she would call them up and find out
if the dreams were true or not. SALLY could recall saying "drop
dead" to her older brother but not to her mother. The leader
informed her that very often children found it easier to let out
anger openly onto brothers and sisters than onto parents.

SALLY wondered why she, as a child, was the only one in her
family to curse. The leader suggested that perhaps her feelings
had been so intense that just ordinary words wouldn't do; perhaps she had more intense feelings as a child than she was aware
of. MOLLY asserted that her home had always been full of vio-
lence, but that somehow or other, she could never say "drop
dead" to her mother. JEAN observed that she had expressed
herself openly as a child, yet she still had guilt feelings. What
was a happy medium, she wondered. The leader replied that this
was a hard question to answer. SHERMAN also remembered
"feelings like this," and he too felt badly about them. ROXANNE
recalled that it was drummed into her mind to respect older
people. The leader recalled similar experiences in relation to re-
specting his father. MABEL wondered whether fears that one's
parents might die could be disguised death wishes. The leader
simply replied that this was possible. The film was then resumed.

At the conclusion of the film, the leader restated its theme that angry feelings were a part of being human, and that children needed help in not feeling like monsters because of these feelings. He then asked the members to consider what kinds of parents they were to themselves. Instead of responding to this question, BELLE asked one of her own: "Suppose you are able to express feelings, and it is permitted, but you feel guilty. What do you do with the other feeling after it is expressed?" The leader side-stepped the question by suggesting that some light might be thrown on it as they went along. REGINA said she now realized that her hatred for her younger sister was really hatred for her mother whom she regarded as being too soft.

Returning to the leader's question, "What kind of parent are you to yourself?" MABEL could see that she punished herself for not being able to meet the sky-high goals she set for herself. ROXANNE observed that she was four different kinds of parents to herself, pushing, guilty, submissive, and inadequate. JEAN was aware of her difficulty in breaking away from being the kind of parent her mother was. REGINA noted that at times she was a critical parent to herself, and at times she was amused to find herself being like her own mother. PEGGY wondered whether her striving to be an individual could be related to her own mother's not being an individual, but just a mother. LARRY speculated that one part of him was like his critical father, and another part of him like his overindulgent mother.

The leader asked the members if they had any ideas as to why this question, "What kind of parent are you to yourself?" was a difficult one for most people to think about. REGINA declared that they could not see themselves as parents to themselves because this brought to mind that they were judging their own parents. ROXANNE realized that seeing oneself as one's own parent meant taking responsibility for oneself, and how could one then blame one's parents. ROSA agreed, "We want somebody we can blame. As parents we would have to blame ourselves." IDA recollected that her mother's death was a great shock, "I felt that even though we didn't get along, I had no one to excuse what I did . . . I felt all alone even though I'm married and have a baby . . . I think that's a process of standing on our own two feet, the loss of parents." BETTY burst out, "Mother still feels that I am her baby. I resent her telling me what to do, and I tell her I'm grown up, and yet my biggest failing is that I know I lean on her."

At the end of the session the leader asked the group to bring in balloons for an experiment in the next session. ROSA interrupted him to ask whether the picture they had of themselves had been put there by their parents, and if it had been a worthless picture, then was it not disloyal now to think of themselves as worthwhile. The leader replied that this was a difficult question whose answer took time to achieve.

Commentary. The readiness of the group for this session was shown especially in the plethora of childhood recollections and the self-application which the psychodrama and the film stimulated. Particularly noteworthy was the courage with which intimate data were shared with the group and interpreted. The fact that they were able to discuss actively and productively feelings of anger and hate, and even death wishes in relation to their own parents, and that some members came face to face with the extreme difficulty of working out conflicts concerning their own identity, suggests that either the group's capacity for tolerating intense anxiety was far greater than one might ordinarily expect, or that defenses were automatically set into motion as traumatic material arose, somehow restricting the level of anxiety within tolerable limits. This session underscores a growing conviction in us, namely, that future Workshop leaders need to be reassured and warned that they ought not to sell their prospective Workshop members short with respect to their capacity to tolerate anxiety or to their capacity for automatically bringing into tolerable balance the intensity of threat and the level of defense.

When a leader succeeds in getting a group this far in talking about their parents, he ought to be aware that inevitably members will be stirred to intense reactions, and before the session ends he should explore with them how they have felt about having talked so frankly about their mothers and fathers. Indeed, at the very end of this session, ROSA guiltily wondered about being disloyal to her parents. The leader might have profitably left more time for bringing to the surface any other unexpressed feelings which might have been generated in the group by the open expression of hostile attitudes toward parents. As a matter of fact, what is involved here may be stated as a general principle: Whenever Workshop members have been stimulated to express private, particularly hitherto unrecognized negative feelings towards one or another significant person, opportunity must be given for expression of any associated feelings of guilt.

In rereading the text of this session, we found ourselves reacting with vague feelings of discontent whenever some knotty question posed by a Workshop member was put off by the leader with some such statement as, "This is a difficult question to answer," or, "As the Workshop progresses, I hope that you will come to some clarification of this question." If the leader really had no answer in these instances, and it may well have been that there was no generally applicable answer, the better part of valor would have been simply to say, "I just don't know."

On the other hand, some questions deserve more detailed handling. ROSALIE's question concerning the propriety of giving expression to feelings immediately on their being experienced is important since it raised the issue of acting out which is bound to come up in every Workshop. The leader might have acknowledged that uninhibited expression of feelings can be harmful and gone on to discuss the issue in accordance with points on page 23.

In response to BELLE's question about what one does with guilt feelings which emerge after one has expressed angry feelings, the leader might have said, "Belle, in such a situation, it seems to me that you have to decide whether your anger was appropriate or not. If you feel that your anger was appropriate and should have been expressed, then the *guilt feelings* that you had afterwards could become a subject for further exploration. On the other hand, if you feel that your guilt was warranted, that the angry outburst was not appropriate, that your parents did not warrant this much anger, then your *anger* becomes something for you to explore."

The leader's use of the challenge, "What kind of parent are you to yourself?", was an interesting attempt to relate members' self-attitudes to the attitudes their parents had toward them, and to concretize the concepts of identification and superego. ROX-

ANNE's statement, that seeing oneself as one's own parent means taking responsibility for oneself and also giving up a basis for blaming one's parents, presented the leader with an excellent opportunity to explore the meaning of taking responsibility, and the difficulties involved in doing so. At some appropriate point he might have thrown out such questions as the following: What does taking responsibility for your life mean to you? Do you find it easier to take responsibility for yourself more at some times than at others? What makes for the difference? What do you think it means to take responsibility for yourself in this Workshop?

Session Ten

Summary. As requested, members brought in balloons and were clearly in a playful, expectant mood. The leader briefly introduced the Balloons Experiment as still another procedure for stimulating the members' curiosity about themselves. He asked the members how they had gone about getting their balloons. BELLE reported that she had not brought a balloon because she had forgotten the assignment. JUNE, on the other hand, had brought an extra balloon for just such an eventuality. The act of buying balloons made JEAN feel ridiculous, but "tickled" ETTA. ROSA related that she had offered to buy balloons for PEGGY and felt hurt when PEGGY preferred to buy her own package. PEGGY felt that she had to get her own balloon as part of her struggle to be independent. The leader pointed out the wide range of individual differences around the simple act of obtaining a balloon and suggested that these differences reflected significant needs, wishes, and conflicts.

Now the leader asked the members to blow up their balloons as far as they wished, to tie a knot at the end, and to observe what they experienced as they went about this task. After completing the assignment, some members reported feeling good that the task had proved easier than anticipated. Some had feared that they would be inadequate to the task, while others had feared they would go too far and break the balloon. The leader then asked the participants if they could see any parallel between what they had experienced as they blew up their balloons and their experiences outside the Workshop. PEGGY recognized that it was typical of her to feel surprised when a task proved easier for her than she had anticipated. JEAN admitted that her reaction to the balloon task, that of trying hard to do it and then getting disgusted when it didn't work out, was a familiar one for her.

The leader requested the members to rub their blown-up balloons gently against their cheeks, keeping their eyes closed as they did so, and allowing some image to pop into mind. After a silent minute or two of preoccupation with this task, MABEL said she thought of a fur coat. ROSA saw a velvet curtain that she was holding onto. SHERMAN could only experience a numb feeling. The leader, who had joined the group in this task, confided that the balloon against his cheek reminded him of a soft woman's breast. For JEAN, it brought to mind the act of rubbing her face against her infant son's. JUNE recalled the way her father used to rub his cheek against hers. Though PEGGY found this task distasteful, she nonetheless thought of love and of something soft.

The leader wondered what these various images might mean. SHERMAN related his numb feeling to something which eased pain. The leader suggested that he might want to escape feelings that hurt a lot. DAWN announced that her face still felt irritated. The leader offered the thought that perhaps somebody coming close to her was irritating, to which DAWN blurted out, "My mother!" REGINA at first felt that she wouldn't get any image and that the task was all nonsense, but to her surprise, especially since she didn't like cats, she saw a picture of a pretty pussycat. IDA failed to get an image but kept rubbing and thinking, "Where is it? Where is it? The leader commented that perhaps this was like a child asking, "Where is that meaningful contact that I need?" ROXANNE thought of kittens, and went on to suggest that the reported images of fur coats, kittens, soft cheeks, and velvet express desires for comfort, warmth, and safety.

The leader wondered what might be reflected in the fact that some images involved human beings, and others did not. ROSA announced that her balloon was beginning to seem so significant that she was becoming frightened of it. JUNE recalled that it was father rather than mother who was always her solace. ROXANNE said bitterly that she used to like dogs when she was young because unlike humans they did not give with one hand and slap with the other.

The leader now instructed the members to make noises with their balloons in any way they wished and to notice what these noises reminded them of. For a minute or two, a minor bedlam broke out in the group as balloons were slapped, punched, and scraped. The noise reminded SHERMAN of his childhood home. This brought to mind how much he always looked for quiet, and this, in turn, he related to his earlier sensation of numbness. IDA heard radio static. ETTA, a queaky door and footsteps. REGINA, a motorcycle backfiring. ROXANNE, a Japanese gong. The leader stated that his noise sounded like someone trying to clear his throat.

The group then discussed what personal meanings these sounds might have. ETTA wondered whether her creaky door and footsteps indicated that she was more fearful than she could admit to herself. Interpreting his own sound, the leader confided that he had a cold and, not feeling too well, he was conscious of needing to overcome a wish to withdraw. He suggested that members might find it useful in therapy to be as receptive there as they were being here to whatever thoughts, images, and feelings popped into mind.

Upon the leader's inquiry, a number of members confessed already having had the urge to break their balloons, while others denied having had such wishes. ROSALIE said she would like to make the balloon suffer, while SHERMAN asserted that he would simply like to get rid of it. BELLE stated that the balloon gave her a specific, vivid impression which annoyed her and also made her want to get rid of it as quickly as possible. When invited to share this impression with the group, she refused to do so. Though she could not admit this before, PEGGY now confided that the sound reminded her of something sexual. DAWN reported that she preferred to hurt herself rather than the balloon, and that similar feelings existed in her relationship to mother. IDA ashamedly confessed that she didn't feel like breaking the balloon because it reminded her of a woman's breast, and she wished to play with it. She added that she couldn't understand why she felt a little ashamed. The leader suggested that it was hard to overcome what one had been taught about sex.

The leader now invited the group to break their balloons in any way they wished, and to observe themselves as they did so. SALLY reported that she preferred to step on the balloon rather than to break it with her hands. When it broke by itself, however, she found herself relieved not to have been "an instrument in its destruction." At first, ROSALIE found satisfaction in breaking the balloon, but then was sorry: "In real life, too, I'll yell and do something, and after it's over, I'm sorry." ROSA wondered whether this task reflected different ways of handling hostility. IDA, who had hidden the balloon under her chair, wondered whether this reflected a tendency to avoid openly hostile acts. When REGINA suddenly realized that she was breaking the balloon with her hands, she promptly sat on it. The leader suggested that perhaps this was like sitting on one's anger.

The leader next presented the film, "Aggression and Destruction Games: Balloons," which portrays how the contrasting personalities of two children are reflected in their style of breaking balloons. At the conclusion of the film, JEAN said that she had felt like helping the boy break the balloons. IDA, on the other hand, asserted that she would have been angry at the boy had he been breaking the balloons in her house. MABEL enjoyed the balloon destruction so much that she wondered whether she had more anger in herself than she was aware of.

The leader invited the members to throw out any questions or thoughts about themselves that had been stimulated by the experiment. IDA stated that she had felt like running out of the room to break the balloon. This reminded ROXANNE of letting one's anger out in private. ROXANNE then added that her own failure to break the balloon reminded her of her tendency to build up resentment inside until it exploded, much to the offending party's surprise. DAWN wondered why she was still tearing the balloon shreds apart. JEAN suggested that this could be an extension of DAWN's feeling about mother. ROSALIE wondered whether DAWN felt that she had been broken into little pieces, and was now getting back at the balloon.

PEGGY felt that sex was involved in this experiment, but she would not be the only one to talk about it. This prompted IDA to confide that although she was brought up to view sex as shameful, she could not understand why she felt completely different about it with her husband. LARRY wondered if PEGGY might not be experiencing some feeling of inadequacy in relation to sex. JEAN suggested that PEGGY might have unsatisfied needs for love. The leader invited PEGGY to respond to these conjectures, but she preferred not to lest her reactions become "too involved."

Holding the balloon in her hands gave ROSA a feeling of power as if she were holding the globe. She added that she experienced pride in being able to break the balloon easily, and that she was able to do it with ease because the leader had given his permission. The leader suggested that ROSA's feelings of power might be related to past feelings of weakness and helplessness. She responded, "I had been kept from what I would have chosen to do as a child so long, that maybe I don't know at this point what I would do without getting anyone's permission."

The leader asked the members for their thoughts about themselves, each other, or him. JEAN felt that the group was getting closer. IDA felt the members made a lot of keen observations about each other. She added that she was shocked and surprised by some of the things that she had done and would think them over more. MABEL reported that she was holding back, and she sensed that the group was too. SHERMAN complained that he always had a feeling that he would be misunderstood. He added that the last three sessions had been "very low down" for him and that he might be recreating a problem that had taken him a long time to overcome. LARRY noted that he, too, had been closing up more and more in the last few sessions, perhaps because they had touched on something which he didn't want exposed to the whole group.

ETTA admitted that she had been considering dropping out of the group: "I felt that I was digging too much. . . . I picked up the rock, and now I am seeing everything underneath it." MABEL felt that the group was approaching a great big door which had to be opened, and they were afraid to do so. DAWN said she was shaking like a leaf because she feared getting to feel so close to everyone that she would reveal her problems here.

JUNE feared what she would find if she searched herself more deeply.

The leader suggested that the group was going through a phase which every group goes through, one in which they feel both a wish to get closer to themselves and to each other, and a fear that they will. DAWN expressed some anxiety about the number of sessions remaining. ETTA declared that she felt guilty about betraying her parents when she talked too much about them. IDA announced that she had been getting a great deal out of the Workshop. She was beginning to enjoy life and could see positive changes at home. SHERMAN thought that he might be closing up because the Workshop was coming to a close. ROSALIE asserted that she didn't want everybody to know her secrets. The leader closed the session with the statement that the feelings they had been expressing were very important and worth exploring further.

Commentary. This session constituted the first instance of the application of a motoric technique, and it was indeed an impressive experience. Never before had there been in this group more emotional involvement and crackling tension, such a sense of provocative stimulation, and so swift a flow of currents and crosscurrents. One significant event followed on the heels of another with breath-taking rapidity. No previous session was so fraught with the feeling of revelation. From the very beginning of the session, there developed an ever-increasing readiness to communicate personal reactions even though each member must have been aware that such communications would expose him to the analytical and perhaps critical attention of the other members.

A number of factors seemed to have contributed to the stirring quality of the session. For one thing, the very novelty of the activity virtually guaranteed a wide diversity of individual reactions, and the group by this time had learned to use such reactions as starting points for self-exploration. Involvement in the doing of specific motoric tasks served to emphasize feelings and impulses hitherto so covert as often to be beyond awareness. The members caught themselves, so to speak, in the act, and found themselves face to face with unsuspected commitments from which, particularly because of the public staging of the experience, there was no escape. Another consideration has to do with the fact that the balloon experience aroused sensuous, sexual, and aggressive feelings and impulses in rather dramatically direct ways. It is at least open to question whether motoric techniques such as the Balloons Experiment could have quite so emphatic an impact if they did not evoke so directly and dramatically drives which are regularly implicated in neurotic difficulties.

This experiment's vigorous approach to significant material evidently aroused dependency needs and an acute need for reassurance. The urge to let go and to surrender more completely was strong, but the members' fears were even greater. Their fears had to do with uncertainty as to how far fellow Workshop members could be trusted, and particularly with doubt that the Workshop, by its very structure, and the leader by the limitation of his function, could supply the necessary reassurance. MABEL's comment was pertinent: "We are approaching a big door that has to be opened, and we are afraid." Other members acknowledged the temptation to explore further, but ruefully, and perhaps chidingly, called attention to the impending termination of the Workshop. What good would it do to stir up problems, however uneasily they lay concealed behind unsatisfying defenses, if the Workshop's termination were to leave them in a state of dreadful irresolution?

One could raise a question as to the timing of the Balloons Experiment. Given the intensity of the impact it is capable of stirring up, an intensity which should be preserved and not diminished, should this experiment not have come at a later point, one which was closer to their entrance into therapy? It is interesting to note that the Balloons Experiment in the second Workshop, though it was equally effective in stimulating Workshop members to confront some of the covert essentials of their problems, did not arouse anywhere near the same degree of intense anxiety and explicit fears of being left stranded. Obviously, then, there are no properties inherent in the balloon technique itself which invariably lead to the kinds of fears and anxieties expressed in this session. The total Workshop experience up to this point needs to be taken into account if we are to understand better why this particular group's reactions were so intense.

It seems to us that the Balloons Experiment continued a trend that we have seen more or less throughout the Workshop. Members were becoming aware of symptoms (tendencies to comply, difficulties in getting close to people, and the like) before they were able to cope with the associated shame and guilt. They had not yet developed a sufficient appreciation that childhood events made it necessary to develop this or that neurotic behavior pattern, either as a means of self-protection or as a means of obtaining some degree of need satisfaction, however partial or compromising.

Consistent with the foregoing, it would have been useful for the leader, in addition to having drawn the group's attention to individual differences in their ways of responding to this or that balloon task, to have stimulated exploration of how these differences might have related to earlier family histories. For example, those who forgot to bring the balloon might have been queried as to whether they sometimes forgot to do what mother asked them to, and whether this forgetting might not have been a part of a struggle between parent and child. The leader might have asked ROSA whether her hurt at PEGGY's buying her own balloons might have related in some way to past efforts on her part to do things for her parents as a means of winning them, and failing there too. When IDA wondered whether her hiding her balloon under her chair might reflect tendencies to suppress open acts of hostility, the leader might have raised as a possibility to be explored that she might have felt that such open acts would be too dangerous to commit in her family. By raising such questions as these, the leader might have helped members to link their current responses to pertinent recollections of past experience, and thus avoid or work through some of the anxiety that was precipitated.

It strikes us as interesting that in a Workshop devoted to the discovery of one's identity so little ordinarily comes up in relation to sex. The topic rarely comes up on the initiative of Workshop members. When it does, the Workshop leader needs to be prepared with some productive way of coping with it, guiding himself by the readiness of the group to participate while remaining sensitive to the very traumatic potential this subject might have for some members. However, we hardly think that the traumatic threat is so great that, if a substantial number showed a readiness to discuss the topic, they need to be inhibited by the leader. In this session when the subject came up, the leader might have said, "Yes, I'm sure that many of you have seen breasts and nipples and penises and whatnot in the way of sexual things in these balloons. All groups do. And it certainly would be useful to explore how we feel about our bodies and about various things having to do with our sexual relationships."

Session Eleven

Summary. The leader opened the meeting by declaring that it would be useful for the members to discuss what had happened in the previous session, particularly the uneasy feelings they had expressed at the end. ROSA promptly took this opportunity to complain to the leader that he had not helped PEGGY face the truth about herself with reference to PEGGY's refusal to accept ROSA's offer of balloons. REGINA speculated that ROSA had been responding more to her own need than to PEGGY's in wanting to get PEGGY's balloon for her. JEAN and MABEL objected to the notion that the leader was there to say who is right and who is wrong.

The leader suggested to ROSA that she may have unwittingly contributed to the painful outcome of the situation. He continued with a reference to her need to give, but ROSA interrupted him with a question as to whether one friend helping another wasn't simply an act of friendship. The leader did not reply. ROSALIE felt that a person should feel free to reject an invitation. REBECCA, on the other hand, believed that PEGGY should have accepted the balloon. At this point the leader blurted out, "I don't think so." MABEL suggested that ROSA focus on herself and not on PEGGY. TRUDE noted that she herself gave to others in order to keep friends and hinted that ROSA might be like her in this respect. BELLE could see how PEGGY's need for independence might have been so strong as to make it difficult for her to accept. ROSA angrily asserted that it was insincere of PEGGY to have said, "I'm going in to get a pack of cigarettes," instead of,

"I don't want it." PEGGY admitted that she should have simply said that she would rather buy her own, and was at a loss to explain why she didn't.

ROXANNE stated that this situation was more complex than it appeared and that, therefore, it was not fair for ROSA to throw it in their laps and to ask them who was right and who was wrong. The leader commented that this was less a matter of who was right or wrong and more a situation in which compelling needs on the part of each person were clashing with each other. He added that each person could most usefully deal with this situation by trying to understand her own compelling needs.

The leader later suggested that this discussion might have a bearing on why people in the group were fearful of getting closer to themselves or to each other. ROSALIE wondered whether they were afraid to trust each other. ROXANNE stated that they were afraid to reveal themselves to themselves lest they dislike what they find. How then could they expose themselves to strangers who certainly wouldn't like them? JEAN didn't think that the members harbored such terrible things within themselves: "It's only a chain of events that have taken place since childhood." ROSALIE announced that she suddenly saw a possible relationship between her current distrust of people and her not being able to confide in her parents.

The leader asked the members if they could see any relationship between their experiences in the Workshop and past experiences with their families. REGINA confided that sometimes she felt friendly toward the group, but that on other occasions she felt that she had to swim out ahead of the others. The leader suggested that she may have had similar feelings in relation to her family. ROSALIE was startled and dismayed by her contradictory feelings toward her parents, loving them so much on the one hand, and yet having negative feelings on the other. The leader commented that such mixed feelings are part of being a human being. REGINA observed how differently members reacted to the Workshop, some friendly, and some fighting it. The leader suggested that members, without being aware of it, might be reliving some of the central problems of their lives within this very Workshop group.

ROSALIE remarked sadly that she would miss the other members when the group broke up. This comment prompted the leader to suggest that a majority of the group had experienced painful separation from their parents in childhood and that these earlier experiences around separation may be playing their part here and now. BELLE asked the leader if he meant that each person saw the group as his own family. The leader replied that her experiences in the family must in some way be influencing how she was behaving in the group. This was difficult for BELLE to grasp. The leader asked BELLE if, in the interest of making his point a little clearer, she would give him permission to bring up what she had written to him in her letters. BELLE gave her assent. The leader then told the group that BELLE had been resistant at various points to going along with what everybody else was doing, and that she had been exploring her resistant feelings in her letters. He speculated that BELLE, in her earliest childhood experiences, may have felt forced to do things that she had not wanted to do and that she might now be experiencing the Workshop again as a situation in which she was being forced to comply.

This very simple speculation about BELLE's attitudes and their origins obviously struck home. It was followed by a long, thoughtful silence on the part of the group. JEAN, the first to break the silence, wondered if a distrust of others could come from a feeling that one's parents, though they loved you, would not understand you if you came to them with your problems. The leader commented that the family was the only world a child knew and was the first place that one learned about life and about oneself. SALLY wondered whether her tendency to avoid judging other members in the group could relate to her experiences with mother who always turned the other cheek and always tried to be understanding. Again the group fell into a long and thoughtful silence. ROSA suggested that SALLY's mother had guilt feelings and was, therefore, always doing good in the eyes of God. She went on to speculate that SALLY had adopted her mother's attitude and was now afraid to have any spirit and to assert her needs.

TRUDE related her fears of speaking up in the group to her experiences with her dominating father. DAWN noted that she had been very free in the group despite having been taught to distrust everybody, but then she reminded herself that she had fought against the family teachings. IDA reported that TRUDE's talking about her father reminded her of her own mother and brought tears to her eyes. The leader wondered if others, too, had experienced needing somebody desperately, at the same time being frustrated and hurt and angry with this person, yet not being able to fight back or break off. MABEL declared that her relationship to her mother was like this, but she now felt that the situation was caused less by her mother and more by her own inadequacy. SHERMAN stated that if he were TRUDE he would become independent of father by getting a job. The leader suggested that perhaps part of TRUDE's difficulty in breaking away from home had to do with a wish on her part not to break away. MABEL noted that she could not make herself leave mother. TRUDE recalled being afraid to leave home.

The leader asked for any last comments. DAWN declared that her feelings toward the Workshop group were similar to those she had had in the past toward other groups, namely, that the group would not accept her. ROSALIE pointed out, "You said your mother and father said, 'Don't trust anyone in the whole world,' and you said you didn't listen to them, but you did. Right now, that's what *you're* saying." Several other members made sympathetic comments to DAWN.

Commentary. After the balloon session, the leader was in some conflict as to what to do in Session Eleven. On the one hand, he felt that unresolved feelings had piled up at the end of Session Ten which the group could usefully continue to air and explore. Many members had apparently been stirred up to the point of opening the door on an examination of their personal problems. They were feeling intensely anxious by this development and at the same time frustrated by the structured limitations of the Workshop. On the other hand, the leader was inclined to follow his customary procedure, namely to introduce new and pertinent stimulus material, either a movie or another experiment, with full awareness on his part that a great deal had been stirred up that would not be followed through, except possibly in the letter correspondence. In part, the leader's conflict sprang from an ongoing dilemma which will probably confront each Workshop leader at one time or another, namely, how to steer a middle course between the traditionally didactic role of teacher and that of group therapist.

In abandoning the syllabus and in electing to continue discussion of the previous session, the leader moved toward the role of therapist. Yet, in maintaining the discussion on a generalized level, he stopped well short of that role. True, current personal problems did spill out toward the very end with TRUDE and DAWN, but a degree of such spillage is probably unavoidable. The leader simply encouraged the group to explore relationships between their behavior in the Workshop and past family experiences. The group responded productively as though they had, without specific help from the leader, achieved and accepted a balanced conception of the Workshop's circumscribed function.

The ROSA-PEGGY incident is an important one. Conflicts among members can be expected to break out in every Workshop. We believe that the leader should not have taken sides by blurting out, as he did in this session, his opinion that PEGGY should not have accepted the balloon. He should have attempted to turn the situation toward an examination of intrapersonal motives by intervening with a statement somewhat as follows: "Rosa, you felt that Peggy refused your help. What about this bothers you? And, Peggy, for you it was not simply the question of not accepting Rosa's help, but also your inability to reject the help in a more direct way than you did. What in you made it difficult to be more explicit about your wishes?" The leader might then have underscored some of the members' very perceptive comments about this conflict by simply adding, "It seems to me that some of the things that members have said about this argument might be important leads for Rosa and Peggy to follow up." The leader decided not to get more deeply involved in this conflict because he felt that the group's feelings about the Workshop experience to date should have top priority. Also, neither participant showed any readiness for really going into the episode in a self-analytic way.

The leader's speculation about BELLE's earliest experiences

proved to be a turning point in this session, galvanizing the whole group's attention on the significance of the past. The leader's main interest at this point was to find some way of getting the group to consider its role in the Workshop and to explore its past experiences in terms of this role. He latched on to BELLE's situation as a dramatic illustration of this main theme: "What have your main attitudes been here in the Workshop, and how do they relate to your childhood experiences?" By focusing on one person's situation, the meaning of the general principle of continuity between past and present became concretely meaningful and gave the group something they could work with.

Session Twelve

Summary. This session was devoted to the Dreaming About the Class Experiment with the general intention of introducing members to still another method and source of data for self-exploration, and more specifically, to help them become more aware of the implicit attitudes and roles being acted out in the Workshop.

At the end of the sixth session, the leader had instructed the members as follows: "Place a pencil and paper next to your bed tonight. Before going to sleep, think about this class, any aspect of this class, and make up your mind to dream about it. As soon as you wake up in the morning, jot down your dream, even if it seems to have nothing to do with the class. If you don't recall any dreams at all, try again the following night."

Those students who reported that they never dream were instructed to make up dreams about the class and clearly label them as such. Fifteen members handed in actual dreams, and one a made-up dream. These were reviewed by the leader in preparation for this session.

The leader introduced the experiment by first presenting some relatively simple dreams obtained from patients in therapy. He asked the members to try their hand at analyzing them, to consider what each dream suggested about the kind of person the dreamer was. After the group gave its reactions, he shared with them pertinent facts about the patient which led to a deeper clarification of the dream's meaning. He then presented dreams of previous groups and classes for similar analysis and discussion. At various points he indicated ways in which one could approach the interpretation of dreams and suggested how dreams could be useful in therapy.

Following this preparation, the leader returned the members' dreams and invited each participant to write out his interpretation to his own dream. He advised that any member who did not wish to have his dream read and discussed in class should note this at the top of the sheet. He emphasized that members be as open as possible to the thoughts and feelings which occurred to them as they listened to the reading of a dream, disregarding whether these thoughts and feelings seemed logical, sensible, or relevant. At the same time, he reminded the group that its speculations were, at best, guesses.

The leader started the experiment by presenting his own dream, openly acknowledging at the outset that he was the dreamer: "I dreamt that right in the middle of the session LARRY turned to me, and he asked me if I would help him on a certain matter. I told him that I was sorry, but I couldn't give him the kind of help he wanted. He burst out, 'You're just like all the others,' and he walked away angrily which made me feel very bad." DAWN speculated that LARRY, in adopting an attitude that no one can help him, does not let the leader help him in any way. ETTA declared that they all have to accept that the leader cannot tell them how to live, but that he feels pain when he sees someone struggling. ROSALIE felt that the leader was sorry that he could not give the mothering and fathering that they wanted.

The leader acknowledged the conflict between a need to please in order to be liked and a need to stand by his belief that the really useful answers to their problems would have to come from within them. SHERMAN expressed puzzlement as to why the leader could not give help, which prompted ETTA to cross-examine SHERMAN angrily about how he would teach his children to walk. BETTY pointed out that even in therapy one did not get answers. PEGGY asked the leader point-blank whether it might not be dangerous for a group not to have any answers of some sort. Would this not stop members from looking and groping? The leader replied that he felt that this was no more dangerous than anything else, and, in fact, there might be dangers in not going through this process. He added that in past Workshops, while a few members might have become discouraged, the overwhelming majority had felt that they had profited by the experience. REGINA asserted vehemently that she was like the leader in giving, giving, giving, and then feeling quite unappreciated if she were criticized: "If it doesn't agree with me, why don't I stop it? . . . And there's a problem I have to answer myself." JEAN asked the leader if it hurt him to hear people in the group say things against him. He replied that his main feeling was one of pleasure at members trusting him enough to tell him how they really felt.

The remainder of this session was devoted to the anonymous presentation in succession of several other dreams submitted by a number of members, and their interpretations. Examples of dream discussions follow.

DENISE's dream: "As Dr. ——* was returning our letters, he announced that he wanted to speak to certain people in the group individually. I was looking forward to seeing my letter, and that was all." PEGGY said that the dreamer wanted to be one of the persons that would be seen by the leader later. ROSALIE stated that the dreamer felt that other members were favored over her. BETTY saw the dreamer as one who hoped, but did not expect, that the leader would take an interest in her. In her own written comment, DENISE stated: "This dream definitely expresses my desire to be noticed and treated as an individual. The ending 'and that was all' probably expresses my insecurity and self-distrust. I am afraid to put an end to it."

The leader expressed the wish that he could help DENISE with her need to break through and get into contact with him and the group. ETTA thought that DENISE must have felt attacked in the past and that her only defense was to withdraw. IDA declared that as far as she herself was concerned, she would rather be criticized than ignored. To this, DENISE declared, "There's criticism and criticism." ROSALIE pointed out that it

*Dr. —— refers to the leader.

was DENISE who was ignoring the group rather than vice versa. DENISE recalled that she became afraid to voice her opinion ever since she encountered a high school teacher who picked on her constantly. She added that while she did not associate the leader with that teacher, she did feel that she was not important enough, nor was her need great enough, for him to single her out.

In response to a question from the leader, she acknowledged that these feelings were very similar to those she had in her own family situation. The leader then asked for her permission to relate some facts from her personal history to the group. He told the members about her parents having died when DENISE was quite young, how DENISE had to live with her sister who had her own children, and how, under such circumstances, a child might easily feel that she was not as important as the other children. The group listened intently to this account but made no comment when invited to do so.

BELLE's dream: "Some other girls and I were chosen by various means, from different places, to be in a special class under the care of a male psychiatrist. There were constant assignments on the board to be done by each of us. Either I came in late and didn't understand what was to be done, and it needed to be explained to me separately, or—and here the instructor changed to female—I couldn't find the place where the assignment was in a notebook. The teacher kept prodding me to find it, even though the other girls had already started what became a contest. She was sure I could win and kept prodding or poking me to start anyway. I was sure I couldn't do it, because I hate crosswords or competitive games (ping pong) and didn't want to enter the competition even though I felt her confidence in me. Then I saw Kevin eating from a plate of delicious looking bacon and bragging that he knew the man behind the counter in the drug store, and he gave him special service. I kept wondering what kind of a set-up this was where the girls had to get meals from a drug store instead of an inside restaurant like in an institution. When I found it was a drug store, I kept thinking of an ice cream cone."

JEAN perceived the dreamer as a person who wants to be different from other people and who lacks self-confidence. LARRY speculated that men must be very important to her.

ETTA thought that the dreamer was saying that there would need to be a lot of pulling on the leader's part before she would give out with anything. IDA speculated that the female teacher was possibly the dreamer's mother who constantly kept after her. JEAN sensed a strong desire to eat in the dreamer. The leader wondered if the drug store represented the Workshop. MABEL speculated that there was competition between the dreamer and her husband. IDA saw the dreamer as someone who needed encouragement and who had to be the best. LARRY suggested that this dream reflected her changing concept of the Workshop, in a downgrading direction. ETTA sensed a definite dragging of feet on the part of the dreamer. The leader wondered if the ice cream cone referred to the dreamer's wish to have some of the pleasures of childhood again.

In her written interpretation, BELLE stated: "This group became the earlier school atmosphere in my childhood. The female was my mother who urged me to compete with the other children. I skipped many times, and the propriety of my going ahead of my age group was never questioned by my mother. Apparently, I had some doubts about keeping up with or adjusting to the group. By the time I was in high school and was again accelerated, I did question my own desire to do so, but my mother was so disdainful of my reasons that they were quickly overruled. Inwardly, I suffered much insecurity. I was fifteen at the time of my graduation. My friends were older and behind me in school. I had to face college alone. The only reassurance was that I might show them the ropes when they got to college. Kevin's special treatment was the attention he got in class?" When invited by the leader to give her reactions to the group's comments, BELLE stated that she would rather not.

Commentary. The device of suggesting to the members that they dream on order about a particular subject, in this case the Workshop, seemed generally effective in acquainting them with the symbolic significance of dream content. This was particularly true in those instances where members did not dream specifically about the Workshop but referred to it in disguised symbolic form. The participants showed considerable perceptiveness and ingenuity in their interpretations of each other's dreams, reflecting in this what was probably some growth of psychological sophistication and some reduction in resistance to facing their own inner feelings. It is also more than likely that the interpretations offered by individual members were highly selective and, as such, in large measure projectively determined.

Again, the leader set the ball rolling by using his own dream as an example. The discussion which followed elicited a plethora of transference material in the sense that both hostile and protective attitudes toward the leader were expressed. The whole issue of what the Workshop was all about, how the leader related to the group, and what the group expected of the leader came to the surface. Future leaders should be aware of the possibility of using one or another device, such as their own first memories or dreams in order to precipitate this kind of transference material.

In PEGGY's point-blank question of the leader as to whether it would be dangerous to continue in the group without any answers, she seemed to be saying something like this: "Sure we are ready to explore, but don't expect us to explore without the assurance that we will be supported or kept in line. Give us something to hang onto." The leader might have responded more effectively in any of a half-dozen ways, but his main intent was to move on with the experiment. Had he had a strong feeling that she was expressing an attitude that was widely shared at the moment, he would have decided to drop everything and to go into a more extended discussion of what she was raising.

The leader's reassuring response to JEAN, that he was pleased at being trusted enough to be told by the members how they really felt about him, raises some interesting considerations. It certainly tended to bring the leader right into the group. The leader needs to be ready to shift flexibly from the role of the inquiring explorer to that of fellow member, albeit a fellow member with a special function in the group. His response confronted JEAN with an alternative way of looking at a situation, and challenged certain rigid expectations that she might have had. In effect, he was saying, "Look, Jean, don't assume that speaking out your feelings to another person will always hurt or trouble this other person. Sometimes, telling him how you really feel can represent a very satisfying communication of confidence."

Another leader might have felt in this situation that he could be more useful to JEAN had he elicited more of her feelings rather than sharing his own. He would have recognized that JEAN was probably asking for a reassurance from him that, despite the attack on him, he still loved them. He would have withheld reassurance in order not to evade a larger issue. It is fine to express hostile feelings toward people who will be gratified at this satisfying communication of confidence, but what about saying what one thinks as an expression of confidence in oneself?

DENISE's dream and the situation which evolved around it seem worth singling out for comment. Her dream and the interpretations of it characterized her as a long-suffering, self-effacing person. This self-image evoked a sympathetic appreciation from the group. Especially important, in view of DENISE's having grown up in an atmosphere of alienation from substitute parent figures and substitute sibling figures, was the leader's sympathetic reception of her plight. In his reaction to the dream, in his going out of his way to express interest, he flatly contradicted the dream's statement that he would ignore her. That this experience had a salutary effect on DENISE was indicated a few sessions later when she behaved in a very uncharacteristically self-assertive manner.

Session Thirteen

Summary. The leader introduced the film, "Angry Boy," dealing with the problem of hidden hostility in a child and with how, through the help of therapy, this hostility is traced back to his home life. The leader stopped the film at the end of the scene in which a therapist interviews the mother. He asked the members what their reactions would have been toward the therapist had they been in the screen mother's shoes. JUNE doubted that she would have been able to speak as openly as the screen mother did. ROSALIE thought the therapist was curt and had cut the mother short in a very brief interview. BETTY defended the therapist, stating that she had refrained from pushing the mother too fast. Had the therapist been more sympathetic, thought ETTA, the mother would have felt relief but without any incentive to change her ways. PEGGY felt like hitting the therapist for not really listening and being too blasé. ROSA saw the therapist's face as compassionate and intelligent, but ROXANNE regarded the therapist as a bit too humoring. JUNE was pleased that the interview was short and the therapist impersonal.

At the end of the movie, the leader asked the members what thoughts the film had stimulated about themselves. IDA felt less guilty and "back in the human race" when she saw the movie mother raising her voice to her child as she herself has done. ROSALIE announced that she had become more tolerant and understanding with her child since attending the Workshop. JUNE informed the group that her behavior was unchanged but that now she felt twice as guilty as she used to. This prompted BELLE to declare that this is why she wondered whether being aware helped. ROSALIE replied that awareness helped by putting you on guard and making you think twice.

PEGGY said that the discussions were fine intellectually, but that it was still difficult for them to do the right thing in a real situation. The film frightened JEAN because she recognized some of mother's traits in herself, and even though she was aware of these traits, she worried as to what harm she might do to others because of them. DAWN complained that with all this knowledge, she still could not accept anything good in her life.

The leader asked the members for any hitherto unexpressed or unfinished thoughts about the group, themselves, or himself. ROXANNE began talking about the group's shortcomings. She felt that she would not reveal herself to be judged and picked apart by the other members whose own problems made it impossible for them to judge good or bad. SHERMAN agreed with ROXANNE's point of view but believed that the group would eventually become more liberal in its judgment. ETTA speculated that there must have been a lot of people in the past who had told ROXANNE what to do and, under similar circumstances, ETTA would feel the same way. However, she added that she didn't regard the others' comments as vindictive, nor did she feel she had to accept others' criticisms uncritically.

ROXANNE replied that she did not feel that anyone in the group was vindictive, but she did feel that each member's judgments of other people were weighed down by his background. She had done some reading in psychology and was convinced that she would be able to understand her problem completely only if she arrived at these understandings herself. No one in the group could actually tell her what to do. This was a general short-coming of the group: you have a lot of people with a lot of problems, and you have to deal with all of them at once. The leader commented that others in the group probably felt as ROXANNE did and that some people probably felt quite differently, and that both factions were entitled to feel the way they did. He suggested that it would be valuable for ROXANNE to be aware that her feelings were not inevitable reactions to the situation, and that it would be useful to explore how come she had these particular feelings in this situation while other people had quite different reactions. And with this remark, he closed the session.

Commentary. An important unit in this session was the use made of the sequence in the film depicting a therapy interview between the mother and the social worker. The technique of asking the members to visualize themselves as parents in a similar situation was successful in eliciting a variety of attitudes toward therapy and therapists. There was even spontaneous recognition that individual differences of reaction reflected important personality differences among the members themselves. The leader might have highlighted this point by singling out for further examination two specific members' contrasting reactions. For example, at one point he might have said, "Did you notice that JUNE was glad that the interview was short while, in contrast, the brevity of the interview made ROSALIE mad? I wonder why ROSALIE and JUNE might feel so differently about this? What kinds of past experiences might relate to their different reactions?" The leader might have further exploited the opportunity that this situation presented by next suggesting that the members must have very different reactions toward him, as they did toward the social worker, and that these reactions too would be very important to explore.

When members were invited to tell what thoughts the movie stimulated, they responded productively. Yet, their very productivity led to the outbreak of complaints, namely, what was the use of awareness if it led only to more guilt feelings. The concept

of awareness in these members' minds seemed limited to awareness of their "bad" behavior and of failing to meet other people's
needs. Obviously, the concept of awareness in the leader's mind
was a broader one, including one's mode of being, values and
goals, relationship to self, the very human origins of their patterns
of living, and a perception of the possibility of changing.

This conflict of aims, it seems to us, confronts every mental
health educator, for, in part at least, the educator stresses one set
of values, and the population he works with another. Workshop
members in general tend to be other-directed and passive recep-
tacles and agents for conventional values, often of a competitive
and materialistic sort. The mental health educator is likely, on
the other hand, to value authenticity in self-perception and in
self-expression, and hence in the clarification of those mechanisms
which stand in the way. This major underlying discrepancy is
often an unverbalized obstacle to the leader's and the group's
efforts to communicate with each other.

ROXANNE's outburst probably expressed an attitude shared
by others in the Workshop, yet, in its intensity, she was undoubtedly in the minority. Still the leader could not help but feel a
mixture of despair and irritation, feelings which were only dimly
conscious at the moment. Should the leader have shared these
feelings with the group rather than cover them up in order to
act like an accepting leader? Should ROXANNE's outburst have
been taken as a signal for the need to structure once again the
aims of the Workshop? Should ROXANNE's intellectual arro-
gance in the service of a bitter and cynical, masochistic injustice-
collecting have been exposed? What would have been best for
ROXANNE? What would have been best for the Workshop?

After mulling this incident over, we believe it might have been
very useful for the leader to have challenged ROXANNE at this
very moment, when she was most eloquent in her resistance to
the group, in a way which might have helped to bring her up
short and, hopefully, encourage a reevaluation of what she was
unwittingly doing. The challenge might have run along the
following lines: "Roxanne, you seem to be trying to discourage
me and the group from helping you. I know it doesn't feel that
way to you, but as I listen to you saying over and over again that

this is wrong, and that is inadequate, and the members can't help, and the Workshop is limited, I keep feeling heavier and heavier, and I'm beginning to wonder if this is not the effect you are aiming at without realizing it. Is that possible? I wish you wouldn't hastily dismiss this possibility, for if there is anything to it, then we have put our finger on something of central importance in your life, that is, a need to reject the very help that you seek out."

This brings up the general point that the leader needs to feel free on appropriate occasions to challenge members, to confront them with divergent points of view, or even to share his negative feelings toward them. In the latter instance, the leader maintains a sensitivity to his subjective reactions as possible clues to the unconscious intentions of the member or group. Of course, such challenging should be used carefully and sparingly, only at very crucial moments, and especially when there are no members in the group to assume this role.

Session Fourteen

Summary. The leader broke up the group into five smaller groups. He instructed each subgroup to make a collective effort at creating a story, an imaginative fantasy about the Workshop with a title and a surprise ending, and between five and ten sentences in length. It was suggested that each group elect a chairman who would encourage everyone in his group to contribute to the story and who would write the story down as it developed. Through this experiment the leader hoped to draw the members' attention to their competitive and collaborative behavior in groups. By focusing the task on creating a fantasy, he hoped to get a picture of what the Workshop experience had meant to them to date. Also, by separating them into small groups, he intended to prepare them for the imminent separation from the Workshop and contribute a transitional experience to later group therapy.

The groups scattered to different parts of the room. The leader and the professional staff formed a sixth group and assumed the same task assigned to the others. After some twenty minutes, the leader halted the proceedings and asked all the groups to exchange their stories. Each group was then asked to write out an interpretation of the story received from one of the other groups, treating the story as if it had come from a single individual. Five minutes later all the papers were handed in, and the groups came together. The leader then read all the stories, of which two are given below, inviting the group to comment at any point.

> *A Trip to Mars:* The Workshop got together for an emergency session. We were told it was imperative to bring balloons. As our discussion commenced, we learned that there was great chaos in the planets around us. We were appointed psychological ambassadors to Mars. We blew up our balloons and took off. We landed and set up Workshop beachheads. Suddenly we found ourselves surrounded by hostile Martians. Up rose a great man on a brown horse dressed all in brown. He lifted up his hands and announced, "I am ———*, the Great Marshal of Mars." He then pointed his fingers at us and said, "Don't I know you all?"

> *Fish Tail (Tale), by Five Fish:* Thirty little fish living in the water having all the oceans, seas, rivers, and lakes as their realm are given the magic ability to change at will into a herringbone tweed carpet. This is to transport their beloved teacher and guide, Father ——— Neptune on his tours of inspection around the earth in the upper atmosphere. One day on one of his frequent sorties, Father ——— Neptune, who was a fishchiatrist, circled too low on his carpet and ran into a peculiar phenomenon that struck him a traumatic blow. Years after he discovered that this phenomenon was a mortal called in mortal terminology, "Psychiatrist." As they passed each other the Psychiatrist said to Neptune, "Good Morning." To this day Father ——— Neptune is haunted by the thought, "What did he mean by that?"

The leader asked the group what similarities and differences they noticed in these stories. ROSALIE said that everybody seemed to be looking to get away from where they were. MOLLY thought that all the members were looking for comfort and help. LARRY saw in these stories some critical skepticism of the leader,

---

*The leader's name is referred to here and in subsequent dashes in these stories.

but ROSALIE, ROSA, and IAN denied that any criticism was intended. ETTA could see antagonism toward the leader only in the Fish Tail story.

The leader asked the members what they noticed about themselves in the small group situations. IDA complained that she felt slapped down by ROSALIE when she objected to ROSALIE's taking over the group. ROSALIE defended herself by declaring that she took over the leadership from LARRY because he was haphazard, and this seemed the quickest way of getting the task over with. LARRY accused ROSALIE of taking the paper away from him. IVAN pointed out that nobody raised any objections when she did.

ROSA declared that her group's story wasn't as good as it could have been, but she didn't want to hog the show. She also observed that SHERMAN wasn't satisfied with the group's wording, yet contributed none of his own. SHERMAN, defending himself, said that he didn't even feel that he was being heard.

The leader wondered what needs might develop in us when we get in a group and what we do in relation to other members to satisfy our needs. IDA said that she didn't like the way authority was being imposed on her in the group. It felt like being slapped. The leader commented that this reminded him of IDA's relationship with her mother. IDA responded that this was her relationship with people generally. She added that she clammed up toward the end of the small-group meeting because she felt it would be futile to say anything, and this was frustrating to her because heretofore she felt that the Workshop group was one place where she could express herself freely. IAN asserted that any self-appointed boss like ROSALIE would bring on hard feelings in him.

The leader commented that members' needs differed in every group and that it would be surprising if conflicts didn't inevitably crop up. JEAN was puzzled as to why one group got along so harmoniously, and another was full of hostility. ROSALIE was surprised that DENISE who never said or did anything in class took a stand in the small group by taking over the paper very nicely and writing the analysis. DENISE explained that she simply wanted to avert group dissension. ETTA speculated that IDA was beginning to realize how important she was as a person and was not going to take being knocked flat.

BELLE said in a meaningful tone of voice that everyone was extremely polite in her group, but she did not care to elaborate this. SALLY declared that she had become aware of being a dominating person and was wondering whether she should have accepted being the leader, but she had to admit that she enjoyed the role. REGINA agreed with BELLE that there was politeness in the group, but felt that there was freedom too. She added that SALLY and she had compromised about the length of the sentences and "there was feeling there." SALLY quickly exclaimed that these feelings did not have to be bad feelings. ETTA observed that one could never get BELLE to say anything specific, even in a casual conversation.

REGINA recalled that in the beginning BELLE had asked her to lead, and she had gotten that old feeling of everything being loaded onto her back again, but she immediately recognized that this was really her own feeling. The leader commented that members must have come into the group situation with a lot of their own feelings. BELLE asserted that she did not feel it was fair to discuss her group. She would rather discuss what she did. However, when the leader expressed interest in hearing about what happened to her, she put him off with, "You probably will."

Commentary. There was something of a parlor game character about this experiment, yet it was productive in a number of ways. In the first place, the stories made up by the group offered the Workshop members yet another symbolic means of access to their underlying attitudes of helplessness and of searching for comfort and support. However much the leader may have aimed at an equalitarian relationship, the group seems far indeed from an autonomy in which they can see life without father. Except for the staff's story, there is a fairly uniform deification of the leader in the fantasies. The leader might well have focused on this aspect of the stories, once again underscoring the persistence of the transference attitudes which cast him in the role of a great father endowed with magical powers.

Though the leader recognized the rich projective implications of the stories, he deliberately chose not to press the discussion along those lines, in part because he considered that it would be more important to get at the members' interactional experiences, and in part because the group itself did not seem to catch fire around discussion of the story content. Certainly, participation in the small groups was an extremely involving experience. It provided a splendid opportunity for self-observation in respect to the role that each participant played within the small group of which he was a member.

Though the discussion brought into focus typical interpersonal roles on the part of different members, the leader chose not to focus the discussion in a way which might have crystallized useful generalizations. The members were reviewing their interpersonal roles. Although they did not resolve various issues and differences that arose, the leader's feeling was that they were experiencing something important and that their experiences in themselves had ample stimulus value for those who were inclined to engage in later mulling over.

The IDA situation, however, might have been a useful one to focus on from many different angles. IDA was apparently involved in a situation of conflict with a maternal authority figure to whom she had surrendered her autonomy, only to react with opposition and anger. The leader might have directed IDA's attention to what she was feeling at crucial moments in her relationship to ROSALIE. He might have wondered whether her reaction was typical of her life style. He might have commented, "It seems noteworthy, Ida, that you didn't fight back or talk up until too late. You let Rosalie take over at the same time that your doing so distressed you. Can it be that you welcome frustration by a dominating mother in order to escape responsibility and to keep your anger alive? I wonder."

The leader felt definitely annoyed at BELLE's hinting that there was plenty she could say if she only wanted to, but that she didn't wish to let the group in on it. It would have been desirable if the leader had felt free to express these feelings. Perhaps his feelings were partly irrational. Perhaps there are some members who would make almost anybody feel hostile. Perhaps there

are times when group members need to be challenged and confronted directly with some vigor, even irritated vigor, in order
to keep them from continuing to reinforce what they take for
granted about themselves and the Workshop. Had the leader
expressed his feelings about BELLE, he might have said something like this: "Belle, I feel myself getting annoyed with your
teasing kind of withdrawal. It strikes me that perhaps this is,
without your realizing it, exactly how you want me to react.
What do you think?"

This session, with its emphasis on role-taking in small groups,
may well have made a contribution to the growing readiness of
the members to accept group therapy. We say this even though
we recognize that conflicts were generated which were not picked
up and which were certainly not resolved in the remainder of the
session. We suspect that by this time the group members had
developed some awareness and acceptance of the fact that the
development of conflict among members is part of the sum and
substance with which they must work.

Session Fifteen

Summary. This session's experiment aimed at introducing the
members to the productive potentialities of group therapy. The
leader broke up the group into four subgroups carefully composed with the idea in mind of facilitating an optimal group experience for each member. Each subgroup was assigned to a staff
member who acted as group leader. The Workshop leader simply
instructed the members to discuss anything that they wished in
these groups. After meeting for about an hour, the subgroups
were called together by the leader who had up to this point wandered from one group to the other simply listening in without
participating.

The leader asked for the members' reactions to this experience.
JUNE, with considerable excitement, declared that she was the
focus of discussion in her group, that "the wall had been pene-
trated a little," and that many ideas had occurred to her during
this small-group meeting that she had never thought of before.
IDA asserted that she found the group more helpful, polite, and
serious with a responsible leader than when the group met on its

own in the previous session. BELLE learned that although she wanted approval from the group, she felt happier when she was more assertive. SALLY thought that BELLE's greater friendliness and relaxation this week helped to relax the rest of the group. The leader wondered how aware members were of the impact they had on each other. REGINA stated that at first when she heard that the group was going to be broken up again, her "stomach was on the floor," and she felt that she would not talk, but MABEL's and BELLE's attitudes helped to relax her.

IDA, too, at first was not going to say anything in the group, but she did. ETTA stated that while at first she thought she would sit the group out, despite herself she became interested in JUNE's problems. IVAN figured his problem was unique, but in the group he loosened up as he perceived that everyone had a problem. ROXANNE reacted typically. She was disappointed because the group had to end. It was unfair to be given just a taste of what was beginning to be such a fruitful experience. The leader responded that he could not blame her for being disappointed.

TRUDE was shocked to discover that DAWN's relationship with her mother still affected her though DAWN had not seen her mother for many years. DINAH conjectured that DAWN's longing for mother might be her chief trouble. DAWN admitted that she would like a mother to love, but not her own. SALLY suggested that DAWN might be using whatever mother did as some kind of an excuse. IDA declared that she used to blame her mother for everything, but after her mother died, she realized that she was the same miserable person as before, that it wasn't mother's fault entirely, and that she herself was partly responsible for having become the way she was.

The leader observed that they were focusing on the topic of mother and wondered whether this might be related in any way to the fact that this was the last Workshop session. JUNE felt that this must be since mother was the most important character in their lives. REGINA observed that they began by discussing their relationships in the group and then got stuck on mothers. The leader asked whether they might feel safer in talking about mothers than about what had happened among themselves in their small groups. But this comment in no way swayed the group from its intense preoccupation with parents.

ETTA confided how her feelings toward her father had undergone successive changes from feeling at first that he was God, later "a dog," and now someone to pity. She added that recognizing that mother and father had flaws was one thing, but the question still remained as to whether she was going to become any different. Turning to ETTA, REGINA stated that we don't always see other people as clearly as we might because we inject our own feeling about them. SALLY stated that she, too, understood her father a little more now. As a child, she felt that he didn't understand her, but now as an adult, she thought he might have meant well. ROSALIE declared that parents have feelings too.

Commentary. The impact of members on each other in the small groups was felt much more intimately than hitherto, with the effect that feelings of mutual identification deepened. The emergence of more intimate personal problems in the small groups developed a momentum which carried over to the group as a whole. At first glance, the cementing of identification in a more intimately involving experience would seem scarcely well calculated to help the participants taper off their Workshop commitments. Yet this very cementing paved the way for their later entrance into therapy groups composed of fellow Workshop members.*

The leader might have encouraged the group to probe more intensively into what the small-group experience meant to them. After all, being placed into a smaller group altered the usual Workshop format very radically and brought into play in the fourteenth session what happens when the "parent" is away altogether and in the fifteenth session what happens when a "foster parent" takes over. Certainly members in the group differed markedly about being assigned to a small group. For some, like REGINA, it was a terrible threat at first. It would have been worthwhile for the leader to inquire more into how the members felt about being in a small group as compared with a large group,

---

*This type of session would ordinarily be limited to Workshops in clinical settings.

about being with the people they were with, about the leader being absent, and about being with the new leader.

It is very interesting to note how typically ROXANNE reacted in this session. Everything was bad for her, and in this session it was bad because it was so good. Note that the leader responded to ROXANNE in what now had become for him a typically appeasing manner.

The latter part of this session was of special interest. Here appeared the beginnings of a new perspective in looking at parents as people in their own right and with their own problems. There was a general spirit of, "Forgive them, for they had their troubles too." It is hard to see just how this happened to develop or what led into it. It seemed almost to come out of the blue. Surely, however, there had been certain inconspicuous events in previous sessions which pointed in this direction, for example, the recognition in one session that TRUDE herself might have needs to hold onto father, or the "Angry Boy" session in which the film mother is portrayed as a person with problems of her own. It may be, too, that members received such a high degree of acceptance in their respective small groups in this session that this experience in itself enabled them to look with a similarly accepting and benign attitude toward their parents.

The leader aimed in this session to discuss the small group interplay among members as well as separation anxiety. The group, however, had its own notions of what was important, and fortunately the leader did not press his preoccupations.

CHAPTER 3

~~~~~~

THE SECOND WORKSHOP

T HIS CHAPTER is devoted to descriptive summaries and analyses of the sessions of Workshop II. In the interest of economy, these summaries focus on novel and significant variations and developments, while omitting material too similar to that already offered in the context of Workshop I.

The second Workshop represented an effort to rectify what was felt to be a deficiency in the first Workshop, namely, a too rapid pacing of challenges and confrontations. The second leader, guided by the staff analysis of the first Workshop experience, was persuaded to use an approach which was more slowly paced and which was much more closely attuned to the dependency needs of the group and their need for reassurance. From the very beginning, he very consciously operated on the assumption that an initial experience of a warm, supportive character was very necessary if Workshop members were to be spared unnecessary anxiety and won to the cause of self-examination and self-acceptance. However, in the effort to rectify what was an admitted error in the first Workshop, the pendulum may have swung too far.

Session One

Summary. The leader opened the session by asking the members what thoughts they had on their way to the Workshop. MIRANDA said that she was surprised at the intelligent appearance of the members. MIRIAM was impressed with the members' eagerness to help themselves. The leader queried the group as to what they expected would be done in the Workshop to help them. LOIS anticipated that everybody would report their problems. MIRANDA felt her problems were too personal. JOSHUA stated that he might help somebody else in the group but that group therapy was not for him. CARLA declared that she would not come if she had to tell her problems. She had expected that the group would be helped through impersonal discussions.

The leader informed the group that they would not be called upon to reveal themselves, but he wondered what frightened people about self-revelation. MIRANDA promptly denied feeling afraid. It was simply a matter of the group not being able to help as a psychiatrist could. JOSHUA said that they feared being ridiculed instead of understood. MARGIE admitted being ashamed to tell her friends about attending the Workshop. GLADYS, on the other hand, felt that she could probably talk about her problems more easily in the group than at home. MIRIAM, a member of the leader's concurrent therapy group, suggested that they feared others' disapproval were they to expose horrible feelings such as hating one's mother.

The leader agreed that many people are fearful of exposing what might be disapproved, but he expressed the belief that the group would lose much of its shame and sense of uniqueness when they came to understand the reasons for their behavior. He then pointed out that members could help themselves by relating each topic under discussion to their own lives, that they all had more assets than they gave themselves credit for, and that he himself would try to assist in whatever way he could. He also recommended that they read the book, *Personal Problems of Everyday Life*[29] as a supplement to the course.

The leader introduced the Kick-the-Dog slides with the recommendation that the members observe the slide characters' strengths as well as their faults and consider what past experiences might underlie their behavior. At one point in the discussion, the leader asked how many felt it would have been better if the slide characters had refrained from expressing their anger. MIRANDA asserted that she would like to control herself, but that she couldn't. LOUISE thought that self-contained people must be born that way. JOSHUA felt the man was justified in yelling at his wife because she was uncooperative. PAULA objected to JOSHUA's idea that it was the woman's place to take abuse from her husband. JOSHUA insisted that the wife should have kept quiet until she realized she was wrong. This prompted much group derision. JOSHUA, perhaps as much pleased as discomforted by the jeering, said that he was outnumbered.

SIBYL believed that the kind of situation presented in the slides could not happen with emotionally mature people, but MIRANDA disagreed. MIRIAM expressed the opinion that one needn't react with anger if one didn't take it as a personal attack. The leader commented that there could be appropriate times for being angry, but that when we became mad it was important to find out what made us feel this way. In this way we could learn to handle more effectively situations in which anger was inappropriate.

Commentary. By contrast with the opening session of the first Workshop, this session was less pressured in its pace and less euphoric at its conclusion. Whereas the first Workshop's opening session tended to slip from one topic to another, from slides to movies, to the group's own reactions, this meeting was much more sharply focused around a single activity, the slides, and a single theme, that of anger and its displacement. The first Workshop's session ended up in the air, without any effort on the part of the leader to pull things together. This session ended with a comment from the leader which underscored the value of using one's anger and other emotional reactions as springboards for exploration. The presence of the group therapy patients also seemed to make a substantial difference from the very first. They made their presence felt through sophisticated interpretations, somewhat paternalistic reassurances, and on occasion, the posing of psychodynamically oriented challenges to various other members.

The leader's opening questions about the group's immediate preoccupations and anticipations about the Workshop proved to be productive in eliciting the fears and anxieties about self-exposure that all members have at the outset in varying degrees. Once having brought their anxieties out into the open, the leader gave direct, straightforward reassurance. It seems very likely that the definiteness and clarity of his reassuring position helped to pave the way for the marked relaxation, degree of participation, and frequency of personal references which occurred in this session. The atmosphere that developed even permitted a very early outbreak of open conflict between JOSHUA and some female members, a conflict which all the participants seemed to take more or less in their stride. No matter what words the leader used, it seems that the most important thing that got communicated to the members was that, as far as he was concerned, "No matter what, I don't condemn. You have no need to feel ashamed."

The leader was warm and friendly and appeared quite relaxed. He listened acceptingly and limited his interventions to those required for encouraging further discussion. However, when he felt that it would be useful, especially at the beginning of the session and at the very end, he shared his viewpoints in a didactic fashion. In general, he radiated the feeling that, under his permissive, yet protective and knowledgeable wing, the participants would learn about themselves and make significant strides toward resolving their problems.

Session Two

Summary. In order to encourage a relatively unthreatened group exploration of some elementary dynamics of human relationships, the leader presented the film, "This Charming Couple." Midway through the discussion, ALLAN noted that people in the group were ready to pounce on JOSHUA whenever he spoke. GLADYS said that JOSHUA needed help even though he saw himself as being there to help everyone else. LISA thought he was a nice guy. LENA regarded his assertiveness as thought-provoking. LOIS insisted that JOSHUA needed help in his cynical attitude toward women. JOSHUA, who seemed to be enjoying the attention, said that he disagreed as a means of getting others to justify their stand, and that this helped him. GENEVA and LOIS exclaimed that here he was admitting getting help after all! The leader commented that JOSHUA was saying something important, namely, that it was difficult for him to agree. LOIS wondered whether it was necessary always to disagree in order to get help. RITA felt that JOSHUA was learning despite his difficulty in admitting that he was wrong. LOIS declared that since she loved everybody, she would love him too.

PHOEBE thought that the members of the group should be able to disagree without being jumped on. The leader said that PHOEBE's statement was worth thinking about. DOLLY expressed admiration for JOSHUA's honesty and forthrightness. The leader expressed agreement with this. He then asked the group if they shared DOLLY's opinion, and a number of members replied, "Yes, definitely." He added that sometimes a person's behavior might be motivated by factors which we need not take personally. The leader went on to state that the members should feel free to continue arguing with JOSHUA and that JOSHUA should feel free to express his opinions. LENA thought that the members objected to JOSHUA because his thoughts were so different from their thoughts, but that there really was no right or wrong. The leader agreed. He added that, in his opinion, JOSHUA liked coming to the group very much and would benefit by attending. The film was then resumed.

At the conclusion of the film LOIS asserted that she now felt sorry for Winnie, the film's heroine, rather than angry; that she now saw her as someone who as a child had to live up to too high expectations, and that in this respect she herself resembled Winnie. MIRANDA said that she now realized that her dislike for Winnie's domination was related to her irritation at her own weak father for letting her mother dominate him. PHOEBE said the film reminded her of her brother and sister-in-law, both nice people, who never quite came close to each other. The leader stated that we are all nice people but that self-defeating things drive us. He added that there was no question but that, if the two young people in the movie could learn about their self-defeating ways, they could change and become happier. Neither EFFIE nor MIRANDA could see the couple as ever really being happy together. The leader commented, "You mean unless something were done about it."

Commentary. This session continued the smooth, easy-going, emotionally involved tone of the previous one. The film proved to be extremely provocative in eliciting a fair amount of psycho-dynamically oriented speculation concerning the motivations of its protagonists. A number of participants went so far as to speculate rather freely on similarities between the film characters and themselves.

The outstanding example of interaction among the members was the incident in which JOSHUA suddenly became the center of attention, and the group divided itself into his supporters and detractors. This was a very important event. It was a kind of test case in which members discovered through their own experience (an experience, by the way, which the leader himself in no way prompted) that they could talk about each other with a fair degree of frankness and come out of such discussions unscathed. This incident clearly paved the way for later frank exchanges among the members. The leader's handling of this situation was consistent with his emphasis on the positive, and on fostering a safe, warm, harmonious group atmosphere.

Another leader, less intent on keeping threat to a minimum, might have been more open to the expression of negative as well as positive feelings toward JOSHUA and then have given the group more time to explore the possible significance of its diverse reactions. Instead of focusing the members' attention on understanding JOSHUA so that they could forgive him and not feel so hurt, he would have centered their exploration on their own part in the interaction with JOSHUA: "Why do I feel hurt? Why do I feel threatened by him when other people don't react this way?"

The leader's confident manner, his emphasis on there being no right or wrong, his buoyant optimism, seem to have been effective in making most members feel relaxed and accepted to a considerable degree. It seems important to note, however, that underlying the leader's approach was a feeling tone that strikes us as being somewhat overoptimistic. For example, he stated that there was no question but that the hero and heroine could become happier if they only learned what it was that they were doing that was self-defeating. When MIRANDA expressed doubt that this marriage could ever be happy, the leader seemed to insist on his optimistic vision when he rejoined with, "You mean unless something were done about it." Here it would have been more useful, it seems to us, to have asked, "What's on your mind, Miranda?" This would have been better than imposing a conviction that could have meaning for the members only if it arose out of their own experience, perhaps bitter experience.

Session Three

Summary. The leader, continuing his policy of easing the group into self-examination, and wishing to remain alert to any subjective obstacles that might have arisen, opened the session by asking for the members' reactions to the Workshop thus far. LOUISE complained that the leader answered her questions in her letters with still other questions. LENA declared that no one could answer one's problems but oneself. LOUISE retorted that she wouldn't be in the group if she could answer her own questions. The group laughed appreciatively. The leader agreed that members needed help but pointed out that they might be getting a kind of help from him that was different from the kind they expected. MIRANDA stated that she would love to get answers from the leader but didn't feel that the leader should give them. The leader recognized sympathetically that it was frustrating to be asked questions but felt that the members would benefit most by learning how to think for themselves.

The leader then stated that one way of learning about ourselves was to try to understand others. With this in mind, he read to the group excerpts from letters written to him by members at the end of the preceding session. In one such excerpt, the writer asserted that she always came on time to the sessions and was irritated by latecomers. The leader invited the group's reactions. MARY felt that the writer was very strict with herself and others. PHOEBE confided that she couldn't relax sufficiently to come late even when she wanted to, nor could she relaxedly accept others being late. RENEE angrily wondered who had shaped the writer's personality to be so exact. GENEVA recalled that her mother always kept appointments on time, and that now she was teaching her own children to do the same. HOPE regarded this trait as a sign of weakness in a very anxious-to-please person. The leader suggested thinking of behavior in terms of whys instead of strengths and weaknesses.

MIRANDA acknowledged the letter excerpt as her own and expressed amazement at the variety of comments. She told the group that it was true that she had been trained to be punctual, but that she had never before thought of this in such terms. While she has always been battling her mother's domination, she had to admit that mother, nonetheless, had had this influence on her. LENA declared that she could see absolutely no reason in her own background for her punctuality, especially since her father was compulsively late. The leader commented that there was no one answer to everything, but that little by little they would pick up the pieces which would make a bigger whole. RITA could see a tie-up between her own punctuality and her relationship to her sister.

In line with his intention of introducing relatively nonthreatening yet challenging material, the leader presented the film, "Choosing for Happiness." This movie tells the story of Eve, a normal, attractive college girl who finds some flaw in each boy she meets. As usual, the leader stopped the film at various points for group discussion. Some highlights of these discussions follow: MARY observed that Eve would not accept people for what they were. This prompted MARY to confide that she tried to change her husband but couldn't. LOIS observed that she resembled Eve in having to do everything herself. JOSHUA announced that the session had helped him a lot, for he now realized that he had always been trying to change the other person. He resolved to change himself from now on. EFFIE wondered why she tried so hard to change herself in order to accommodate others. SELMA thought that Eve had many fine qualities but was maladjusted. MIRANDA asserted that we all have some good in us, and the leader heartily agreed.

JAY stated that Mary's therapy (Mary was Eve's cousin in the film) had destroyed her individuality and that he feared this outcome for himself. Upon the leader's inquiry, some people agreed with JAY about this possible outcome in therapy, but others flatly disagreed. RENEE stated that she had read that one emerged from therapy the very same person, but that one saw things more clearly. EFFIE said that one's real individuality came through in therapy and that only the conflicts were eliminated. The leader

compared therapy to a process in which the crabgrass is eliminated in order to allow the good grass to grow. GENEVA announced that she had experienced a completely new feeling in
this session, the strange reaction of feeling like two people, one
person feeling the things that she needed, and the other, the
things that her husband needed.

Commentary. This was another lively, spirited session in which
the members appeared to move forward perceptibly in their trust
of the leader and of the group, in their willingness to enter into
frank and direct exchanges with each other, and in the beginnings
of analytic self-examination. Not least in importance, they
seemed to be enjoying the experience. The friendly spirit in the
group enabled the members to feel more free than they otherwise
might have been to communicate personal aspects of themselves
and to interact with each other, even to the point of occasional
expressions of irritation and disagreement.

The group's relaxed atmosphere seemed to be related to the
leader's decisive and reassuring handling of three crucial and
anxiety-laden events. In the first session, the leader dealt sympathetically with the fear of exposing oneself. In the second session,
fears of direct, frank interaction with fellow members appeared
to have been considerably allayed by the leader's protective and
supportive handling of the JOSHUA incident. In the present
session, the frustrations relating to the lack of definite answers
emerged, and was again handled in an accepting way, with an
affirmation by the leader that members would benefit most by
learning how to think for themselves. These three issues arise in
every Workshop, and leaders need to be clear in their positions
with respect to each and with respect to techniques for meeting
them.

At the outset of the session, LOUISE objected that her questions were answered by the leader with other questions, and that
if she herself knew the answers, she would never have come to
the Workshop. What is interesting is that the demand for answers
was very strikingly a limited one. Not many people joined in.
On the contrary, the leader's position that "people benefit most
by learning to think for themselves" was supported vigorously by

a number of members. Could it be that the participants, already basking in the leader's warmth, needed to deny their dependence in order to please the leader and maintain his favor? Would it not have been wise, for the sake of the camp represented by LOUISE as well as for the camp represented by MIRANDA, to have come to grips in some way with the members' unresolved wishes and conflicts, perhaps only dimly conscious in some, concerning their disposition to seek pat answers for their personal problems?

This session marked the introduction of a device not hitherto used, namely, the reading of excerpts from letters written by members to the leader. The device proved to be an excellent one. Members proved to be ready in this way to expose more intimate aspects of themselves than they might have had the courage to do orally before the group. Material of topical value, in the sense that it was concerned with members' reactions to what was going on here and now in the group, was thus readily introduced.

The incident in which JAY expressed his fear of losing his individuality in therapy is a noteworthy one. It is interesting that members who might well have shared his fear themselves hastened to reassure JAY that his worries were groundless. JAY's feeling of threat at having to give up himself as he knew himself in order to find himself is perhaps a major essence of resistance in any learning that deeply involves the self. It seems to us that the leader evaded this very significant issue by giving reassurance prematurely. JAY first needed recognition from the leader that his was an important feeling, that it was good he was aware of it, that it was not an unusual feeling, and that it was a feeling which might well be pertinent to his immediate here-and-now reaction to the Workshop. To the extent that JAY articulated what must have been implicit in the feelings of large numbers of Workshop members, to that extent would it have been important to inquire into the fears that other members had about therapy and into the possible meaning and origins of such fears in their lives. In fact, it seems axiomatic to us that any covert anxiety concerning the process of change in the Workshop ought to be encouraged to come into consciousness and to be shared by the members of the group with each other.

Session Four

Summary. The use of letter excerpts having proved to be quite productive in the previous session, the leader devoted a portion of this session to the reading of additional letters expressing significant feelings relating to the group experience. In the first letter excerpt, the writer stated that a lot was said in the group for effect and that, in his opinion, the members could progress more by thinking before commenting. MARY and MIRANDA disagreed with the writer, for they felt that spontaneous reactions were best. The leader wondered why the writer felt as he did. PHOEBE suggested that the writer distrusted others because he himself had not spoken honestly. MIRIAM thought that the person had a need to be perfect. HOPE speculated that the author was afraid of expressing feelings freely, while DOLLY believed he feared ridicule. The writer, PETER, acknowledged his letter, agreed that he sought perfection, and explained that he felt the group's comments were insincere because they were given without much thought.

In another letter excerpt, the writer expressed resentment at members whose personal "tirades" strayed from where the discussion was being led by the leader, and at the leader himself for rudely telling members to keep their oral comments short. The group almost immediately divided itself into defenders of the leader and a minority who agreed with the attack on him. MIRIAM suggested that the writer felt that the leader, as the authority, should be the one to shut people up. MARY suggested that the leader may represent the parent who had shut the writer up. The leader stated that the writer might feel that he, the leader, was the most important one in the group, and, therefore, the writer was impatient with members who did not do what the leader wanted them to do. The writer might also have the wish that the leader listen to him and not shut him up as perhaps mother did. RENEE acknowledged her letter, admitting her impatience with the group's progress, but denied feeling shut up by the leader.

The next unit was the First Names Experiment. After the members had written the names of as many other members as they could recall, they were asked to consider their approach to this task. PHOEBE said that she panicked initially, as she did when she had to introduce people to each other. MARGIE said that she didn't remember names because she kept away from people. MIRANDA observed that she remembered LENA's name up until the very moment that names were asked for. MARY did it systematically because, typically, she felt that she must do this task right.

The leader focused the group's attention on the number of names recalled. MIRANDA and HOPE reported that they remembered twenty-nine and twenty-five names, respectively, while LOIS and JOSHUA remembered but five and four names each. The leader asked for the group's reaction to these contrasting extremes. EFFIE speculated that those who remembered more names were more outgoing. SIBYL suggested that some people might simply have photographic memories. HOPE thought that her high name count might indicate that she was less preoccupied with herself than usual.

The leader wondered whether a person who remembered many names might be one who wants to please people or be well thought of. Agreeing with the leader, MARY pointed out that it was flattering to have one's name remembered. PHOEBE observed that while the other members fascinated her, she didn't remember anybody's name, whereas a politician might remember everybody's name because it was the thing to do. JOSHUA admitted that he made a lot of comments because he wanted to get himself in the limelight and to be known by everybody. MIRANDA expressed her irritation at JOSHUA for complimenting her on her looks and yet not remembering her name. EDNA declared that the extent to which she wanted a person to remember her name depended upon how much this person meant to her.

Commentary. This session moved swiftly, with many people participating in a very emotionally involved way. There was a lot of food for thought in it: feelings about the leader, feelings about each other, and a wide variety of feelings about the failure to remember or to be remembered. Worth noting is the fact that this, the fourth session, was virtually altogether free from the depression and anxiety which characterized the fourth session of the first Workshop. Either these were very different people, indeed, or the reassuring tactics and the benevolently authoritarian role adopted by the leader were having their effect.

This session is the second in which excerpts from letters written by one of their number were read back to the group for its comments. Obviously, the choice of excerpts to be read is of primary significance. Our experience suggests that the best ones are those which are neither too long nor too short, involve expression of feelings, deal with a provocative issue likely to be meaningful to the group as a whole, and relate in some way to a commonly shared Workshop experience. The second excerpt, in which the writer expressed the feeling that the leader behaved rudely in cutting people short, presented a wonderful opportunity for exploring attitudes toward authority. The leader's remark that his curtailment of a participant's verbalization might have been experienced as similar to, "Mama shutting him up," was a step in the direction of exploiting this opportunity.

Session Five

Summary. The leader felt that the group had achieved a degree of relaxed cohesiveness and had explored some of the problems that adults come up against in their relationship with each other as reflected in the films or in the Workshop itself. In this session the leader planned to draw the attention of the group to the childhood origins of such adult problems. For this purpose he introduced the First Memory Experiment. Since sample memories and their discussion are illustrated in the report of the first Workshop, only two especially interesting first memories from this group will be given here.

MIRANDA's memory: "I was about five years old and in the street playing. My mother left me in the care of a neighbor, and she had gone up to prepare dinner. I remember seeing my father across the street as he was coming from business, and I called to him, and in my excitement I began to cross the street. He called to me to wait, and it seemed in a split second he ran (or flew) into the gutter grabbing me to avoid being hit by a tremendous sized truck. One so large that the driver probably would never have seen me in time if my father hadn't intervened."

PAULA speculated that the person might feel neglected by mother and more protected by father. RITA declared that the writer was saying, in effect, that father was so wonderful that even a tremendous truck couldn't harm her. JOHN suggested that the writer saw a lot of hostile, frightening forces in the world. LOIS said that the memory indicated that all his life the writer would need someone to help him.

MIRANDA acknowledged the memory as her own. Never before had she thought of father as being the important person in her life and of mother as being the one who left her. In all these past weeks, she had been saying how weak father was, and now the discussion of this memory confused her. When she went on to recall that her father had never kissed her or played too much with her, MIKE pointed out that, nonetheless, he ran when he saw that his child might be hurt. MIRANDA admitted that her father had jeopardized himself for her but ended up again expressing confusion about what all this meant.

JAY's memory: "My earliest recollection is of a day in nursery school at age four. It had been a difficult day. The food there was frightful, and the inmates unimaginative and immature. At 2:00 the kiddies were forced to retire for the afternoon respite. The shades were pulled, and a sinister silence fell. Instinctively I crept, unobserved, to the (Christmas) tree which seemed to be the focus of all the sickening, sentimental horror of the day. On arriving, I found Harvey already there and nearly finished with his work. The tree, about five feet tall, was picked clean of its needles. It stood, self-consciously, a scrawny witless scarecrow, more absurd with its raffish grotesque decorations. It seemed in effect to unfrock the totality of spiritual absurdities which curse the holiday period. . . ."

Much group response, many "Oh's," punctuated the reading of this memory. RITA said that this child saw the world as a horrible dungeon. EDNA thought the child had been sent away from home and felt rejected. DOLLY speculated that the writer associated the tree with some terrible person. REBA stated that the writer used this memory as a protection against seeing kindness and warmth in the world. PHOEBE saw in this memory much loneliness, resistance to discipline, and hostility. DOLLY saw a sadistic quality. SELMA speculated that he came from a broken home.

The leader said that the members must have had much sympathy for the child in listening to this memory. He added how impressed he was with the good quality of the writing. JAY acknowledged his memory, stated that the group's comments were "pretty accurate," observed that someone other than himself had taken action in the memory, and that possibly he felt that he wasn't aggressive enough. He also thought that the memory suggested that he didn't believe in other people's values.

Commentary. This session began with a favorite Workshop procedure, namely, the discussion by the group of anonymously communicated first memories of individual participants. Past discussions of such material on the part of Workshop laity have long since demonstrated to us that members can, in their own interpretations of symbolic material, generate a rich dynamic yield without the leader's help.

Altogether, this meeting contributed to bringing the group closer together, particularly as some of the memory fragments contained material of an especially poignant sort. The sympathetic warmth of the group's response to JAY must have had much to do with the fact that JAY, in future sessions, was perceptibly more outgoing. This session seemed to have a special impact on other members too. For example, the realization that her father had cared so much for her that he had jeopardized his very life to save her apparently shook up MIRANDA and left her quite confused.

It seems important that the leader did not set time aside at the end of this session to inquire into the group's reactions to the experiment. It was an unprecedented experience for most members. The transactions had been obviously very stirring, but what did engaging in this experience mean to different members? Certainly, it is impossible to pursue, in the course of a session, every potentially significant event. As a matter of fact, it is highly unlikely that any leader can be so wise as to detect which of these experiences is the most important to pursue or which of these various events the members are ready to pursue. What he can do is give them an opportunity to make their own choice by setting aside time at the end of each session for such selective expression.

Session Six

Summary. By popular demand, the leader continued with the First Memory Experiment. Toward the end of the session, PAULA and GLADYS wondered why their memories were not read. The leader said that those who had been left out would have their chance in a future experiment involving dreams.

The leader stated that ten minutes remained for them to say anything they wished. EFFIE asked whether a mother should stay home when a child cried about her leaving. The leader replied, "Please don't be mad at me for not answering your question because what I want to do today is to talk about the reactions we are having today. . . ." GENEVA stated that these sessions had crystallized what was wrong with her, but now she wondered where one went from there. The leader replied that in a future session, he would devote some time to consideration of how one might use insight effectively to modify behavior. MARGIE stated that her inability to discuss her memory indicated that she could not take everything as she had thought. Reassuringly, the leader stated that she might be stronger than she realized.

DOLLY stated that she had felt briefly depressed after the previous week's session. PHOEBE confided that she often had the feeling that if she had had this or that in life, she would have been happier, but today she saw that one could have perfectly "lovely" brothers and still end up with problems. RITA felt optimistic because if she could see someone else's memory correctly, then perhaps eventually she could understand her own too. EDNA stated that she had had insights for a long time but that she didn't think she could do anything about her problems by herself. SELMA also felt that she needed proper guidance.

LOUISE stated that it was painful to begin to see oneself truly. The leader stated that even though it was painful, the more we looked at things in ourselves, the less frightened we would be. He compared the process to a splinter which hurt when one first pulled it out: "But when you get it out, you feel wonderful. So this is a process which takes a little time, but don't be afraid of it. You'll survive it, and I think you'll feel a lot better."

JOSHUA and LOUISE felt that this session couldn't help

them because their problems were more physical than mental. PHOEBE stated that, up until the Workshop, she had been trying to behave in the right way so that her daughter would be less resentful, but she had begun to realize that she needed to change her feelings and not simply her behavior. LUCY reported that even when she left a session feeling that she didn't get anything from it, she noted that she acted differently. MIRANDA asked how this could help them when they didn't even know what they needed. The leader replied that sometimes one was helped even though one didn't know it. He went on to compare the members to farmers who removed rocks so that something could grow: "And I think this is what we are trying to do here at this point, to allow you to function better, and to allow you to see that you can do things in a way which you never thought you could do before."

Commentary. When PAULA and GLADYS complained that they had not been included in the memories, the leader simply noted their names down with a view toward bringing their dreams before the group later. It is our opinion that the leader acted quite properly in this instance. To be sure, he did not go into the attitudes and feelings which lay behind their complaints, but something else got communicated to them which we feel was more important. By satisfying their needs, he communicated a respect for their right to have made the demand. There are times to analyze, and there are times to satisfy. It certainly is true that the Workshop process is oriented toward clarification and toward self-understanding. Yet we believe that constantly throwing back to a member such questions as, "Why?" or "I wonder what lies behind that?," can be quite a castrating experience and can make members feel, justifiably, "Good God, is there nothing I do that can remain unquestioned and can be taken at face value?" Had PAULA and GLADYS been very demanding members who were engaging in power struggles with the leader, then he might well have made an interpretive comment.

Toward the end of the session there was an outbreak of feelings of frustration and skepticism about the Workshop's benefits. This outbreak of feeling, though by no means as intense or as widely experienced, resembled the outbreak of discouragement and anxiety at the end of the first Workshop's fourth session. Though these reactions in the second Workshop may have been delayed by the strong support, reassurance, and implicit promise given by the leader, they would appear to be reactions that can be anticipated at some time or other in any Workshop. No matter how emphatically Workshop leaders underscore the self-understanding or the preparation for therapy function of the Workshop, a substantial number of members will insist on converting the experience into a resource from which they can extract definite answers or remedial courses of action with reference to their personal problems. A leader needs to be very clear in his own mind about his views toward such reactions and how he might best cope with them.

In this instance the leader muffled the members' confusions and misgivings by vigorously asserting the possibility that they were being helped even though they didn't know it, that he would help them even more in the future by giving specific directions on making use of one's acquired insights, that this is a process analogous to getting rid of "splinters," "takes a little time," and need not be feared, and that at the end of the process, they will feel a lot better. Comparing one's growth to getting rid of a splinter strikes us as oversimplified. Self-defeating attitudes, inner conflicts, and unrealistic goals are not simply external things which have implanted themselves in us through no fault of our own. Neurotic development is a much more complex affair than this analogy suggests.

The leader's need to generate pleasant feelings in the group in an atmosphere of harmony appeared to limit the group's freedom of expression of negative feelings. For example, when EFFIE raised the question about what to do with a child who cried about mother's leaving, the leader asked her not to be mad at him for not answering the question. When MARGIE stated that she wasn't as strong as she thought she was, the leader emphasized that he thought she was. Another leader, less concerned with accentuating the positive, might have elicited a fuller expression of MIRANDA's and DOLLY's depressed feelings to which they referred only passingly.

Session Seven

Summary. The leader introduced the Birth Order Experiment
as another means of exploring the influence of childhood experiences on personality development. After about twenty-five minutes, the leader called all the subgroups together. He then asked
the members if they could see any connections between their past
experiences and their current feelings toward themselves and
others. PHOEBE learned that her hostility toward her mother
was tied up with her relationship to her daughter. RITA felt that
she was teaching her children to stand on their own two feet, as
she herself had been taught to do. MIRIAM said that she now
avoids having her children do what she herself resented having
had to do as a child. LOUISE said, "I am neat, and my sister
isn't neat . . . I never thought of looking at it that way . . . when
I yell at my children for not picking up their toys . . . that maybe
I'm angry with my sister. . . . " PAULA recalled that she always
wanted to be better than her older sister. RITA stated that the
film made her aware that her oldest child must have felt somewhat neglected when her youngest was sick. JOSHUA expressed
confusion because he noticed that everyone was trying to blame
someone else for his troubles, and he wondered whether their
own personalities could not have caused these troubles. The
leader reminded JOSHUA that the darkest hour was just before
the dawn.

LISA asked the leader whether their children were better off
for being able to say, "I hate you," or should they be slapped
down. The leader asked what the other mothers in the group
thought. Before coming to the Workshop, PAULA said she would
have felt rejected had her child said this, but now she tried to
find out why he felt that way. Several others reported similar
reactions. MIRANDA, however, declared that when her daughter
complained of stomach aches in order to get out of going to
school, it was better to simply tell her to go instead of to probe for
the whys and wherefores. The leader suggested, "The best thing
is to take a look and see what is going on and see what we can do
to correct it. Do you think that you would go along with this?"
The group members chorused an emphatic, "Yes!"

JOSHUA protested that we were not here to figure out our

children but ourselves, for as we became better, our children would. The leader agreed, but added that he was sure there was a relationship between the way we felt and the way our children felt. GLADYS confided that in therapy she discovered that she herself was the problem and not her son. ELLEN thought that it was a great mistake that she had not been in therapy at the same time that her son had been. The leader commented, "It's never too late."

LOUISE said that she knew why she told her child that she hated him, but how could she stop? The leader stated that in one of the future sessions, he would show her how to stop. This caused an excited hubbub in the group. RITA exclaimed, "The golden formula!" The leader added that if they could become clear on the reasons behind what they do, then, "I can show you a formula that will work to get rid of it, but you will have to really know what it is, otherwise it doesn't work."

Commentary. Ostensibly, this was to be a meeting devoted to the Birth Order Experiment. The groups were, indeed, separated according to birth order with the usual instructions, but relatively little developed in the subsequent discussion which focused on birth order problems. While there was some oscillation between two themes: (a) of their own experiences as children, and (b) of the bearing of childhood experiences on their role as parents, the prevailing preoccupation seemed to be with the evil things they felt they were doing as parents. The leader tended to fall in with this preoccupation, especially when he invited other mothers in the group to comment on LISA's question as to whether children were better off or not for being able to say, "I hate you." At this crucial moment, the leader might have better directed attention to LISA's underlying anxiety, or, recognizing her anxiety over her role as a parent, related it to her own developmental experiences by making some comment such as, "I wonder what your experiences were in this connection in relation to your own mother," or, "Maybe you could answer that question for youself if you were to become clearer on what effect saying or not being able to say, 'I hate you' to your own mother had on you."

The leader continued his reassuring, inspirational approach. Thus, when JOSHUA expressed confusion, the leader asserted optimistically that the darkest hour came just before the dawn. If anything, his didactic comments in this session seemed lengthier and more frequent. This trend reached its climax when the leader allowed himself to get caught up in the group's concern for controlling their behavior and to repeat his promise that he would impart to the group a formula that would work. The risks involved in extending such promises should be obvious. The enthusiasm which greeted the promise attests to the intensity and the generality of the needs, wishes, and hopes that were involved.

Confronted by the group's pressure for answers, and sharply aware that time was running out, and convinced that he did have some concrete recommendations to make to the group which could facilitate and shortcut their groping, the leader decided to give a talk in the next session outlining these concrete suggestions. In the regular post-session staff discussion this plan of the leader was carefully reviewed. We had definite reservations about the appropriateness of devoting a substantial part of a session to a lecture. We feared that a lecture would confirm the members' expectation that they would be told what to do, rather than that they would be helped to investigate what they do. The confirmation of transference rather than an encouragement of an attitude of investigation toward it could scarcely be regarded as a contribution in preparation for later therapy, at least that of an insight-oriented type. Nonetheless, we confess we were curious to observe what effects would ensue upon the introduction of such a device. Furthermore, we believe that there is no one and only way of conducting a Workshop, and we wished to give the second leader the widest possible latitude in the testing out of his own ideas. The staff concurred with his proposal.

Session Eight

Summary. In fulfillment of the promise he made in the last two sessions, the leader gave a twenty-five minute talk designed to reassure the group that compulsively self-defeating behavior can be modified and to offer them guidance in their efforts to control and modify such behavior. His talk emphasized the view of both effective and ineffective behavior as products of a largely unconscious process of conditioned learning, and the crucial importance in the learning process of early life interpersonal experiences, particularly within the family and in relation to the mother.

The core of his suggestions regarding methods of modifying behavior may be paraphrased as follows: "Analyze and try to understand the causes of your behavior, the hidden personal meaning to you of those stimulus situations which have habitually led to compulsive and ineffective conditioned responses. As you repeatedly recognize the subjective interpretations that you place upon these stimulus situations, you can gradually expect to behave more and more intelligently so as to achieve more and more effective gratification of your needs."

The leader's talk, despite the complexity of his material, was simply worded and interlarded with many telling epigrams and numerous homely examples drawn from familiar patterns of everyday life. At the same time he was careful to convey a sympathetic appreciation for the arduousness and the disappointing slowness of any process of behavior modification. He warned the group to expect disappointing setbacks, but urged them not to be discouraged.

At the conclusion of the leader's talk, JOSHUA exclaimed enthusiastically that the leader had done a wonderful job, and that he now understood himself better. Dominated by his father, he had felt inferior and dependent, had found it difficult to break away from his parents, and now felt a strong need to be the center of attraction. He speculated that when he pushed his own family around, he was really pushing his mother and father. PHOEBE wondered how she could get the strength to stop doing things that she knew would hurt her. MARGIE said that she had the same trouble, and EFFIE added that they all did. DOLLY advised PHOEBE to look for and work on the cause. PHOEBE replied that she had done this but was overwhelmed by the many possibilities that occurred to her.

CARLA asked what one did if one had already applied the leader's method, and it hadn't worked. The leader wondered whether deep down she really knew her problem. CARLA replied that one couldn't go into all the many causes. The leader stated, "This is something that you have to begin to think about. . . . JOSHUA happened to see something immediately, but it doesn't have to happen that way. . . . This is sort of a tool to use." LUCY complained that she had tried this, but couldn't tell when she finally got to what was really basic. MIRANDA doubted that such knowledge would help her. Though she knew that she shouldn't do something, she couldn't stop herself. The leader suggested that she consider afterwards, "Why did I do this?" MIRANDA said that she let out her anger on her children for no reason. The leader asserted that there were reasons. REBA suggested that MIRANDA might not have figured out the right reason. MIRANDA asked how one finds it. The leader answered, "By thinking . . ."

In introducing the film, "Feelings of Rejection," the leader suggested that watching this film might make it easier for them to think about themselves. The film was shown without interruption. After the film, MIRANDA expressed the opinion that the movie was too pat. PHOEBE resented the movie because the film heroine, Margaret, knew what her problem was, when most of them didn't. RENEE thought that the answer came too quickly in the movie. JOSHUA said that the film didn't show him the causes of his psychosomatic symptoms. The leader told JOSHUA that if we forget about the symptoms and concentrate on removing difficulties in disturbed relationships, the symptoms frequently disappear. LUCY declared that she had gotten a lot out of this session. She had always been looking for some complex answer to her problem, but now realized that it could be something as simple as her mother having told her that she would not be loved unless she were a good girl. SIBYL recalled that she had tried looking for the cause of her guilt complex, but still didn't know how to conquer it. CARLA complained that she didn't know how to conquer the feeling of being hurt at her failure to win mother's love. The leader stated that he would go into it a little bit later.

LUCY recalled that her parents would say that little girls should be seen and not heard, and that as she grew older she withdrew and stopped talking. LENA stated that she became an extremely bad child in reaction to her parents' repeated statements that children should be seen and not heard. The leader commented that here were two different ways of reacting to the same thing. LUCY stated that she was in tremendous conflict between needing to be good to everyone and not really wanting to be this way. She added that she didn't know how to be herself because she didn't really know who she was.

JAY expressed skepticism about being able to cure oneself by understanding the cause. MIKE said he knew what was right, but he wondered why he couldn't do it. The leader replied that, as in learning how to skate, there was a lot of slipping and falling before one got the knack. MIKE retorted, "It's easy to see what should be done, but how?" The leader answered, "Little by little." MIRANDA wondered how she could leave things in the past if her mother kept upsetting her. The leader answered that mother wouldn't bother her were she able to change her own reaction. When MIRANDA asked how one did this, the leader answered that she had to find out why. CARLA pointed out that trying to find out why might arouse anxiety, which some people couldn't take. The leader agreed, but added that he didn't think it ever killed anybody, and that in the end it paid off.

Commentary. The leader's talk stirred up a ferment of reactions and, as such, it was effective. But the reactions were expressions of discontent, disbelief, disappointment. An argumentative, demanding atmosphere was generated in which the leader was maneuvered into a defensive position. The group reaction seemed a culmination of a hitherto muted but progressively developing process of disaffection and restiveness which had begun in the sixth session. This process developed as expectation gave way to impatience, and as impatient protest and demand maneuvered the leader into making a definite promise, and as delivery of the promise gave rise to disappointment with the gift.

We list in what follows a number of considerations pertinent to the psychological processes underlying the events of the session, as well as to their implications:

1) Perhaps the greatest risk inherent in the benevolent authority approach as exemplified by this leader is that it may intensify

dependency attitudes, and dependency, unanalyzed, tends to be insatiable.

2) Though apparently giving in response to their wish, and thus confirming their dependence, the leader was actually making an exhortation to independence. His gift was a general formula, and, as such, it left the members alone and frightened before the implicit demand that they apply it to themselves effectively. The discrepancy between the leader's expression of faith in their potential for independence and the inner self-feeling of dependence probably led to confusion in some members.

3) The formula was experienced by a number as an oversimplification altogether discrepant with the felt complexities of the problems confronting them. For these members it made a mockery of their suffering.

4) The leader's promise was consistent with the magical powers the members attributed to him. The more his wisdom, the more wise the anticipated gift. Disappointment was probably inevitable.

5) A crisis of disappointment and depression, as magical fantasies arising out of dependency needs are relentlessly dissipated through deflation of the leader, may well be inevitable and a necessary phase both for the group and the leader before genuine progress can be made.

As later sessions proved, the wave of disappointment did not disastrously inundate the group. Whatever the transformations, probably humanizing, to which the image of the leader was subjected, his image as a good, though now less, all-powerful father seemed to persist. It was a shock to be thrown on their own when they had expected a more magical gift. But, as will be seen in the very next session, many members took up with renewed vigor the task of self-examination. What must have stood out in the group's perception of this session is that the leader had tried to help.

We need now to face a number of important methodological questions implicit in the events of this session. First, one wonders why a lecture was needed at all. When members pressed the leader to tell them how to stop their unacceptable behavior, would it not have been more appropriate for him to have used the occasion to elicit the members' reactions to the Workshop process, and to have again structured the aims and methods of the course? Even if he wished to communicate the content of his lecture, could he have not done so in a much less formal way, by simply using the numerous here-and-now events which developed in the Workshop as illustrative instances of this or that principle, thus minimizing the risk of encouraging a conventional teacher-pupil relationship?

The lecture, even assuming that it was well done and was free from oversimplification, would at best constitute a conventionally didactic lesson. Only as Workshop participants reacted to the lecture and to the leader, only as they gave expression to their disappointment, only as they shared their bewilderment and perplexity did they actually become involved in an experience whose investigation would have restored the spirit of Workshop methodology. Unfortunately, the didactic, intellectualistic point of view from which the lecture was given made it difficult to use the participants' reactions for investigative purpose. Instead, the leader was driven into a defense of his position. He had to deny that he had any intention of conveying an oversimplified view of the complexities of life. He had to repeat that the control of behavior, so poignantly sought by the members, would come through repeated application of rational understanding.

Instead of simply accepting JOSHUA's announcement that he now saw the light, would it not have been more in the Workshop spirit for the leader to have said, "This is very interesting, Josh. Now perhaps we can understand more of what's been happening between the two of us," or, "Josh, now that you can see a line of relationship there, I wonder how this might refer to our relationship here?" (In the group and in his letters, JOSHUA had been very active in his efforts at seeking attention, either by dominating or by withdrawing and sulking.) Or, in response to LUCY, the leader might have said, "Lucy, do you suppose that this need to be good in order to please mother might have carried over here into the Workshop too?"

We wish to make clear that we do not oppose the use of lecturettes in the Workshop. A didactic statement or a lecturette does not in itself violate the Workshop spirit as we conceive it, but when a leader does use this device, we would recommend that it be brief, carefully timed, and avoid oversimplification. The leader needs to dissociate himself from the content of the lecturette, leaving the door wide open for members to accept or reject it. He presents material in the following spirit: "Here is what has been found empirically, or some authorities believe, and so forth, and this may be pertinent to what just happened here. You may wish to consider it." We would especially suggest that a leader stop his lecturette at various points, and then ask the group to feedback what they thought they heard him say, and what their reactions were to the content of what he said, and to the very fact and manner of his having given a lecturette and placed them in the position of being an audience.

Session Nine

Summary. The leader, in doubt about the consequences of his directive approach in the previous session, now felt the need to provide the group with an experience which would give them maximum opportunity for self-directive exploration of feeling and behavior. For this purpose, the Balloons Experiment was selected. After informing the group that in this experiment they would be playing with balloons, shortly to be distributed to them as a way of learning about themselves, he asked for their reaction to engaging in this kind of activity. REBA declared that she did not like to do things which would remind her of her unhappy childhood, but MIKE, who never had played much when he was young, enjoyed the idea. PHOEBE and MIRANDA admitted some anxiety about doing something that might be embarrassing.

The leader now instructed the group to blow up their balloons. He himself blew one up and then confided his surprise at how easy the task proved to be. He asked the group how they felt during this task. REBA said that she avoided blowing up her balloon more fully than she did out of a fear of breaking it. MIRANDA couldn't see what there was to think about in blowing up a balloon. LISA at first looked forward to the task, but then found that the actual doing was no fun at all. She added that this was the story of her life. MARY saw this as a novel experience which might relate to how they accepted something unusual. REBA told MIRANDA that she would come out with answers if she asked herself why she reacted the way she did. MIRANDA retorted peevishly that this would take her a lifetime. MIKE said that balloons always made him think of a female nipple.

The leader stated that whatever we do can be looked at fruitfully in terms of its personal meaning. He then asked the members to close their eyes, rub their balloons along their faces, and see what images popped into mind. DOLLY described the experience as pacifying and soothing. LUCY felt a soft feeling, such as a child might get from its mother. The leader stated that he had a feeling of lying against something soft and cuddly. JOSHUA wanted to crush his balloon but feared that the noise would annoy everybody. REBA declared that she was doing what she had to do but didn't like it.

The leader invited members to comment on each other's reactions. MIRIAM observed that she had been anxious even before rubbing the balloon, and speculated that this might reflect a fear of physical contact. MARY suggested a fear of getting close. MIRANDA declared that she had followed REBA's suggestion and had thought, but without results. LUCY speculated that members who did not like this task were fearful of pleasure or of releasing themselves. JOSHUA was confused about what relationship there could be between balloons and one's feelings.

MARY stated that they didn't want to relate their sexual associations. LUCY then confessed that she liked to touch the balloon, and had nobody been around, she would have put it in her mouth. The leader stated that the balloons could mean more than just a balloon to them, that it could reveal something about their deepest feelings. MIRANDA then exclaimed that the thought had just crossed her mind that she might be a frigid woman. The leader responded, "So you see that there are associations you can get. Very good."

SELMA excitedly observed that whereas she has always had difficulty in stopping herself from smoking, she would not put her balloon down now, not even to smoke a cigarette. She added that her balloon brought back a childhood memory of an adult holding her little hand. MIKE stated that the balloon was a pacifier without being put in the mouth. For LUCY, breaking the balloon would be like doing something sadistic to another person. LISA complained that she got no reaction whatsoever from playing with the balloon and wondered if there was anything wrong with her. The leader suggested that she might feel very uneasy about letting herself feel emotion out of a fear of getting hurt. MIRANDA observed a peculiar sensation in her arms and a shakiness in her hand, both of which she related to the idea of breaking the balloon.

The leader wondered what might be behind either the fear of breaking the balloon or the wish to do so. Much to the amusement of the group, CARLA declared that she had always wanted to squeeze somebody's throat. (She was gripping the balloon at this point as if she were choking somebody.) REBA objected to breaking her balloon out of a feeling that things shouldn't be wasted. JOSHUA admitted that many times he had wanted to be destructive, and he now wished that he had dozens of balloons to break.

MIRANDA stated that she had felt completely relaxed when she walked into class this morning, but now the business of breaking balloons was unnerving her. SELMA thought that MIRANDA was blaming her mood on the balloons. The leader said that this might be true, that MIRANDA might be externalizing, that is, putting the blame for what was bothering her onto some outside thing in order to keep from looking at what within herself might be causing her feelings. LUCY suggested that those who feared breaking the balloon were afraid of losing control or of hurting something.

The leader now asked the group to break its balloons. Bedlam broke out for a few minutes. LUCY said that she would use a lighted cigarette. MIKE said that he would be willing to break somebody else's balloon, but not his own. The leader asked how they felt as they broke their balloons. SELMA said she didn't really want to break it, but did so because she didn't want to make an issue of it. RENEE said that the broken balloon looked repulsive to her. This statement brought the image of a "spent condom" to MARY's mind. The leader commented that it might be easier to bring out such thoughts if one kept in mind that everyone else was having similar thoughts. REBA declared that she had a headache, and the leader invited her to think about what the cause could be. Now that her balloon was broken, SELMA observed that she felt nervous and shaky whereas before she had felt like a child in a hypnotic trance. REBA noticed that SELMA had replaced her balloon with a cigarette. PAULA observed that she was so concerned about getting approval that she couldn't react with true reactions to the balloon. She then speculated that her need for approval might be interfering with her getting to know her real feelings.

PHOEBE saw REBA as pampering herself in not breaking her balloon. She added that she was annoyed with REBA much as she would become annoyed with her daughter. REBA declared that she got her headache because the others broke their balloons despite her disapproval of it. The leader suggested that she got the headache because she couldn't express her anger at not being able to make the others do what she wanted them to do. MIRANDA said she felt annoyed at REBA for sitting in judgment on her today, and yet, at the same time, she wondered if she were looking for REBA's approval.

JOSHUA declared suddenly that he realized now the reason for the Balloons Experiment. It was to bring out the issue of sex which, he noted, the group was evading. MIKE observed that nobody had pointed out that the balloon looked like a nipple or a penis. LOUISE was sure that everyone had thought this. PAULA said she was looking for it, and the group burst out laughing. The leader asked if others shared JOSHUA's feeling and were finding it difficult to talk about sex. A number of members nodded their heads affirmatively. The leader then invited members to write their comments about this in their letters so that excerpts on the topic might be read to the group for discussion.

After a five-minute break, the leader invited a free-for-all discussion. MARY reported that her marriage had improved since the textbook and the Workshop had helped her to realize that in pressing her husband to help her in the house, she had been taking away some of his manhood. REBA asserted that, instead of feeling crushed at MIRANDA's remarks as she would have before therapy, her main feeling now was that MIRANDA could use her anger as a tool to find out whom she represented to her.

REBA and MIRANDA then made up, each of them denying any intention to hurt the other. MIRANDA speculated that she was seeking approval and had been disturbed when she didn't get it.

JOSHUA felt that the Workshop had helped him. He no longer felt angry at anybody, realized that he was not alone, and could now accept people's differing from him. LISA doubted the sincerity of this statement since that very morning JOSHUA had told her that the group had not helped him at all. JOSHUA insisted that the group had definitely helped. He added that his physical symptoms had been gradually decreasing, but that he still needed to get rid of his destructive urges. SARA, too, felt that she had been definitely helped. She could now talk to people without holding her head in shame. PHOEBE warned JOSHUA not to be too optimistic, citing her own experience of having relapses following periods in which she felt she was getting some place.

EDNA wondered about her always doing things for others. The leader suggested that she did things for others to make people do things for her. He added that we aren't born to be altruistic, that what we do must necessarily be an expression of something we need. He then presented a hypothetical situation of two men crossing a desert with a supply of water sufficient only for one. He asked the group what they thought was the right thing for the man who possessed the water to do. Should he share the water with the result that they would both die, or should he drink it himself and live and let the other man die? Most of the group said that they would drink the water themselves. The leader then said, "I am glad to see a lot of healthy people here." REBA doubted that this was healthy. The leader said it would be incorrect to give up one's life, that one had a right to survive, that if we exaggeratedly try to please people and do everything for them, we were hoping that they would do something for us.

Commentary. The Balloons Experiment seems very suited to generate at least the following significant experiences and concepts:

1) Even trivial behavior merits close observation since it often

expresses, symbolizes, or projects significant aspects of ourselves, our needs, our coping patterns, and the like. These are worth observing in the microcosms of trivia for we may not have the vision or the courage to perceive them in the macrocosms of life.

2) Hostile, destructive needs often affect our behavior in objectively irrelevant ways and often generate unnecessarily defensive reactions. To understand oneself, it is important to understand one's patterns of frustration, hostility, guilt, and defense.

3) Sensuous and sexual fantasies are more frequently and intensively active in our minds than most of us care to acknowledge. Our inhibitions in accepting sensuous and sexual needs often prevent constructive resolution of conflicts in these areas. It seems virtually inevitable that each Workshop group will have at least one intrepid soul who, bursting with a compulsion to confess, eager to demonstrate his emancipation, or seeking a little bonus of unexpected titillation, will report that one or another aspect of the Balloons Experiment has generated sexual fantasies in him. It is perhaps just as inevitable that the majority of the group will remain inhibited.

4) Spontaneous associations which run through one's mind in response to almost any stimulus can be useful to pursue as clues to self-understanding. Allowing oneself the freedom to let anything pop into mind, to perceive images, to see what one is reminded of in response to this or that occurrence, can all be a valuable part of the student's armamentarium in his efforts at self-understanding, and useful as a training experience for therapy.

The simultaneous presence of an articulate, aggressive, even defiant repressor like MIRANDA, along with a number of people who had gained considerable sophistication in psychodynamics, for example, REBA, seemed particularly fruitful in this session. MIRANDA served as a virtual stooge in her aggressive assertion that a thing is a thing is a thing, and that the past is the past. In her own extreme way, she must have been a champion of everyone else in the group who retained nuclei of emotional resistance against the assimilation of personally meaningful psychodynamic insights. Yet MIRANDA's protestations were often so naive and so manifestly the desperate defensive clawing of a tigress at bay, that they served only to highlight and to lend conviction to the interpretive suggestions and the sophisticated insights which were expressed.

The MIRANDA-REBA episode suggests the generalization that the deliberate juxtaposition of extremes of blunt and aggressive naiveté on the one hand, and of a certain experience and sophistication on the other, offers special promise of productivity. Further, it is suggested that MIRANDA's participation was fruitful for both herself and the group because the Balloons Experiment offered the invitation of a party-like activity at the same time that its motor aspect involved a commitment to action subject to observation by self and to interpretation by others.

The leader's role during most of the Balloons Experiment was very much in line with Workshop spirit and principles. He introduced the whole procedure in a relaxed and unpressing way. He consistently encouraged members to keep expressing their reactions, was accepting of all the different responses that emerged, and stimulated participants to become curious about the different events that occurred. Asking the group to discuss its reactions to the idea of playing with balloons was especially helpful in setting the stage for what followed. His repeating several times that anybody could speculate about anybody else's responses probably had much to do with the fact that there was more reciprocal interpretation of each other's behavior in this session than at any time before.

The Balloons Experiment stimulates a whole array of reactions, including those relating to sex. None of these needs to be dealt with intensively. All a leader need do is encourage each person to think over the meaning of his reaction by himself.

When SELMA pointed out that MIRANDA was blaming her feelings on the balloon, the leader made a brief didactic statement about externalization. Here is an example of how a leader can casually toss off some didactic generalization which has immediate pertinence to a here-and-now event. This is the kind of optimal circumstance under which a principle can be communicated. Things are happening before everybody. Feelings are involved. It's current, and it's plain.

This is, perhaps, the first time in which the leader engaged in an experiment along with the members and confided his own reactions on the same level with those of the group. It is likely that his confession of surprise at how easy it was for him to blow up the balloon stimulated more active group participation and in some way generated significant shifts in attitude toward him. It is often useful for the leader, following such participation, to invite the group to give their reactions to his reactions or to speculate on the meaning of them.

Toward the end of the session the leader resumed a more authoritarian, pedagogical role in an effort to persuade the members of the group to accept without guilt their right to an enlightened self-interest. The authoritative assertion of self-interest as an inalienable right may be reassuring, and even inspiring to some members. Again, it conveys the feeling that the leader is on the side of the members, or at least on the side of how, in his judgment, they need to be if they are to be healthy and free.

On the other hand, leaders who see the Workshop as an approach dedicated to the process of helping members discover the implicit values which govern their behavior will question the wisdom of pressing his values on the group, as well as the validity of his presented values as necessary ingredients in mental health. A leader with this view may be challenged to devise value centered experiments as a means of stimulating the group's exploration of its implicit values with respect to one or another issue. He will confine his efforts to helping the members become more aware of their implicit basic assumptions and of their behavioral consequences, leaving it to them to exercise their own active, explicit choices.

Session Ten

Summary. The leader again used the device of reading letter excerpts to the group as a means of bringing into focus much that had remained unexpressed in the balloon session. In the first letter excerpt the writer stated that she had enjoyed the balloon session because she was able to give vent to angry feelings which she had been inhibiting for the last two years. JOSHUA confided that his angry feelings subsided when he became involved in a hobby. HOPE suggested that he find out the why of his anger instead of simply learning how to bottle up his feelings. LOUISE declared that when she was angry, she felt better after playing Mah-Jongg. MARY asserted that screaming or breaking dishes was childish. DORIS declared that one is better off breaking a dish or taking a walk until one has calmed down and can think the matter through. REBA believed that cooled off anger may still come out in some physical symptom.

MIRANDA asserted vehemently that anger was good and healthy, and that it was not good to give each thought such deep concentration. Open disagreement flared between MIRANDA and MARY, with MARY taking the position that one should be able to have differences of opinion without getting angry. PHOEBE recalled that her parents were angry at each other all the time, and that in her experience, anger was a way of hurting others. RITA observed that her point of view contrasted with that of PHOEBE. In RITA's home, everybody suppressed their anger when a good fight would have cleared the air.

The leader attempted to summarize the discussion: it is a matter for individual decision as to whether or not to let out anger; some anger is constructive, and some anger is self-defeating; letting out anger all the time does not solve things; it is important for us to find out what it is that makes us angry. He asked the group if they could go along with his summary, and the members responded in the affirmative.

The leader next read the following letter excerpt: "My heart started to beat faster, and I was quite anxious when you asked us to rub the balloons on our faces. I thought it showed fear of physical contact that I am consciously not aware of. Mary said that it was a closeness to sex which caused the anxiety. I think she may be right. But what added to my confusion is that the balloon was not just one thing for me. I thought of a breast and a penis." EFFIE thought the writer was taught to suppress sex. The leader then stated that unfulfilled childhood needs to be dependent, loved, and secure were often channeled into sexual areas. For example, a sexual relationship could meet the need to sit on somebody's lap and to be somebody's little girl.

JOSHUA agreed with the leader, confiding that in sex he looked for somebody to hold him affectionately because as a child he didn't have the love he wanted. He added that his wife didn't understand this. PAULA suggested that he wanted a mother and not the sex act. CARLA pointed out that most women were looking for someone to lean on themselves, and that JOSHUA had to understand this about his wife if he wished her to understand him.

MIRANDA asked why all this had to relate back to the love for a parent. The leader declared that even the so-called mature person could not divorce his present from his past. MARY supported the leader with an example of a child whose father expressed love by a slap on her rear end and who as a grown-up wished for that from her husband. MIRANDA still couldn't see how everything related back to childhood. The leader then explained that one's childhood was like a mass of clay and that what has happened has been a pushing and a pulling that have given one all kinds of dimensions. MIRANDA still failed to understand why love couldn't be an adult feeling with another adult. The leader replied, "Because I'll tell you why. You are a personality as a whole, a unit. One part of you cannot act adult and the rest not. It's a holistic concept."

Commentary. The balloon session continued to demonstrate its provocative power by very robustly sustaining further discussion of the experiences involved in it. The coordinated use of the Balloons Experiment and the letter-excerpt technique was an extremely effective technical stroke on the part of the leader.

The persistence of the discussion on anger was impressive. Some of the more sophisticated members kept reiterating the importance of searching for the causes of anger. The leader did well in picking up this emphasis and in confirming its importance. Yet one feels the need for the addition of another ingredient, namely, attention to the immediate reactions being experienced here and now in the meeting. Failure to direct attention to such immediate experience appeared to encourage recourse to intellectualization and advice giving. How useful it would have been to have explored actual angry feelings that members were experiencing or had experienced toward each other or toward the leader! The leader might have invited this kind of discussion by simply saying, "I wonder if you can recall times during this Workshop when you felt angry at another member or at me?"

The leader was plainly impressed with the vigor of the discussion and the importance of the topic of anger, and he was impelled to attempt a summary of the points of view which had been put forward. After giving the summary, he asked the group whether they felt that they could go along with it. It might have been more productive to ask what others thought they had heard him say, what their reactions were to what they had heard, and to invite the expression of opposing or differing points of view.

The value of the balloon session in provoking sensual reactions came to some measure of fruition through the leader's deft use of letter excerpts written by members who took the leader's invitation to express in their letters what they could not express orally before the group with reference to sex. After some initial hesitancy, the group overcame its inhibition and entered into the discussion with a verve and a directness which was quite surprising considering the size of the group. The leader's interpretation that sexuality might sometimes be a means of gratifying simple affectional needs carried over from childhood was a comment with considerable validity and as such possessed useful provocative value. On the other hand, this intervention on his part may have offered a premature escape from anxiety and guilt intrinsic to sexual conflicts per se.

It seemed a questionable technique for the leader to have gotten involved in an argument with MIRANDA in which he tried insistently to press home the point that current sex and other attitudes related to one's past experiences. MIRANDA's persistent doubting, her earnest need to extract some reassurance that manifest behavior has an all significant immediate validity offered an excellent opportunity for the exploration of the group's attitudes toward and understanding of the bearing of childhood experiences on current personality and behavior. Such opportunities seem more fruitfully developed by focusing on the whys of individual differences in belief, with particular reference to the here-and-now sensual and aggressive reactions elicited during the Balloons Experiment, rather than by the authoritarian assertion of one or another point of view.

Session Eleven

Summary. The leader proposed giving the group the opportunity to decide what should be the agenda for the remaining sessions. He asked them how they felt about this proposal. Many members immediately expressed a preference for the leader to make the choice. MIRANDA said that she had to make so many decisions on her own that she liked occasionally to be told what to do. EDNA and JOSHUA expressed the opinion that the leader knew best what problems bothered the majority. LOUISE feared that the members would make selfish choices. RENEE was annoyed with the leader for shirking his job. MIKE, DOLLY, and LUCY approved the leader's asking the group for its choices, but LUCY added that she had nothing to suggest.

MARY stated that it was hard to choose because the sessions had been almost equally effective in stimulating them to think. The leader asked whether anybody had found one particular session that he or she liked better than others. The group was silent. HOPE finally reported that the movie about teenagers had stimulated many helpful recollections. The leader, sensitive to the group's inhibition, assured the members that in offering suggestions they would be helping him, as well as the Workshop staff, in evaluating the relative effectiveness of various techniques. This apparently freed a number of members to refer to this or that session as a favorite one.

SELMA announced that, after the balloon session, she had questioned her mother about her childhood. She learned that her mother never had time to love and fondle her. MIRANDA stated that she felt very badly that the Workshop was ending, for she enjoyed it tremendously. She added that her trend of thought had become very different. SELMA also was upset about the imminent ending. The leader wondered whether this was why they didn't want to make choices for future sessions: "It's almost as if . . ." PAULA finished the sentence: "You are pushing us out." The group laughed.

The leader distributed a listing of various alternative activities for future meetings which the members were then asked to rank in order of preference and to return during the break. The "menu" listing was as follows:

.... A film about a person's dependency on his mother and how this affects his adjustment in marriage and his job.

.... An experiment in which each member in the group explores his impressions of every other member in the group.

.... A chance to reread and discuss all the letters you have written to date.

After the break, the leader read the following letter excerpt: "I wished you had asked LENA not to read in class. I think it shows her rudeness and her feeling of superiority which I resent in her or anyone." HOPE speculated that LENA's reading was a way of bringing attention to herself. LOUISE thought it was unfair for the leader to read this excerpt because LENA was not present to defend herself. PETER thought LENA was rude. Other members too expressed their irritation with her. The leader wondered what could be behind their annoyance. EDNA felt that LENA acted as though she had been the boss of the whole situation, something that the other members envied. HOPE suggested that LENA wanted attention which she had not gotten from her parents. CARLA objected angrily to LENA's being torn apart when she was absent.

MARY acknowledged her letter and declared that LENA symbolized someone who treated her with disrespect. The leader wondered if LENA had been doing things which members felt they should not do but would like to have been able to do. MIRANDA disagreed: "It was simply a matter of courtesy." PAULA said she had not taken LENA's behavior personally because she understood that this behavior related to LENA's problems. MARY suggested that the group represented LENA's parents to her.

The leader next read the following letter excerpt: "REBA annoyed me today. I think she made too much of a fuss with the balloon when you told us to blow them up. We all did, even though we were afraid that they would break. She made quite a fuss about it. When you told us to break them, we didn't want to, but we did, excepting her. I feel that she just wanted to be different, and it bothers me very much. Why?" JOSHUA couldn't understand why members let petty annoyances bother them. DOLLY suggested that we get annoyed with people when we see something in them that we dislike in ourselves. RENEE suggested that when people get annoyed, it might represent family figures, both past and present. LOUISE acknowledged being the writer of the letter and added, in response to MARY's questioning, that she had broken her balloon although she had wanted to bring it home. The leader suggested that we get mad at people who take the apple that we had our eye on.

MIRANDA declared that she just listened out of courtesy to members who acted like analysts. HOPE pointed out to MIRANDA that she preferred to be told what to do by an authority. SELMA stated that one didn't need to be a professional to have common sense. When RITA asked if MIRANDA had REBA in mind, MIRANDA said she did. GLADYS explained that REBA had been trained in group therapy to think about the whys of everything and only wanted to help. DOLLY stated that she disliked REBA's manner and not REBA herself. CARLA thought that some people liked to go around proving their authority. The leader suggested that there might be another reason underlying the one we give for objecting to somebody's playing psychiatrist.

Commentary. This was a very lively session which, dealing with issues of considerable significance, generated much heated interaction. In general, the letter-excerpt technique again more than paid its own way. The excerpts selected involved interactions between people in the group. As such, they stimulated further interaction which probably would never have taken place without the opportunity for members to express their feelings in letters. The letter-excerpt procedure has been so frequently productive in our experience with it thus far that we are impelled to recommend its incorporation as a regular feature of the Workshop.

The group found itself almost completely inhibited, even confused, when the leader invited the members to select for themselves a preferred topic or activity for the subsequent sessions. Almost universally, they called on the leader to continue making the selection. Was their behavior symptomatic of the leader's relationship with the group? It was a relationship in which the leader had not previously hesitated to offer didactic and authoritative generalizations intended to support the self-esteem of members, to supply them with "healthy" values, and to provide condensed formulas whose application would lead to more effective behavior. It may be that such authoritarian leadership roles are bound to impede the growth of the group toward the autonomy they intend to encourage.

The group's resistance to accepting the invitation to participate in charting its course presented the leader with an opportunity to explore with them their anxiety over responsibility for autonomous decision. This might have led to a productive examination of their dependency and of their transference reactions onto an authority figure. Be that as it may, the "menu" procedure was a neat compromise between the leader's hope that the group could take full responsibility for planning its future course and the group's wish that the leader should retain full direction.

A number of generalizations offered by the Workshop participants during the LENA incident were very trenchant and pertinent. For example, DOLLY suggested that one got annoyed with a person when one saw something in him that one disliked in oneself. Did an important comment of this kind generate in each person's individual breast a silent process of self-questioning, a search for examples of such behavior in themselves? Or did such a comment provide a kind of intellectual closure which shut off further inquiry? Would it not have been useful to devote more attention to elaborating and emphasizing DOLLY's generalization? For example, DOLLY might have been asked to give examples of what she was talking about. Was this the reason that she reacted as she did to LENA, and were there other situations, perhaps, including occurrences in the group, in which she found herself developing hostile attitudes toward people displaying behavior she wished to disown in herself? One might also have turned over some of these questions to the group for its consideration. In this way what was left at the level of abstract generalization might become a basis for exploration of concrete personal experience.

The MIRANDA-REBA conflict brings to mind the dispute

between ROSA and PEGGY in the first Workshop. The element
these two situations apparently had in common was a kind of
sibling rivalry for the leader's favor. While the ROSA-PEGGY
incident was not one of rivalry for the leader's attention, there
was a turning to the leader to adjudicate who was right, and who
was wrong. One of the main elements of the MIRANDA-REBA
conflict in the very beginning appeared to be concerned with
MIRANDA's objection to REBA's standing in for the leader.
"Sibling" competition for the leader's favor existed in both Workshops. Yet it occurs to us that in both there was lacking an
explicit discussion of such rivalry situations in relation to the
leader. It is difficult for us to say why this was so. In any case,
future Workshop leaders might well keep in mind the potential
value of bringing such competition out into the open either by
taking advantage of spontaneous opportunities that arise in Workship events or by creating experiments for deliberately highlighting this dynamic situation.

Session Twelve

Summary. The leader presented the film, "Overdependency,"
which had been selected from the "menu" by the group. In the
discussion which followed, SELMA suddenly realized that she
didn't like the wife in the movie leaving food on the table for her
husband because this brought to mind how her working mother
did the same thing when she was a child. ELLEN confided that
she had been overindulgent like the movie wife toward her son.
RITA recalled that she had mothered her husband to the point
where he had resented it. LUCY declared that her face was
blotching up all over, and the leader suggested that perhaps the
film was hitting home personally.

The film was resumed and then stopped again at the point
where Jimmy begins to tell the doctor about his childhood.
JOSHUA could see himself in Jimmy. MIRANDA, in a critical
tone, said that Jimmy reminded her of her father who had had
a breakdown. She recalled having felt very critical toward her
father and of shouting at him, "Snap out of it." MIRANDA
agreed with MIKE that her father could not snap out of it by
himself. EDNA said that Jimmy reminded her of her husband

who used his heart trouble as an excuse. At the end of the film, RITA said the movie brought to mind that she had failed to teach her son to fight and to stand up for his rights. She added that her own mother had taught her to resist passively.

After the break, the leader read the following letter to the group: "I was wondering why I had no comment last week and why I was so quiet during the previous week's session. I thought a great deal about it and concluded that it was because of Miranda's comments. . . . It seems to me that she is constantly battling her mother so that when anyone in class offers her any criticism, she feels it is her mother talking to her. I feel she thinks that in some ways her mother was right, but she'd rather die than admit her mother may have been right. My emotions become disturbed when she talks down to the class by saying, 'I hear you, but I won't listen.' I resent anyone who feels he won't listen and won't extend what we call common courtesy. . . . Again, I repeat that it is not Miranda who irks me, but she's renewing feelings that I have toward at least a dozen people."

MIRANDA said that she knew this was MARY's letter because she had seen her hand it in. JOSHUA admired the writer for he would like to express his feelings toward others just as freely. PHOEBE thought that MARY was doing the same thing that she criticized MIRANDA for, namely, battling with mother. MARY declared that she was intolerant of anybody who did not use every situation to learn about himself, as she herself did. DOLLY wondered if MARY's parents had told her that if she complied with the rules, she would be a nice girl. MARY recalled that her parents were in business when she was a child, and she had to do for herself, and she now felt that others should too. MI-RANDA observed that she didn't feel resentful toward MARY as she had toward REBA, and this struck her as curious.

The leader now read another letter excerpt about MIRANDA, this one written by HOPE: "When Miranda was talking and I answered her and others, I looked at her. I was amazed at her ability to keep her trend of thought going. She seemed to me to be able to follow everything that was going on around her. Were I to be in her position, I know I would miss half of it because I would be thinking other things, like what other people were thinking about me." In reaction to this excerpt, MIKE warned

the group not to get mixed up with MIRANDA's tongue. ELLEN
saw MIRANDA as a tough nut to crack, someone whom you have
to fight all the way. EDNA admitted being jealous of MIRANDA
for being able to cope with certain situations that she herself
couldn't. Much to the amusement of the group, JOSHUA announced that he wouldn't want MIRANDA as a wife because she
was always trying to get the upper hand. MIRANDA admitted
that it was fortunate that her husband was stronger than she was.

Commentary. Once again, the reading of letter excerpts proved
itself an effective device for stimulating significant interactions
among the Workshop participants. What is of special interest is
that the anticipation that one's letter might be chosen to be read
before the group did not seem to inhibit the written communications to the leader. In some curious way, it would seem as
though many members were able to hide behind the thin guise
of pseudo-confidentiality as a means of getting out into the open
feelings they recognized and wanted to but could not express in
a direct and spontaneous way. Of particular value was the leader's exploitation of the adventitious fact that two members wrote
about the same third member, MIRANDA, expressing quite different attitudes.

Session Thirteen

Summary. The leader introduced the Dreaming About the
Class Experiment. (In a previous meeting he had instructed the
group to dream about the class. All the dreams submitted by the
members had been mimeographed, and copies were now distributed to each member.)

This was another session marked by active participation, much
emotional involvement, and high interest on the part of the
members. Nevertheless, since the Dreaming About the Class
Experiment was illustrated in some detail in the report of the first
Workshop, we shall confine ourselves here to the presentation of
a single dream and its discussion.

PHOEBE's dream: "I was in school and drinking a very large
glass of milk. The teacher said, 'Don't drink so much milk, you'll
get fat.' The doctor, who was also there, Dr. ——,* said, 'Oh, she

---

* In this dream, Dr. —— refers to the leader.

makes herself sick, that's why she's thin.' I felt absolutely crushed by that remark. Then the teacher came and said, 'Don't feel so bad. Don't worry. I'll see you get help, and you'll be all right.'"

MARY suggested that the dreamer felt that the leader wasn't giving her the personal help she wished for. SELMA thought that the dreamer might feel the doctor was not good for her, and that she would rather stay with her old ways. RENEE sensed a past conflict in which one of the dreamer's parents said one thing, and the other parent said another. MIRIAM noticed that it was either/or with the dreamer, and that there didn't seem to be any medium. CARLA speculated that the dreamer, after coming to class, now felt that she was not as well as people thought she was and that she needed to be taken care of. PAULA thought that the writer felt guilty about making herself sick all the time.

The leader said that he felt a little bit bad about this dream because he may not have recognized something in the dreamer that he should have. The dreamer, wanting support from him, might have experienced him as saying to her, "You don't need it. As a matter of fact, all your troubles are in you. You are the one who is making yourself thin. . . ." He added that the dreamer may be afraid to tell him that she had a lot of difficulty for fear of appearing like a crybaby. Though she wanted help, she might feel that she had to appear as if she didn't need it yet might be mad and disappointed about not receiving it.

PHOEBE acknowledged the dream and confessed that she did care a great deal about what the leader thought and had feared that he would get angry and not want to help her if she said or did the wrong thing. She felt guilty because, though she felt it was in her power to get better, she somehow didn't really take care of herself. She also admitted that she was looking for someone to lean on but felt that she had to keep this need hidden.

At the end of the session, the following "menu" was distributed to the group:

.... An experiment in which each member in the group explores his impression of every other member in the group in order to learn more about how we tend to see others, and how others tend to see us.

.... A session in which all your letters to date are returned to you so that you can reread them and discuss the leader's written comments and your reactions to them.

.... An experiment in which we make a small change in
our behavior, and we explore our reactions to making
this change.

Commentary. The leader's acknowledgment of PHOEBE's dependent needs stimulated in PHOEBE an extraordinary example
of the expression of intimate and honest feelings involving interaction with the leader. Her acknowledgment of feeling the need
to say and do the right thing lest the leader be angry and reject
her undoubtedly stemmed from a core problem which she
brought with her to the Workshop. Nevertheless, some question
remains as to whether the felt necessity of saying and doing
the right thing was not, in part, the result of an authoritarian element in this Workshop's leader-group relationship. In any case,
PHOEBE's dream was a dramatic and provocative one going to
the heart of leader-member relationships. It presented a wonderful opportunity for the group to explore its feelings with regard
to the Workshop and of its perception of the leader.

Session Fourteen

Summary. The leader introduced the Seat-Changing Experiment, the "menu" item chosen by the group. He began the experiment by first observing aloud that members tended to take
certain fixed seats each week and wondering why this was so.
JOSHUA declared that he always wanted to be in the center.
RENEE speculated that a member's current choice of a seating
position might be related to his place at the family table. MIKE
suggested that some members wanted to sit close to the teacher,
but that others sat far away so that they could hide from him.

The leader now suggested that each member pick a seating
position as different as possible from his habitual one. He asked
for the members' reactions to this suggestion. GENEVA was at a
loss as to where to go. LOUISE complained, "Why make us all
unhappy?" MIRANDA said that she wanted to change as little
as possible. MIKE, on the other hand, felt this was a game and

was ready to play. Then, at the leader's signal and with much merriment (and tension), the members went about their task of changing their seats. The leader moved from the head of the table to a seat in the midst of the group circle.

After the group had finished the seat changing, the leader asked what they had observed in themselves as they went about the task. SELMA stated that she had wandered around feeling lost. LOUISE said that she didn't like the leader for making them uncomfortable. A moment later she added that a few weeks ago she would not have been able to come right out and say that she didn't like him because, to her, a teacher was like a god. SELMA asserted that she was beginning to realize that people tend to stick to the same thing and feared to venture because they felt safer this way. JOSHUA, who had chosen the leader's seat, complained that it was uncomfortable because the sunlight got into his eyes. (Later he returned to his original seat.)

The leader observed that while some members had made only a minor change in their seating position, others had shifted markedly. RITA observed that she usually was very hesitant before making a radical change. MARY speculated that the experiment showed how they reacted to changes in everyday life. RITA suddenly realized that she was very annoyed with her husband because he left the radical decisions to her. The leader suggested that perhaps we really wanted others to make changes or decisions for us. RENEE now admitted that one of the reasons she didn't move from her chair was that the leader had not instructed her where to go, and she could not decide for herself.

The leader asked if any members, in addition to JOSHUA, had thought about taking his chair. RITA observed that it had never occurred to her to take the leader's chair, and though she had changed her seat, she was still somehow in the same relative position to the leader as she had been before. MIRANDA declared that had she been in SELMA's shoes, she would not have let JOSHUA get away with taking the chair without fighting him. RITA couldn't figure out why she was so uncomfortable in her new seat. When some members asked her why she didn't change it, she declared that it was very typical of her to go through with a bargain, even if it turned out to be a bad one, out of a feeling that it was her fault that she made it in the first place. MIRANDA said with some satisfaction that the leader had to turn his eyes away first when their eyes met. The leader responded, "So you licked two of us today." The group burst out laughing.

The leader asked whether anybody had the thought of sitting on the arm of a chair, or on the table, or on the floor. When RITA said that the leader had only asked them to change chairs, he reminded her that he had asked them to change the place where they were sitting and to make it as different as possible, and that this instruction did not actually exclude the floor or the table. LOUISE asserted emphatically that it was not the time nor the place for sitting on floors. RENEE observed that when the leader brought up the possibility of sitting on the floor, she began to slouch more and more and now couldn't get herself up. She couldn't understand why she was so negative today and was really scared.

RITA stated that she would never sit on the table because it was not accepted socially. She then recalled that her father would look very stern if someone put a comb on the table. With some excitement, MIRANDA reported thinking of something that she hadn't thought of for many years, namely, her parents telling her as a little girl not to sit on the table and kick her feet because this meant wishing one's parents were dead. She added that from that day she never sat on a table.

RITA reflected that though she differed from her parents in her religious views, she nonetheless found herself one day preparing a chicken in the religious way her mother did. Feeling very daring, GENEVA changed her seat to the leader's to see what would happen if she made this change. MIRANDA said this discussion was really hitting home because she now recalled that, like her father, she wouldn't touch meat if it didn't come from a kosher butcher.

JOSHUA angrily declared that he couldn't see how all this talk about food related to Workshop business. SELMA said that it was not the food itself but certain underlying things. RITA speculated that JOSHUA was feeling ignored and was trying to gain attention. GENEVA said that this session was very important since it pointed up her typical pattern of saying, "This is better than nothing. Accept it." Today she had tried something new in making a small change to the leader's seat. She had taken a chance and yet nothing had happened to her. In fact, the seat was very comfortable, and it made her feel very important.

The leader now requested the group to return to their old seats, and, once they had done this, he asked them for their reactions to the new change. SELMA said that it was like coming back to the old homestead, but she realized now that she had been happier in the other seat. GENEVA said that she liked the new seat better than her old one, but that she couldn't question the leader's authority. SELMA observed that GENEVA had looked and talked differently when she had sat in the leader's chair. GENEVA declared that tonight she would sit in her husband's seat, and if he were to tell her to change seats, she would refuse. The leader wondered whether a lot of members do things that they really didn't want to do. SELMA reported that for a long time she had been doing the family entertaining on Mother's Day against her will, but that yesterday, for the first time in years, she had left her mother in charge.

The leader opened the discussion to anything the members might have on their minds. MIRANDA asked the leader whether he would miss the group after it ended. He answered that he couldn't honestly say that he would feel bad because he would then feel depressed every time a patient finished therapy. He had certainly enjoyed a very warm and human relationship with them, and if in any way this had been helpful, this made him very happy. MIRANDA said that she felt bad and would miss him.

Commentary. There is no doubt that this session was the most exciting one of the entire Workshop. One opportunity after another arose which the leader could have taken for making didactic interventions or invitations to analytic exploration, but, had he done this, he would have risked halting the surging flow of events which swept the group on to one significant experience after another.

It is noteworthy that the leader in this session and in the next one seemed to have resolved his previous ambivalence between his push to teach and his underlying wish to encourage the group's autonomy. He started out the Workshop with an effort at remaining in the background and doing no more than was necessary to encourage the group to express itself. At some point, however, he seemed to become anxious about whether the group was making sufficient progress, and he became increasingly active and didactic in an effort to speed up the group's forward movement. As he became increasingly aware of ways in which his didactic interventions were cutting off significant expression and exploration of feeling on the part of the group, and as he became more and more aware of the creative potential in the group for productive exploration, he became increasingly able and content to stand on the sidelines and to take no more action than was necessary to encourage the group in its flow of response.

One wonders whether members might not have had considerably more difficulty in meeting the challenge of this session than they did had it not been for the spirit of play surrounding the experiment. It is surely one of the values of the Workshop and the atmosphere it is able to generate that, through the development at such critical points of a spirit of play, anxiety can be diluted to a degree which permits involvement in significant, emotionally-stirring experiences without substantial loss of the seriousness necessary for working through.

It seems worthwhile to review the ways in which this session approached the criteria for a productive Workshop meeting:

1) The members' personal involvement was at a maximum. Each member had to *do* something. He had to make a commitment. He was given the instruction to change, in a trivial enough way to be sure, as radically as possible. But what constituted radical change was not defined. Each person had to construct his own definition, and each one had to decide whether or not, and to what degree, he would conform with the instruction.

2) The requirement of some commitment or decision automatically opened up the prospect of potential conflicts. Each member had developed his own habitual pattern of living, his own level of homeostatic balance, and his own measure of identification with his pattern and his balance. He was now asked to disturb this balance. The disturbance of homeostasis obviously generated varying degrees of anxiety. At the same time, mem-

bers were under varying pressures to conform with the instruction out of their stereotyped attitude toward authority and, perhaps in a deeper sense, out of motives of mastery, growth drives,
or ego ideal, to venture into the realm of the unfamiliar.

3) The experiment brought into sharper and more emphatic
focus problems of relationship to authority than had been true in
the entire prior history of this Workshop. One obvious factor
which precipitated the issue was the fact that the leader left his
chair and took a place among the members sitting at the table.
In eliminating the prestige distance between himself and the
group by vacating his place at the head of the table, he created
conditions which encouraged members to become aware of their
habitual and implicit relationship to the leader as an authority
figure and to attempt at least a tentative reorganization of that
relationship. There can be no questioning the dramatic and significant beginnings of reorientation with respect to authority:
JOSHUA's sitting in the leader's chair; GENEVA's taking the
leader's chair after JOSHUA had vacated it; LOUISE's sudden
outburst that she disliked the leader; MIRANDA's novel experience of meeting the leader's gaze and finally staring him down.

4) The displacement of the leader from his customary position
of authority so disarranged leader-group relationships that the
precipitation of latent rivalries among the members was just about
inevitable. Questions of who would occupy the leader's vacated
seat at the head of the table, who would sit next to him, whom
would he favor in his selection of a seat, naturally arose. Further,
the readjustment of a single member's attitudes toward the leader,
when overtly expressed and exposed to the view of the group, for
example, MIRANDA's reaction to staring the leader down, probably stimulated a number of other members to reexamine, and
perhaps alter, their perception of the member in question, their
perception of their own relationship to the leader, and their perception of the leader himself.

5) The conflicts which the change of a habit pattern entailed
for many members called attention to the vast, unconscious background of adjustments, perceptions, and expectations which support the constantly shifting foreground of focal adjustments. This
background is taken for granted, rarely questioned, rarely ex-

amined. Many aspects of it are hardly even knowable. Focusing on this background of assumptions, as occurred, for example, when the leader asked why members had not thought to sit on the floor, seemed to do two notable things: it identified the violation of these background assumptions as a potential source of anxiety, and it brought into question the validity of these assumptions. Perhaps even more important is that, in however small a compass, a few members found it possible to question the validity of these implicit assumptions. They could ask feelingly and hopefully whether the price they paid in self-restriction was worth the gain they received in comfort and support.

6) Questioning the validity of the assumptions involved in the background of one's moment-to-moment experiencing directed attention to the origin of those assumptions. It was not necessary for the leader to ask, "What early experiences did you have which might account for the assumption that you could not sit on the floor?" Quite spontaneously, various members experienced flashes of reminiscence. Images appeared of familiar scenes in childhood, of statements made by one or the other parent, of experiences which comforted and supported and at the same time set limits. The group had a first-hand experience in the recoverability of unconscious material.

Toward the end of the session when MIRANDA asked the leader whether he would miss the group, the leader responded with respect for the question, simply accepting it at face value. He did not scrutinize this poignant moment but simply let himself become involved in it. Another leader might have wished to use the question as an opportunity for exploring the separation anxiety experienced by the group.

Session Fifteen

Summary. In the previous meeting, the leader had returned all the letters to the group together with a sheet of instructions. This guide sheet instructed the member to review all of his letters at home with an eye to discovering one or more repetitive patterns. It was suggested that special attention be paid to such features as the following: the reaction to the Workshop expressed in the very first letter, changes in the length of letters and in the salutations and closings, and the leader's written responses found to be most and least helpful. Also, members were instructed to underline each feeling expressed in the letters and then to notice the frequency of different feelings.

The leader opened this session by asking the members what they had noticed as they reviewed their letters. PETER said his letters did not seem as if he had written them. PHOEBE said that feelings of pessimism and skepticism ran through all her letters. She thought these feelings might be characteristic. MIRANDA observed that she had moved from self-centeredness in her early letters to an increasing interest in the group and its work. SELMA observed that her letters included no references to anyone but herself.

At the leader's suggestion, the group participated in a go-around in which each member read the first sentence of his very first letter. PAULA noted that both SELMA and she had to say in the opening sentence that they were glad to be there. PHOEBE was struck by how tense and skeptical everybody was when they first came. MIRANDA declared that people had changed, and now there was a closeness.

The leader now proposed that each member in the group read aloud the last sentence and the closing of the first letter. RITA observed that LISA expressed great reverence in her closing, "Respectfully." LISA said she was very upset about having been the only one in the group to close with "Respectfully." This stimulated a fear that she was different from other people. PAULA speculated that LISA was more upset by the tone of subservience to authority in her closing than in her being different. LISA agreed with the statement and recalled that as a child she was surrounded by knowledge at home and experienced acutely her own lack of knowledge. The leader wondered why for LISA being different was something negative rather than positive.

RITA suggested that the closing might reflect a member's feeling toward the leader. MIRANDA noted that her closings became friendlier and less formal. ELLEN observed that she had kept addressing the leader as Mr. —— and had no closings at all. PAULA was annoyed at herself for always closing with "Very truly yours," though she didn't know what she would have preferred to write instead. RENEE observed that she became very hostile in her letters, didn't bother with any closings, and began to abbreviate her name more and more until she finally just signed, "R." She added that in each letter she felt she had revealed too much and that these were ways of taking back what she had written.

MIRANDA reported that once she had spelled the leader's name wrong, and he had written a comment, "Don't you like me today?" following which, not wanting to offend him, she always checked to make sure that she had spelled his name correctly. MARY noted that she treated each letter with respect, always starting, "Dear Dr. ——," and always ending, "Yours truly, Mary."

EDNA observed that she had signed all her letters, "Sincerely, Edna," until one day the leader had made a comment that upset her. Thereafter, she stopped using, "Sincerely," and just signed, "Edna." SELMA said that in one letter she wrote, "Aw, nuts," but not wanting the leader to think too badly of her, she followed this up with, "Pardon me." RENEE confided that in one letter in which she wrote that someone was "full of shit," she just signed her last name because she was ashamed. MIRIAM noted that she broke away from her usual pattern of doing the right thing by signing, "Miri," instead of "Miriam." The leader commented that the feelings they expressed toward him in their letters might reflect their feelings for somebody important in their lives. JOSHUA could see that in some way the leader had played the role of father. He added that he had always wanted someone to help him in time of need.

The leader wondered about the kinds of emotions they had underlined in their letters and with what frequency different emotions occurred. RITA observed a shift from glowing feelings to feelings that were more and more disturbed. MIRANDA declared that she had not realized before what an unhappy person she might be, for in every letter disturbing emotions were expressed. SELMA noticed that in her letters she frequently used phrases such as, "My very little this," or, "My very small that," and speculated that she must be degrading and tearing herself down all the time.

The leader asked whether they found any connections between

what they learned in their letters and how they had felt during the Workshop. MIRIAM was very pleased that she had finally gotten to the point in the Workshop where she no longer felt she had to please the leader by turning out longer letters than she actually felt like writing. RITA stated that had she written MIRANDA's tearing-self-down adjectives, she would have felt like crying, and yet she wondered why MIRANDA was so gay about the whole thing. MIRANDA answered that she did not feel so bad about her faults as she used to before the Workshop.

The leader inquired how they had felt about writing letters. MIKE said that thoughts would open up as he wrote them. MIRIAM had thought that they would be beneficial, but had resented them nonetheless. DOLLY said that the letters helped to clarify her thoughts and gave her an opportunity to express what she could not discuss openly in the session. RITA was inhibited in writing about personal problems lest she encroach on the leader's time. She suddenly realized that the sense of fairness on which she had always prided herself was really a liability and that she would be better off if for once she could be a "real stinker."

The leader said good-by. He wished them well in their future enterprises and warmly shook their hands. With a mixture of sadness and elation. they trooped out the door.

Commentary. Opportunity to review their letters in historical sequence stimulated in some members, who seemed to have had the least capacity for it, an intense intraceptive experience. Various insights and significant self-attitudes emerged even though, under the circumstances of the Workshop, it was not possible to develop their implications. Focusing on the variations in types of closing which occurred in a single member's letter series sensitized the members to the projective implications of habitual, even institutionalized, forms of normally casual behavior, and brought into the foreground both habitual and impulsive situational fluctuations in attitudes toward authority. In both of these respects, this aspect of the experiment had something in common with the Seat-Changing Experiment.

Another productive use to which the experiment lent itself was

demonstrated by the leader's suggestion that the members underline every instance of emotional expression contained in their
letters. A number of rather remarkable self-confrontations occurred. Thus, MIRANDA had not before realized what an unhappy person she might be. In some instances, members revealed
considerable progress in the ability to interpret dynamic modes
of expression. Thus, SELMA, on noticing repeated use of the
phrase, "My very little this," or, "My very small that," observed
that she must be downgrading herself all the time.

The group's display in this session of autonomous exploring and
evaluating underscores what capacities lie latent in the group
which, given the proper conditions, can emerge. In part, this
autonomous group behavior can be credited to the very nature
of the experiment which seemed peculiarly well designed to
release a greater potential for this kind of independent self-
exploration than the group itself realized it had.

CHAPTER 4

~~~~~~

EVALUATION OF WORKSHOP EFFECTS

T HIS CHAPTER focuses on an evaluation of the effects of the two Workshops and addresses itself to the following two questions:

1) To what extent did the Workshop serve as a stimulus to change in members' perceptions, feelings, and behavior?

2) To what extent did the Workshop serve as a useful clinical adjunct?

We used a variety of materials for evaluating the impact of the course with respect to these two questions. Verbatim typescripts of each session and the members' weekly one-page letters provided evidence of ongoing developments within the course itself. The members' responses to questionnaires and interviews* administered at the conclusion of the Workshop provided us with their immediate retrospective evaluations of what the Workshop meant to them. Also, at the end of the Workshop, outside informants, relatives and friends of each member, were invited to write out their independent observations of change in the members. Thirteen spouses, nine friends, and five blood relatives sent in their observations for twenty-four of the members.

In order to learn about each member's post-Workshop history in relation to therapy, the number who entered therapy, the

---

*Virtually all interviews were conducted by the Workshop staff members and not by the leaders themselves. Interviews were recorded verbatim, either with the aid of tape recordings or through stenographic recording. For the most part, interviews followed a structural pattern for which questionnaires were prepared in advance.

degree of persistence in treatment, and how each member viewed the relationship between his Workshop and therapy experiences, we undertook to contact all of the two Workshops' members about a year after the completion of the second Workshop. (This was two years after the completion of the first Workshop.) We succeeded in obtaining such follow-up interviews with all fifty-seven members.

The Workshop as a Stimulus to Change

After exploring alternative approaches to the task of evaluating the Workshop's effects, and taking into account the lack of any control groups, we decided finally to devote our time and energy to evaluations within a predominantly phenomenological frame of reference, that is, to base our judgments of the impact of the Workshop chiefly on the participants' own subjective reports of their experiences. Within the framework of these reports, we devised a system of assessment centering around the concept of "movement." Movement refers to changes in attitudes, feelings, and behavior reported by a member (and his outside informants, if any) as having occurred in him during the course of the Workshop. Our assessment system included carefully defined categories of movement and explicit specification of criteria for rating degree of change in each category. In short, we classified the members' statements with reference to categories we deemed to be psychologically meaningful. At the same time, our approach allowed the participants themselves to be the judges of their own progress.

We are not unaware of the limitations of self-report as a basis for assessment. There is the possibility that a participant may exaggerate, minimize, or overlook changes in himself. A judgment of degree and direction of movement provides no information as to its value, depth, or permanence. Without a control group, it is unknown to what extent the Workshop, rather than other factors, was responsible for a reported movement. Nonetheless, while a subjective standard of personal value is manifestly inappropriate in the case of psychotics and sociopaths, it seems to us an ultimately inescapable, significant part of any criterion of mental health in the case of rational people having a reasonable degree of internalized social morality.

Preliminary to the assessment of movement, it was necessary to organize the vast amount of raw data into categories which would be convenient for handling, yet meaningful in terms of human experience and of the goals of the Workshop. Rather than impose preconceived and arbitrary categories, it was thought best to derive the categories from the content of the reports themselves.

As a first step, then, the letters, questionnaires, interview typescripts, and the reports of relatives and friends were collated for each member and carefully reviewed.* The wide range in degree and kind of change reported was impressive. For example, there were some members who reported growth of insight into the effects of their parental upbringing; some felt generally more optimistic and hopeful; others referred to significant shifts in relationships with parents, spouses, and children. There was hardly an area of human experience that was not touched upon by one or another's set of data.

There emerged from all the diverse instances of reported change three, no doubt interrelated but still clearly distinguishable, categories into which virtually all the data bearing on Workshop effects could be classified. These were labeled Awareness, Sense of Well-being, and Interpersonal Relations. These are categories which will be seen to be reasonably comprehensive in their reference to important areas of human functioning pertinent to criteria of mental health. At the same time, they are very much rooted in concrete data.

Once movement categories were identified, the next step was the development of criteria for rating the degree of movement within each category. Examination of the reports submitted by the participants disclosed that within each category of movement reports of change varied along several lines: the sheer number of changes, the respondent's judgment of the magnitude and direction of each change, and the intensity with which any given change was experienced as inferred from the emotional tone with which it was reported. All these considerations entered

---

*We were gratifyingly impressed by the spontaneity, the tone of earnestness, and the citation of concrete experiences which characterized most of the reports.

into the criteria developed for assessing degree of movement in each category.* Definitions of each category and the specific criteria for rating degree of each type of movement are presented below.

Movement in Awareness

The category of Awareness refers to changes in the extent to which the member becomes conscious of, identifies, or understands descriptive and dynamic aspects of himself and his life history.

The criteria for assessing degree of movement in this category are as follows:

High: One or more new insights are reported in such a way as to indicate a strong emotional impact, a dramatic discovery, or a significant shift in one's previous perceptions or attitudes. There are signs of a greater tendency to locate responsibility for one's life experiences within one's self.

Moderate: Movement consists mostly of a confirmation, sharpening, or elaboration of what was in awareness prior to the Workshop. New insights, when they occur, are reported either very tentatively, or with little specification or emotional involvement. There are signs of a greater tendency to locate responsibility for one's life experiences within one's self.

Low: Various aspects of one's problems or personality may be discovered or confirmed, but there is lacking a recognition of one's own responsible involvement in these. There may be an awareness of the relatedness between one's past experiences and one's current personality or problems, but this awareness falls short of recognizing the responsible part one played in one's own life history. Rather the self is seen as a passive object that has been damaged, weakened, or molded by past experiences along certain lines which persist unchanged into adulthood.

Unmoved: No change is reported.

Of the fifty-seven participants, twenty-four were judged High

---

*Classifications of the members in accordance with these criteria were carried out by the authors, with the relatively few instances of disagreement resolved through discussion.

in Awareness, ten Moderate, nineteen Low, and four Unmoved.*
In brief, a majority of the participants reported a growth in self-
awareness, at least to the extent of experiencing a heightened
sense of responsibility for events in their lives. Following are a
number of concrete examples of movement in this area:

BETTY: *High.* "I probably was blaming myself for years . . .
that my father died only a few months after I told him I didn't
want to see him again . . . and it made me think of other things
—things my mother said to me as a child . . . that made me feel
guilty for the separation of her and my father . . . I never realized I resented my father leaving us as I do now . . . I know
now that a lot of my fears go back to my childhood . . . It seems
to me everything my mother said to me especially unfavorable
. . . has made a great impression on me . . . I realize I look to
my husband as a father and why I feel so badly when he does
. . . something that hurts me. . . ."

DAWN: *High.* She came to recognize that she may not be the
"good-for-nothing person" that mother always said she was: "I
realize now it was because of her ailment more so than mine . . .
As a direct result of my birth she suffered a nervous breakdown.
The best way that she could get back at me was to degrade me
and . . . make me feel like a nothing . . . when I first started
thinking about this, I felt a great lightening within myself . . ."
At the same time, she became sharply aware of existing im-
maturities, especially her unreasonable demands on others: "I
feel as if I am play acting at being a mother and wife. . . . I
feel as if I never passed the age of ten. . . . The Workshop
made me aware of the fact that I am not the sweet, good-
natured, helpful person I thought I was."

DENISE: *High.* In the Workshop she was sharply confronted
with her own passive dependency, especially as reflected in her
need to be "prodded" by the leader to speak up in the group.
"Could this be my crutch? . . . In other words, once someone
forces me to speak, the responsibility for what I say is no longer
mine but the other person's. This seems to me to be an important discovery." She was struck by her inability to remem-

---

*Since no consistent statistically significant differences appeared in the quantitative
findings for the two Workshops, they are treated in combination.

ber her mother and concluded that ". . . it seems to me there must be some terrible feeling about my mother which I am trying to hide." She came to recognize a relationship between her current withdrawal and mistrust of others and her emotional deprivation in her family: "The Workshop has made me realize that . . . all my life I have felt like a lump of clay who must obey . . . because she must not be ungrateful . . . now in my faint flutterings toward independence, I feel very guilty and ungrateful, but the Workshop experience has made me realize that I must establish this independence if I want to be a happier person."

GENEVA: *High.* She came to see for the first time the morbidly dependent character of her relationship to her husband, and began to realize that this dependency originated in her relationship to mother: "I think a picture is beginning to clarify itself . . . it seems to me now that he has always been more important to me than I have been to myself . . . I built him into a superhuman being which, of course, he wasn't. . . . My thoughts are beginning to leave the basic relationship with my husband and are beginning to function on my relationship to my mother. I'm beginning to become aware of a dependency on her . . . I always thought she was docile. Now I'm beginning to realize that she was domineering and did not permit us to stand alone. . . ."

JUNE: *High.* "The Workshop made me realize . . . that I set up impossible standards. Just knowing this has helped, nor did I know just how much resentment boils inside of me, how *much* hate and hurt and disappointment there is toward those one is expected to love—mother, husband, others." She became more aware of the relationship of this current pattern to her past efforts at displacing her brothers in her mother's affection through the attainment of perfection.

JEAN: *High.* She began to connect her distrust of men to mother's earlier warnings, her general fearfulness to mother's threats to put her in a reform school, and her dislike of responsibility to her having been a "pampered youngest." "I can see many things now in regard with my relationship with my mother . . . my confusion in trying to break away from her . . . my feeling of guilt involved . . . my need for her . . ." She came to feel that one of her greatest problems was "that I set very high standards for myself and really those standards weren't for me." Her sense of self-responsibility increased sharply. "Through the Workshop I have learned that this help must come from myself, that . . . only I am my own saviour."

RENEE: *High.* "I used to think I was big-hearted, generous, and doing too much, and in the end I find that I am really just selfish, and I really want things, and when I want them I want them with urgency and I can't wait, like a baby for his bottle." Discovering that it was unreasonable for her mother to have expected her to always love her sister, she was now able to admit previously denied jealousy feelings. A sharpened realization developed of how she was "still trying to get tons of affection" from mother, a "cold and pessimistic" woman.

ROSA: *High.* "Before the Workshop I wasn't aware of being a dependent person and thought of myself as the very opposite . . . I had such a guilty conscience that I felt compelled to be kind to everyone . . . and if I couldn't maintain this impossible standard and went into a fit of anger . . . I suffered keenest remorse . . . I see it was because of my restricting environment where my wishes were seldom if ever considered, so I had no conception of what my wishes were, let alone how to consider them . . . I was able to see where I was under a blanket of fear as a child and that I was somehow carrying that fear as an adult, that there was no need anymore for me to keep that fear."

MIKE: *Moderate.* He began to consider the possibility that he may have been vying unwittingly with his son for his wife's attention. He became a "little more" aware of being a pressuring person and that his family might resent this. For the first time he raised the question, "Why am I striving for betterment and perfection all the time?"

ROSALIE: *Moderate.* She was able to entertain the possibility that she loses patience with her daughter because she finds her own weaknesses reflected in her. She began to see herself as a "bitter" person. She related her current distrust of people to her probable distrust of her parents.

IAN: *Low.* Thinking back on early experiences in his own life failed to clarify his understanding of himself beyond the general thought that his upbringing was not a very good one and that, as a result, he has been hurt in a variety of ways.

PAULA: *Low.* She reported a whole series of ways in which she became more aware of her personality characteristics. However, she did not move beyond a detached, intellectualized listing of her findings.

Movement in Sense of Well-being

The category Sense of Well-being refers to changes in the feeling areas of *esteem, adequacy, mood,* and *physical comfort.* Esteem refers to self-regard and self-acceptance; adequacy refers to one's sense of competence in coping with situations other than those which are directly and manifestly interpersonal in character, for example, "cleaning the house"; mood refers to degree of tension, anxiety, pessimism, and depression; physical comfort refers to the intensity of somatic symptoms.

The criteria for assessing degree of movement in this area are presented below.

High: Positive and marked symptomatic change is reported in at least one of the following areas: self-esteem, adequacy, mood, or physical comfort. A change is considered marked if the member himself regards the reported change as high in magnitude, uses descriptive terms of extreme intensity, and provides some specification in describing his pre-Workshop status or the change which followed. Some positive change is reported in at least one other area. Some incidental or temporary worsening may be reported, but it is decisively outweighed by the positive changes.

Moderate: Positive movement short of marked symptomatic change is reported in at least two of the aforementioned areas: some incidental worsening may be reported, but it is decisively outweighed by the positive changes.

Mixed: Both positive and negative developments are reported, but neither type of change decisively outweighs the other.

Low: Positive movement short of marked symptomatic change is reported in no more than one of the four areas.

Unmoved: No change is reported.

Worsened: Changes in a negative direction are reported exclusively or in clear preponderance over positive changes.

Of the fifty-seven participants, thirteen were judged High in this category, sixteen Moderate, seven Low, six Mixed, twelve Unmoved, and three Worsened.

No psychotic breaks occurred in any of the participants during or immediately after the Workshop period. There is no doubt that in a few members considerable anxiety was aroused as defenses were more or less successfully attacked. However, we know of no instance where anxiety was generated to a degree where it could not be handled by the participant. Almost invariably those people who reported some increase in anxiety, at the same time recognized that such anxiety was essentially constructive in nature, being symptomatic of a closer approach to the truth. Concrete examples of movement in this category are presented below:

BETTY: *High.* Her marked improvement with reference to walking in the street alone was a "source of wonderment" to her family and friends: "I was afraid to walk to the corner alone. Now I come to the Workshop alone when I have to and go other places alone. Also I preferred going by car even if it was more convenient to use a bus or subway, but now I do ... I used to get panicky, but now I try to ignore it, and it goes away."

JEAN: *High.* She reported an improved appetite and a marked reduction in the number of her headaches—an improvement which she regarded as "a great conquest." Her husband felt that the course benefited her tremendously: "She no longer feels that her problems are the most unique and most difficult imposed on mankind."

REGINA: *High.* "I have a habit of every spring, going into a real depression where I hardly function, and this spring I haven't. I feel that the Workshop did this thing. It carried me along ... Some of the overwhelming anger in me has drained off, or dissipated enough that I am almost on a full diet instead of 'eating for my ulcer.' "

ROSA: *High.* "I have begun to be a better 'mother' to myself, less demanding, more understanding, and more willing to be just plain nice to myself ... The thought of suicide is rare now —fleeting, compared with an almost daily former wish for death. Also, I still have anxiety to a great degree, but it's softened by feeling hope where there used to be futility . . . I would definitely say that my confidence in myself has grown to where I am aware of it."

ZIVA: *High*. She reported improvement in emotional stability, in her ability to do housework, and in an ability to think more clearly. A close friend reported: "Her improvement in the last couple of months is so marvelous that it is unbelievable. At the beginning . . . she was terrified of both people and different noises . . . even to go into the car with her husband. Now she goes into the car and is even a back seat driver, and she isn't scared any more to go into a bus."

DAWN: *Moderate*. She declared that she "would have gone to pieces" if it had not been for the Workshop: "I no longer feel suicidal . . . I can laugh at something I think is funny without looking around first to see if others are laughing too . . ." However, she was still far from a self-accepting person: "I keep seeing myself in a different light, but the more I see, the less I like." No longer able to blame her mother, she felt "confusion and helplessness."

DOLLY: *Moderate*. Her depressions and migraine headaches decreased in intensity and frequency. She was able to accept her work: ". . . that is one 'lump in my throat' that is dissolving. Actually I feel much happier for it . . ."

JOSHUA: *Low*. He claimed that since the Workshop he was less excitable and that he had learned to calm himself down more easily.

JUNE: *Mixed*. Since starting the Workshop she found herself becoming quite tense, smoking and knitting more, and no longer able to diet. She was more frightened and guilty about her hostile fantasies toward her children. However, she noted that prior to the Workshop her self-picture was so hateful she simply could not face herself at all. Also, she believed she was becoming stronger in being able to recognize what sent her into agonizing depressions, and her depressions were not as suicidal as in the past.

MIKE: *Mixed*. His discomfort grew as he became convinced that there may be some things about his relationship to his son that he did not want to face. At the same time, he sensed somewhat that there may be something hopeful in this very recognition on his part.

EDNA: *Worsened.* Her failure to clarify her problems left her feeling that they might be more deep-seated than she had thought, and this, in turn, made her feel "more frightened than I ever have been."

Movement in Interpersonal Relations

The category of Interpersonal Relations refers to changes in the participant's degree of *assertion, self-control,* or *affiliation* in his relations with others. Assertion refers to the ability to behave independently, to express one's real feelings, thoughts, and wishes, or to resist the demands and exploitations of others; self-control refers to the conscious exercise of restraint upon impulses or feelings judged by the member himself to be unwarranted or disproportionate to a situation, for example, impulses to retaliate, feelings of hurt, and demanding behavior; affiliation refers to the degree of movement toward people be it in the form of feelings of warmth and sympathy, communication, or actual association.

The criteria for assessing degree of movement in this area are described below:

High: A marked degree of change is reported in one or more of the following areas: assertion, self-control, or affiliation. A change may be considered marked if it involves more than one other person, the member himself regards the shift as high in magnitude, uses descriptive terms of extreme intensity, and provides some specification in describing his pre-Workshop status or the change which followed.

Moderate: Positive movement short of marked change is reported in at least two areas.

Low: Positive movement short of marked change is reported in one of the three areas.

The criteria for Mixed and Unmoved are the same as those cited in the Sense of Well-Being category. There were no instances of Worsened change in this category.

Of the fifty-seven participants, fourteen were judged High in this category, twenty Moderate, sixteen Low, two Mixed, and five

Unmoved. Concrete examples of various types of movement in this category follow:

DENISE: *High.* She has begun to take independent steps, has become more open and communicative, and is decidedly more self-assertive, especially in relation to her family: "I always asked my sister to shop with me. A short while ago I shopped . . . without seeking her advice at all. This was a great step forward for me . . . Since I allowed my husband to read my letters to Dr. ——— (the leader), he has become much more sympathetic and understanding, and, in turn, he has confided his feelings most intimately to me . . . an unforeseen development which has . . . bound us closer together than ever before in our marriage." According to her sister, "She has always been tightly locked up inside herself . . . but recently she seems to have matured to a point where I can really discuss things with her on equal terms. She is more outgoing and much friendlier to other people."

LOUISE: *High.* Instead of persisting in stubborn arguments with her husband, she began to curb her temper and "give in more . . . overlook certain things that he does and not feel sorry that I overlooked it . . . I feel that's a major step." She stopped beating her children: "On one occasion I had a difference with my sister. Later that same day my son did something . . . which irritated me. Instead of hitting him, I talked to myself and said he didn't do anything so really bad, so why should I beat him up because of my sister? I didn't hit him, and I felt very good." According to her husband, she became more self-assertive in relation to her dominating mother: "It has been many years since she answered her mother back without feeling (later) that she had committed a heinous crime . . ."

MARY: *High.* She was no longer angry with her husband if he did not offer to help with household chores: "I respect his manhood and am waiting for him to feel so sure of himself that he can offer his help to me. If he feels that attending golf instruction courses are important to him, I should accept it and not feel it as a personal rejection." For the first time she was able to discuss his youth with him, and, as a result, they learned more about each other. She took out her anger less often on her children. She no longer felt she had to please her brother, and for the first time she could say "no" to him.

MIRANDA: *High*. For a year prior to the Workshop she rarely left her home, but now she had a fairly active social life. She no longer complied compulsively with mother's wishes, and for the first time she asserted herself with her husband, though this meant opposing his wishes. She reported fewer flareups with her children: "When my older daughter is irritated with me and says that she hates me, I don't feel badly at all anymore . . . I try to pacify her and tell her that we all feel this way toward our parents sometimes, and I am certain she will love me again later . . . had a marvellous effect . . . I don't think I would have done that without the Workshop."

ROSA: *High*. She no longer feels a necessity to comply automatically to the needs of others at the expense of her own: "Life consists of time, and I prefer to spend my life in my own way . . . I no longer phone or visit my parents daily . . . which was a custom of years' standing . . . Telephone calls which would waste a lot of time used to arouse resentment and frustration in me. I didn't seem to know how to shorten the call gracefully . . . Maybe it sounds terrible, but I can fib nicely now and even tell the truth when I am busy, as I did before, but without feeling mean or guilty."

GENEVA: *Moderate*. She refrained from efforts at changing her husband and stood up to him more when they disagreed. Able to see mother now as a bitter, frustrated person, she reported becoming more tolerant of her, and less vulnerable to her "belittling sneers." She was more "tolerant" of her children.

MIKE: *Moderate*. He still felt like pushing his son out of the house in order to get him on his own: ". . . yet I feel real pity and sympathy for him whereas before the Workshop I felt so hard that I did not want him ever to come back." He was trying to be more aware of his family's feelings: "I'm ready to stop quickly if they back up . . . and I see it quickly, whereas before, I would forget it."

PAULA: *Moderate*. She had fewer arguments with her husband. "My husband did say something that I got very upset about . . . when I had time to think about it, I realized that my husband hadn't meant it to do with me. If it was ten other people, he would have said the same thing." She found less need to justify herself. For example, when asked by her sister-in-law if she were going to buy a kitchen set, instead of telling a whole story about how she would have liked to but her husband didn't want to, she now answered with a simple "no."

ZIVA: *Moderate*. She felt more relaxed toward her husband, "In every way, including sex." She was less impatient, nagging, strict, and overprotective with her son. "I learned to control myself a little bit . . ." Her close friend and neighbor confirms that "she is much easier to live with . . ."

CARLA: *Low*. She attributed to the Workshop efforts on her part to be "a bit more understanding" toward her family and to see things from the other person's view from time to time.

SHERMAN: *Mixed*. He felt that his problems with his mother worsened because he was being "very cruel to her and can't help it." However, he felt a strong compassion for her because of her hard life and her willingness "to satisfy." He was much less concerned about what other people say about him. He felt more capable of understanding and helping his wife.

Movement Profiles

The combination of ratings for a given member with respect to movement in each of the three categories constitutes that member's movement profile or pattern of reported change. For example, one member's movement profile was Low-High-Moderate, that is, she was rated low in Awareness, High in Sense of Well-being, and Moderate in Interpersonal Relations. Thirty-three different profiles occurred in our group of fifty-seven participants. In order to communicate more economically what the major types of movement were, we classified these thirty-three profiles into five subtypes. The five subtypes, their definitions, and the number of members in each are presented below:

Global: Positive change is reported in every category of movement, to a High degree in at least two of the three categories, with Awareness rated at least Moderate. There were fourteen members with this movement profile.

Insight: Positive change is reported in every category, to a High degree in Awareness, with no higher than a Moderate rating in the remaining two categories. Twelve members fell into this category.

Intermediate: A Moderate rating in Awareness and in one other category; at least an Unmoved rating in the remaining category. Eight members showed this pattern.

Functional: A Low rating in Awareness, at least a Moderate rating in one other category, and any rating but Mixed or Worsened in the remaining category. (Since in this grouping, movement is most prominent in the Eense of Well-being and/or Interpersonal Relations categories, and since these two categories refer to a person's action and their emotional concomitants, that is, to his actual functioning, we decided to label this subtype as the Functional one.) Eight members showed this pattern.

Low-Unmoved: No higher than a Low rating in all categories, or any pattern which falls short of meeting the criteria of the four profile subtypes above. Fifteen members showed this pattern.

Forty-two of the fifty-seven participants had movement profiles falling into the Global, Insight, Intermediate, and Functional groupings, indicating that an overwhelming majority of the participants reported that they experienced the Workshop as beneficial in varying ways and to varying degrees. The dynamics underlying their claimed benefits varied for these forty-two members. For some the chief dynamic appeared to be a significant growth in awareness which opened a door to new ways of seeing oneself and to new possibilities in living. For others the relationship to the leader appeared to play a central role in stimulating them to try out different patterns of relating to self and others. In still others, the sheer experience of participating in a group of a kind that was unprecedented in their lives seemed to be the crucial factor.

A number of reports, though often articulate and dramatic, left us with some reservations or doubts as to the meaning, depth, or utility of their claimed gains. In nine instances we had reason to question whether the reported gains would outlive the members' contact with the leader since their claimed progress may have been generated by an intense wish to please him. There were two whose reports seemed to be exaggerated as a result of a transient excess of enthusiasm, perhaps more indicative of their emotional lability or of exhibitionistic need than of genuine progress. In the case of one member, we were left with some doubt as to whether the gains she reported might not have reflected a reenforcement of her propensity for acting out in egocentric ways. A follow-up study one to two years following the end of the Workshop revealed evidence in support of our doubts for five of these members in that they left therapy before its completion. However, to our surprise, we found that six members in this dubious group had persisted in therapy to its completion or were still in it at the time of follow-up. The remaining member even claimed maintenance of her declared gains for two years without therapy.

There were 15 Workshop participants whom we classified in the Low-Unmoved group. We have no reason to question the sincerity of these patients' reports. Most members of this group tended to be negativistic, rigid, or unreflective persons.

The Workshop as a Clinical Adjunct

In proposing a study of the Workshop within a clinical setting we anticipated that such a course might be useful as (a) a stopgap form of help for prospective patients while they were awaiting psychotherapy, (b) a means of facilitating the process of entry into therapy, and (c) an experience contributing to the effectiveness of patients' participation in the therapy process itself. Below we consider the effects of the Workshop from each of these points of view.

Stopgap Help

It was our hope that the Workshop, while not purporting to meet their expressed need for treatment, would be perceived by prospective patients as relevant to their emotional problems and intrinsically related to future therapy. As such, it might serve as a temporary expedient to ease the tension of waiting to be called and to make more bearable the difficulties which first spurred them to apply for therapy.

Certainly, the Workshop provided most members with a satisfying form of attention, involved them emotionally, and engaged their deep interest. Attendance was remarkably faithful. The Workshop was frequently described as a supportive experience. Statements such as the following were common: "I couldn't wait 'til the day came that I could go." "It got me through the week."

The Workshop, however, was not just busy work to fill up the waiting time, nor an entertaining activity to distract them from their worries, nor a tranquilizing pat on the back. As the reader now knows, the course was regarded by a definite majority of the participants as providing benefits that went decisively beyond merely "holding the emotional line." Their reports as well as our observations indicate that for many the class was a highly meaningful, even compelling weekly period of honest reflection about the self, during which significant aspects of one's being were confronted and explored, and one's capacity for learning and change was demonstrated through first-hand experience.

That the Workshop was experienced as more than mere stopgap help is evidenced by seven members who, following the course, felt little or no need for treatment, and did not request it. Five of this subgroup had been applicants for therapy before the Workshop. At the time of the follow-up interview, four of the five declared they had maintained their claimed gains for two years, and one member for one year. Below we present capsule summaries of the main developments of each of these five participants:

Though EFFIE attended the Workshop for only eight sessions, she claimed to have achieved many insights bearing on her difficulties, for example, that she had berated her husband for not being her father, and had been "impossible" with her son because she had identified him with her husband.

MOLLY claimed that following the Workshop she seldom experienced her feelings of inferiority and loneliness. She stopped arguing with her mother. A very obese woman, she even managed to lose ninety pounds.

ABE reported that he was no longer subject to the compulsion to write pornographic stories, his chief complaint prior to the Workshop. His outstanding discovery in the Workshop was that his childhood experiences "which I did not consider . . . important . . . have a great bearing on my life as I am today."

After listening to other people in the Workshop discuss their personal problems, DINAH concluded that she shouldn't make every pain "such a tragedy" in life and that she should "grow up."

Although his main symptom, leg pains, persisted, IVAN felt that the Workshop "showed me to be satisfied with what you got . . . it could be worse."

Two members of this subgroup were guests who, prior to the Workshop, had been experiencing considerable subjective distress. They felt sufficiently benefited by the Workshop to continue doing without therapy. According to them, their Workshop gains were still being maintained at the time of the follow-up interviews:

ROSA had come as a guest, but had been intensely oppressed with feelings of loneliness and suicidal thoughts. She stated, "Suicidal tendencies, thank God, are a thing of the past . . . I'm too busy now. Being in that group of people . . . gave me more courage . . . I have been woven into firmer cloth."

One member, DOLLY, came to the Workshop partly as SARA's protector, and partly out of intellectual curiosity. She claimed that as a result of the Workshop she was able to speak her mind, her migraine headaches had stopped, and she was able to feel forgiving toward her grandmother whom she formerly had disliked.

It is difficult to make any generalizations about the meaning of this unexpected development for these seven persons. For some in the group, this may have represented a "flight into health," an unhygienic fortification of defenses, or a kind of protective evasiveness. From this point of view their failure to enter therapy may be regarded as a negative development, a mere postponement of their need to come to grips with their problems.* On the other hand, it cannot be ignored that these members experienced the Workshop as beneficial and that this outcome has a certain validity in terms of the goals which they set for themselves. We might also add that the gains claimed by the two guests strike us as possessing a genuine quality. They imply that the Workshop experience may be all that some people find necessary to become better able to cope with their problems, or that in some instances the Workshop might serve as a useful first-aid measure which can obviate the need for therapy.

Facilitating Entry into Therapy

We anticipated that the Workshop experience might facilitate the process of entry into therapy: (a) by sustaining or sharpening

---

*We recently learned that two members of this group, EFFIE and MOLLY, have reapplied for therapy since the follow-up interview.

incentive for therapy, and (b) in overcoming resistance to group therapy when this is either the therapy of choice or the one most available. Below we consider the evidence related to each of these types of facilitation.

Sustaining or Sharpening Incentive for Therapy.   Two groups are of interest with respect to therapy incentive, the forty-three members who had applied for therapy, and seven guests who, prior to the Workshop, were consciously oppressed in varying degrees by their psychological problems but who, for one reason or another, had not applied for therapy.*   In the case of each group we were interested in the number who, still experiencing the need for help following the Workshop, entered therapy.

Of the forty-three members who originally applied for therapy, five persons following the Workshop felt that their need for therapy had diminished so markedly that they no longer sought it. These members have already been discussed. Of the remaining thirty-eight applicants, thirty-six entered therapy following the Workshop, and one member, at the time of follow-up, was waiting to be called by the family agency to which she had applied. The remaining member, despite a conscious and continuing need for help, decided not to enter therapy. The Workshop helped him to achieve a sharper awareness of his overdependency and of his need to impress others. These developments shook him up and left him fearful that continuing the self-exploratory process might interfere with his ambition to become a writer by making him complacent and comforming.**

Putting these data more sharply, we find that, out of thirty-eight applicants for therapy who continued to experience their need for help following the Workshop, all but one (97%) entered therapy or were waiting for it to become available. Without a control group or base figures of the attrition rate in the average clinic waiting list, it is difficult to interpret this finding. We do not know how many of the forty-three applicants, had they not

---

*Seven members are not considered in this analysis, five who were concurrently in group therapy, and two guests who did not experience themselves as having psychological problems either before or after the Workshop.

**Since this writing, we learned that he has entered therapy.

had the Workshop experience, would have sustained their sub-jectively felt need and incentive for therapy and how many would have removed themselves from the waiting list either because their personal situations had improved sufficiently, or because they had become discouraged by the wait without an abatement of their need, or for some other reason. At the very least, we can say this—that the maintenance of incentive for therapy in Workshop member-applicants who experienced a continuing need for it was extremely high, as reflected in the fact that almost 100 percent of this group entered into treatment.

Of the seven guests who were experiencing the burden of their psychological problems yet who had not applied for therapy, five members entered therapy after the Workshop. The Workshop apparently served as a transitional experience for this group, easing their entry into therapy.

It is our impression that the maintenance or sharpening of incentive for therapy in applicants and guests came about in various ways. Some members, as they became more aware of the locus of responsibility for their problems in themselves, became more motivated to achieve deeper self-understanding. For others, increased incentive was linked to an increase in hopefulness about their capacity for change. Such hopefulness developed out of their own first-hand experiences in the Workshop, their growth in self-awareness, and the beginnings of various constructive changes. The wish for therapy was fortified in still others as they came to recognize that becoming a patient does not signify insanity.

Overcoming Resistance to Group Therapy. The role of group therapy in the armamentarium of the psychotherapist is receiving increasing recognition, especially in the face of the enormous need for therapy and the impossibility of making a serious dent in this need by means of individual therapy. In addition, we are coming to recognize that group therapy has intrinsic merit, and, in some instances, may be even more valuable than individual therapy. Unfortunately, it has been our experience, and we are sure that it is shared by many others, that the majority of patients can conceive of therapy for themselves only in individual terms, that is, as taking place in a private one-to-one relationship with a therapist. Consequently, any experience such as the Workshop which can give them a preliminary encounter with a group process, allay their anxieties over the revelation of personal secrets, and motivate them to an acceptance of group therapy would represent an important clinical contribution.

In order to obtain data bearing on shifts in receptivity to group therapy, we included in our post-Workshop questionnaires such queries as: (a) whether or not the member wished to enter therapy and, if so, which type of treatment, individual or group, he would prefer; (b) whether he would accept group therapy if individual therapy were his first choice and it were not available, and (c) what changes, if any, occurred in his attitude or receptivity toward either form of treatment.* Forty-two members wished to enter therapy at the end of the Workshop. Of these, three members failed to answer the above questions. Our main findings for the remaining thirty-nine are presented below.

Of the thirty-nine members considered in relation to this topic, thirty-two entered group therapy. Of these thirty-two, thirteen had overcome their pre-Workshop rejection of this form of therapy,** and seven, who prior to the Workshop would have accepted group therapy, reported a shift from preferring individual therapy to preferring group therapy.***

One member of the thirty-nine was still waiting to be called for therapy at the time of her follow-up interview. She reported shifting from a pre-Workshop rejection of group therapy to an acceptance of it.

Six of the thirty-nine members entered individual therapy after the Workshop. Only one of these six reported that she shifted

---

*In evaluating shifts in therapy attitudes as expressed at the conclusion of the Workshop, we were compelled to rely on retrospective accounts of pre-Workshop attitudes. Although we have no reason to believe that any systematic bias might have distorted the results obtained, these findings would have been more manifestly valid if we had made a survey of attitudes toward therapy prior to each Workshop for comparison with an independent survey after the Workshop.

**Nine of these thirteen attended group therapy for over a year. Two of the thirteen shifted from group therapy to individual therapy and persisted in the latter form of therapy. Two of the thirteen first entered individual therapy, but then shifted to group therapy which they attended for more than a year.

***Four of these seven attended group therapy for more than a year.

from a pre-Workshop acceptance of group therapy to a rejection of it. Two members rejected group therapy before and after the Workshop. One in the group shifted from a rejection of group therapy to a preference for it, but apparently group therapy was not available at the family agency where she had applied.

In brief, of the thirty-nine members considered in relation to this question, fifteen had overcome their rejecting attitude toward group therapy to the point where thirteen entered it when given the opportunity to do so. Seven members who were receptive to group therapy prior to the Workshop shifted their preference for individual therapy to group therapy and entered group therapy. Only one member out of the thirty-nine shifted from a positive to a rejecting attitude toward group therapy. These findings suggest that, insofar as receptivity to group therapy is concerned, the Workshop succeeded to a considerable extent in overcoming fears of exposure, and perhaps other narcissistic anxieties, and in developing a more optimistic attitude with regard to the usefulness of group treatment.

Facilitating the Patient's Role in Therapy

We conceived of the Workshop in a clinical setting as being a "training" experience in the process of self-exploration which could be useful either as a preparation for therapy for prospective patients or as a source of catalytic stimulation for patients already in concurrent therapy. Below we present our findings with reference to this variable of facilitation of the therapy process for two groups: those 41 members who entered therapy following the Workshop, and five participants who were in concurrent group therapy.

Preparation for Therapy. We have two sets of data bearing on the Workshop's effectiveness in preparing members for therapy: statistics on persistence in therapy, and the members' own views on the matter after having experienced the therapy process.

We wish it had been possible to set up an experiment in which the same therapist would work with two groups of people, one post-Workshop members, the other non-Workshop people. The two groups would have been equated from the standpoint of psychological characteristics pertinent to their potential participation in group psychotherapeutic process. It would then be possible to compare the two groups with reference to such variables as the rapidity and directness with which significant personal problems had been addressed, the rigidity and persistence of resistances, readiness of access to transference reactions, as well as the rapidity and depth of therapeutic change. In the absence of such a comprehensive and controlled study, the findings below, while of definite interest and value in their own right, must be considered as hardly more than suggestive.

PERSISTENCE IN THERAPY. Forty-one members entered therapy following the Workshop. This group can be divided into Persisters and Dropouts. The subgroup of Persisters includes those whose therapy was ongoing or completed at the time of follow-up. Dropouts are patients who left therapy before its completion.

Of the forty-one members, thirty were Persisters, and eleven were Dropouts.

Of the thirty Persisters, twenty-six members were in treatment at the time of their follow-up interview, twelve having attended sessions for two years or more, twelve for over a year, and two for less than six months. Four members had completed therapy to their satisfaction, two having attended sessions for over a year, one for about nine months, and one for less than six months.

The eleven Dropouts gave various reasons for stopping therapy. Seven members left because they found the therapist or the therapy situation unhelpful or unsatisfying in one or another respect. Four members gave excuses apparently unrelated to the therapy situation per se, for example, getting a job, difficulty in leaving the children. Of this group of eleven, one left therapy after a year, four after approximately nine months, and six after only a few sessions.

The above findings suggest that the vast majority of those who entered therapy did so with seriousness of purpose, with an obvious persistence of their original motivation, and with some ability to meet the difficulties and anxieties involved in therapy. What is not possible to say with definiteness, is how much the Workshop may have contributed to this capacity for persistent application to the therapeutic process. Here, of course, we are sadly lacking in statistics from control groups.

THE MEMBERS' VIEWS OF THE WORKSHOP'S PREPARATORY FUNCTION. Of forty-one members who entered therapy following the Workshop, thirty-four made some clear-cut reference in their interviews to whether or not they felt the Workshop had prepared them for therapy. Of this group of thirty-four patients, twenty-eight felt that, in varying ways and degrees, the Workshop had served a useful preparatory function; three felt that the Workshop had not prepared them in any way, and three were even disappointed to find that therapy did not live up to their expectation that it would resemble the Workshop in one or another respect. In brief, the majority of members who entered therapy felt that the Workshop had made some positive contribution toward preparing them for therapy.

The fact that there were only three members who went to therapy expecting that it would be rather like the Workshop and who were consequently disappointed is of special significance. We had some concern that anticipations might be aroused in the Workshop whose disappointment in the therapy relationship might delay its progress. This evidently did not happen, except with a very small minority.

We can hardly expect that the reader would accept the judgment, "I have been better prepared for therapy by the Workshop," as substantial evidence for the fact of the matter. We would, therefore, like to present some of the actual statements which the members made. The reader can judge for himself whether the character of these statements lends credibility to the validity of the members' judgments in this area. In reviewing the members' own responses, we were able to differentiate between two major types of preparation.

1) One way in which preparation is perceived by the Workshop members is in terms of clarification of the process of therapy. A number of persons came to the Workshop with very hazy, if not downright false, notions about therapy. For example, some expected that treatment would be a matter of a few sessions and would simply involve being given advice by the therapist. In the

main, these patients appeared to experience markedly diminished expectations that the therapist would solve their problems for them, that treatment would be speedy, or that miraculous changes would occur. They also came to appreciate better the degree of responsible collaboration that would be required of them.

2) The Workshop also served as a significant preparation for various patients by clarifying just what problems or areas they would need to work on in therapy, by underscoring the importance of exploring the origins of these problem areas in one's childhood experiences, and by opening eyes to a whole world of intraceptive experience previously ignored or only vaguely sensed at best. Sessions such as those on birth order, first memories, and dreams appeared to be particularly effective in orienting members to the kinds of data that can be usefully brought up and examined in therapy, and in giving them some notion as to how one may go about exploring such data in searching, analytic ways.

Examples of these types of preparation are given below in the members' own words:

> CARLA: "I'm quite sure I came into therapy with more insight into my problem, and I was aware of the fact that the problem I had actually started out with wasn't the real problem . . . I think it was a film . . . the lady that started having headaches . . . I started thinking . . . if it could manifest itself in a headache like it did in this lady, why couldn't it manifest itself the way it did with me? . . ."

> GENEVA: "When he (the leader) refused to give answers to my questions, I was first annoyed. I felt that he was disinterested, and I was hurt and felt crushed. Then I began to think about why he didn't answer, and I had to face the biggest truth I didn't want to, that a problem such as I live with has no one-two answer. The answer lies within me, and what I want when I finally look at myself with respect and understanding as to my needs."

> GIGI: "I think it helped me a great deal, where if I hadn't come to the Workshop and just went into therapy, I don't think I would have progressed too well . . . My attitude changed, and I thought, gee, mental hygiene doesn't mean people are crazy, actually . . . Then I realized they were actually normal people with just problems that had to be ironed out, and I

started feeling more comfortable in coming. Now I don't feel bad at all. Before, I didn't dare tell anybody I was going to a mental clinic . . . it made me realize that there actually wasn't any reason for me to be afraid of it, and if I try hard enough, I can overcome these fears."

MIKE: "The Workshop is like an eye-opener . . . I've never been in therapy before, but in the Workshop I began to see that these things required time, patience . . . we must go back and review . . . Without the Workshop I wouldn't know quite what to do to begin with . . . That definitely has made things easier for me . . . Different thoughts which we had explored before because of the Workshop. Somehow to have brought this out has helped me in my group therapy."

PEGGY: "Well, it gives you a better understanding about things, so perhaps you can eliminate a lot of time in therapy . . . I know in the Workshop you learn that dreams are just a reflection of yourself, and, therefore, if you go to the therapist and talk about dreams, you talk about it in a more intelligent way . . . Perhaps if I didn't have the Workshop and sat down cold in therapy, I imagine that this woman (in the therapy group) who did all the talking might have upset me much more than she did . . . I might not have been able to try to get as much out of her as I tried to do because I was being more relaxed and more understanding, or tolerant."

PHOEBE: "It gave me the feeling, a little bit of preparation for the fact that I was going to be with other people and that these people were going to have personalities that I might or might not particularly like, but that I could find very useful and that I could identify with . . . and I think it taught me a certain humility about people too. Well, it's something that I've always intellectually accepted, that we are all equal . . . but I don't think I really believed it until I met a lot of people that I might never have bumped into in the course of my life, but that I found were thinking and fine people. When I finally got to therapy, I was more prepared to relax with the group that I was with and recognized that I would have something in common with them."

RENEE: "(Before the Workshop) I expected it (therapy) was all a whole lot of shit. And now I really believe that it will help me, or rather that I will be able to help myself, let me put it that way. That's the shift. I got the knowledge that I

have to do it myself . . . At the time I went to the Workshop
I went under pressure. Lenny told me I had to go. I did not
want to. Now I see how helpful it is, and I want it . . . I
learned about the things that govern people are not what you
think they are . . . I just didn't know anything about therapy."

ROSALIE: "I found that the Workshop carried me through
to therapy very beautifully . . . if my therapist brought up a
subject I did not immediately disagree. I would think about it
. . . because in the Workshop I found that before you let your
tongue move, your head must think . . . I learned in the Workshop that you could talk to somebody, the therapist, without
being ashamed, without being afraid, without feeling that somebody is going to look down on you . . . I got from the Workshop that when you do something wrong, there's always an
underlying reason why you did it."

SHERMAN: "This preparation is a big thing . . . A new guy
comes into the group, and he says to the group, 'I don't feel
that you people can help me. You're lay people, you can't help
me, only an authority like a doctor can help me.' Right away I
know this guy didn't attend the Workshop . . . He wasn't aware
of the fact that people can help each other, and that's what you
get from the Workshop . . . The understanding . . . that they
have to be honest with themselves . . . I guess it's built up in the
Workshop. Honesty is the start of it . . . I think that's where I
got my true conception of therapy . . . That (Balloon Experiment) was the start of my understanding a lot about my fear,
my fear of things that go on all around me all the time . . . Like
being afraid . . . somebody is going to kill me . . . It gives you
something to work on . . . This experiment wasn't done for
nothing . . . It left me with a feeling that this isn't a lot of
malarkey."

ZIVA: "I know it gave me the start, and I knew that I had to
work on myself, which I didn't know before. I didn't know it
was me. I thought the whole world was—you know, it was
everybody's fault but mine . . . The Workshop was just the
beginning, and it helped me to realize what we have to do in
therapy . . . It's like when you come to school, and you go to
Kindergarten . . . it made it much easier . . . it gave me to
think about myself, and things came out which applied to me
. . . I didn't feel as strange toward therapy. It was like I knew
something already. I knew what Dr. ——— meant, whereas

people who come without a Workshop, it takes them quite some time to understand what they have to do in order to work and to get better."

We have presented two sets of data for judging whether or not the Workshop was effective in preparing members for therapy. One has to do with whether they persisted in therapy. The second has to do with whether the members themselves felt that as a result of the Workshop they were better prepared to participate effectively in therapy than they had been prior to the course. Insofar as these data can serve as valid criteria, the Workshop seems to have been of substantial value as preparation for therapy.

The Workshop as a Catalyst for Patients in Concurrent Therapy. It was our belief that the Workshop has some distinctive attributes, as compared with therapy, which might be turned to advantage for the therapy patient who concurrently attends the course. The Workshop is more structured, follows a syllabus, albeit a flexible one, and is semi-didactic. It involves a far more comprehensive sampling of personalities and psychological problems, and it tends to generate less intense or intimate transferences. The second Workshop provided us with an opportunity to explore, at least in a preliminary way, some effects of concurrent participation in the Workshop and in group therapy. This Workshop contained five members who were also attending a therapy group with the Workshop leader as therapist. These were experienced patients having been in therapy for a year or more. The effects of their Workshop experiences as reported by each of them may be summarized as follows:

HOPE felt that the Workshop stimulated her progress in the therapy group. It gave her leads to bring to the group to work on. In the Workshop her perception of her childhood shifted from "happy" to "sad." She became aware of a "too close attachment to mother," and how missing a real father made her seek one in her husband. Noticing that her reactions differed from others in the Workshop, she could now plainly see that in many instances "my thinking is my very own and not what is plainly the situation . . ."

MIRIAM stated that facets of her personality were revealed to her in the Workshop that she did not know about even after four years of group therapy. She became aware of the influence of her "middle child" role, of how her father's desire for a son made her angry at herself for being a girl, and how much she has always needed to prove herself.

RITA became more aware in the Workshop of her self-protective facade, her impatience with weakness out of a need to be strong, and her expectation that others should change rather than herself. She felt that the Workshop brought her a little closer to the other therapy group members and made it easier for her to talk in her therapy group.

The Workshop experience tended to confirm and extend TINA's awareness of the influence of her past experiences in her family. Thus, when she found herself reacting with anger to a domineering girl in one of the movies, she was able to relate this to her own domination as a child at the hands of her father. When she observed herself reacting with fright at the prospect of one of her letters being read openly in the group, she concluded after some reflection that ". . . perhaps it is all due to my background of feeling stupid when I was a child and ridiculed when I did say something . . ." TINA stated in her follow-up interview, "I think the Workshop enhanced therapy, added to it. It prepared me for certain things to discuss, things that came up in the Workshop itself."

GLADYS dropped out of her concurrent therapy group following the completion of the Workshop. She claimed the Workshop gave her sufficient relief from her guilt feelings and somehow increased her sense of well-being to the point where she felt she no longer needed therapy.

The evidence suggests the potential value of the Workshop as a catalytic agent when pursued concurrently with group therapy. MIRIAM offers an example of the crystallization of a significant focal insight during the Workshop which had eluded her through four years of psychotherapy. TINA introduces the possibility that the Workshop may serve a very useful function as a catalyzer of latent processes which group therapy has set in motion, and also as a stimulus to opening up new paths of self-exploration. RITA exemplifies the possibility of the Workshop helping one

group therapy member to become more communicative with fellow group therapy members. For most of those concurrently in
therapy, the Workshop apparently provided the opportunity to
take new learnings back to the therapy group for active exploration. In addition, the experienced patients were of special value
to the Workshop group in stimulating the other members by the
example they set in freely exploring themselves and each other.

Summary
We have evaluated the effects of the Workshop from two
general points of view. The first is concerned with the role of the
Workshop as a stimulus to change in members' perceptions, feelings, and behavior. The second concerns the Workshop's role as a
clinical adjunct.

In the effort to evaluate the Workshop as a stimulus to change,
we classified and rated evidence, consisting for the most part of
Workshop members' own communications in letters, questionnaires, and interviews bearing on movement in three major categories, Awareness, Sense of Well-being, and Interpersonal Relations.

Thirty-four of the fifty-seven members reported a growth in
Awareness, at least to the extent of experiencing a heightened
sense of responsibility for events in their lives. A wide diversity
of insights, some quite dramatic, were reported, including the discovery of unrealistic assumptions or expectations underlying one's
style of life, and the realization of childhood origins of current
personality patterns.

Twenty-nine of the fifty-seven participants were judged to have
experienced at least a moderate degree of movement in Sense of
Well-being. Especially striking were the reports of symptomatic
improvements. These included abatement of phobic reactions,
psychosomatic complaints, and severely depressive moods.

Thirty-four of the fifty-seven participants were judged to have
experienced at least a moderate degree of movement in the area
of Interpersonal Relations. There seemed to be three main ways
in which movement in this category was expressed. Some members were able to restrain hitherto explosive outbursts of anger
against their children. Others were now relating in a more warm,

honest, and communicative way with their spouses. Many stated that they were now able to assert themselves effectively against the intimidating pressures of others, especially parents.

In order to evaluate the Workshop as an adjunct to therapy, we had follow-up interviews with all of the fifty-seven Workshop members about a year after the completion of the second Workshop. This was two years after the completion of the first Workshop.

Statistics on post-Workshop entry into and persistence in therapy, while difficult to evaluate in the absence of control data, nonetheless, strongly suggest that the Workshop helped to sustain and in many instances sharpen the original incentive for therapy. The efficacy of the Workshop in generating receptivity and even preference for group as against individual psychotherapy seems well established by the data. Based again on the testimony of the members themselves, expressed often in words and tones of dramatic conviction, we are encouraged to believe that the Workshop offers genuine possibilities as preparation for the process of therapy and as a catalyst for patients in concurrent therapy.

The above findings indicate that the course was regarded by a definite majority of participants as providing benefits that went decisively beyond merely serving as a stopgap expedient to ease the tension of waiting for therapy. In fact, seven members who prior to the course had been considerably distressed by their personal problems felt little or no need for help at its conclusion and did not request therapy.

Part Two

LEADING A WORKSHOP

~~~~~~

CHAPTER 5

NOTES ON PROCEDURE

To date we have conducted over 100 Workshops, mostly with classes of adult education students, but including also groups of nursing students, executive secretaries, and labor union members. The foregoing review of the two clinical Workshops against the background of this experience with other Workshop groups has brought into focus a number of recurrent issues and specific, frequently occurring situations. Our purpose here is to identify these issues and situations and, in relation to them, to offer some technical suggestions embodying what we have learned from our experiences. Our hope is that future Workshop leaders may derive therefrom suggestions useful in their own work. Our recommendations are naturally subject to modification in light of the context in which a particular Workshop is conducted.

The notes below have benefited from a review of past Workshop experiences which were satisfactory, as well as others which turned out not so well, of leader behavior which we can continue to support, and of events which we wish had been handled differently. Our aims and methods in the Workshop have undergone successive modifications as our experience with different groups and situations has grown. The reader should, therefore, not be surprised if all the views expressed in what follows have not been exemplified in the Workshops reported in detail in this report.

Structuring

There is at the very outset of the Workshop an air of mystery about it. Members know that it will be in the nature of a class and yet not like any they have ever had before. Just because of this uncertainty and the anxiety which attends this as most other novel situations, structuring on the part of the leader is clearly a necessity.

People enter the Workshop with a diversity of conscious and unconscious expectations and hopes. Probably all share, some with naiveté, and some with underlying cynicism, hope of getting something beneficial out of the course with respect to those aspects of themselves which first aroused their curiosity or concern. It is very likely that this common expectation is far in excess of what any Workshop can hope to fulfill. As a result, the Workshop leader can anticipate periods of depression and disappointment. Whatever the educational value of actually going through such periods, it seems desirable to keep frustrations, arising out of a misconception of what the Workshop is about, within bounds optimal for the facilitation of learning.

In structuring the Workshop for the members, the leader needs to make quite clear that it is not oriented toward solving members' personal problems. On the positive side, he needs to communicate that the Workshop is concerned with the extension of self-awareness, and that this represents not only an enriching experience in its own right but is also a necessary phase in the process of growth toward more effective use of one's own resources. He needs to point out that Workshop methods are very different from those in the conventional classroom situation, that in the Workshop no one need be concerned with examinations or grades, that no one is going to be called upon, that no one needs to talk if he does not feel like it, and that here one has every opportunity to be one's self.

The leader of the first Workshop attempted an initial structuring of the course through a lecturette covering the aforementioned details. The second leader opened the first session with questions designed immediately to elicit the group's initial feelings and anticipations about the Workshop, so that he could at appropriate points provide clarifications, corrections, or reassurances as indicated. Still other approaches will suggest themselves to the reader which may be more suitably adapted to the needs and goals of a particular group.

Structuring is not an intellectual task which, once done in the beginning, can be forgotten thenceforth by the leader. It is a function that has to be performed repeatedly at those times when members indicate, by virtue of their comments and reactions, that they harbor misconceptions and unrealistic expectations.

Initial Emphasis on Simple Awareness of Experience

It may be assumed that relaxation of the students' habitual guardedness will be a necessary aim of the initial sessions of most Workshops. If the student is to be interested in exploring those personal events he ordinarily overlooks or takes for granted, he must first become aware of them. The leader, therefore, encourages the students to notice their behavior and their inner experiences with a minimum of obstructive self-judging, defensiveness, or ambitious straining for results. Thus, the leader's initial communication to the Workshop members includes some statement such as the following: "I shall invite you to participate in various kinds of group experiments. I ask you simply to see what happens as you become involved in each situation. You need not press for anything in particular to happen. Nor need you concern yourself with why you reacted as you did or with the rightness, wrongness, goodness, or badness of your reaction. Simply notice how you do react, the thoughts that occur to you, and what feelings you experience." During the initial experiments the leader encourages members to share their reactions without pressing them to analyze what happened. He is content to draw the group's attention to the dramatic diversity of responses that are reported and to the varied difficulties experienced by members in their efforts at "simply seeing what happens."

The game-like spirit of many experiments is encouraged deliberately as a way of generating this new attitude toward normally guarded behaviors, feelings, and ideas: "Play with this. You need not be serious at the moment. Just let yourself go. See what occurs." This spirit is a sort of analogue of the free-associative attitude in which the patient strives to suspend his conventional goal directedness, reality orientation, and habitual, critical censorship. Yet, at the same time, unlike a party game, there is retention of a serious purpose. The ego is in the wings, observing itself. The member needs to be both an observer who is disciplined to a degree and oriented in some kind of purpose, and a relaxed participant free to let himself go and produce something, either something quite unique in his experience or something familiar at which a fresh look can be taken.

As the reader might expect, the "see-what-happens" orientation is virtually impossible at the outset for most students to follow. Typically, the Workshop member is himself the chief source of obstruction, partly because of a persistent need to accomplish, to get answers, and to learn something tangible and immediately useful, and partly because he is committed to values such as perfection in his behavior, and the indiscriminate approval of others. Value-impregnated attitudes such as these, shared by the Workshop member with most people in our culture, deflect attention away from, and serve as active defense against, the extension of awareness on a simple observational level.

Invaribly, members revert to the habitual, achievement orientation that is characteristic of life in our culture. They begin to ask such questions as, "What am I supposed to feel?" "My reaction was different from most of the others. Is that bad?" "Why don't you tell us what all this means so we can learn something and not waste time?" The leader responds to such questions by varying versions of the following: "Do you notice how caught up we are in our ambition to get results and with our concern about our reactions being right or wrong, good or bad? I know we can't help it. There is not even any point in our trying to force ourselves to be different, but at least notice how hard it is for us to get away from these habitual ways of reacting and experiencing and to simply see what happens."

Eliciting Latent Background Material

The leader recognizes that any reaction on the part of a member is hardly more than a minor, scarcely representative sample of all the important feelings, attitudes, and other background factors in which the reaction is embedded. To be sure, it is impossible to get everything that is relevant to the reaction, but the leader needs to be alert to these implicit, covert aspects and to the desirability of bringing out a measure of these in order to make members aware that there is a rich background of unexpressed meaning which lies beyond the first observed, verbalized, or felt response.

Some members' comments may be couched in objective, analytic, intellectual terms. The leader, who assumes that behind the intellectualistic observations there lies some background of personal feeling, can elicit such feelings by questions such as, "You explained the character's motives in the movie in such and such a way. Could you also tell us your feelings about him?" On the other hand where students initially report their feelings, the leader may inquire about the thoughts accompanying these feelings. Also every expression of feeling is potentially embedded in an ambivalence which the leader may wish to elicit at times: "You say you feel so and so. Could it be that you have other feelings as well, perhaps even opposite to those you just expressed?" Expressions of feelings and of attitudes with reference to the Workshop can be explored: "Can you recall situations outside the Workshop that seem to arouse similar reactions?" Communications may also be explored along a temporal dimension: "You say you feel this way now. Have you felt this way in the past?" Or, "You say you felt this way in the past. Do you still sometimes feel this way now, perhaps even in this class?"

The leader may adopt the following eliciting procedure as members report their reactions to an experimental task: He listens carefully to the member's response, selects some salient feature in it, and then throws out a question for the member to think about and report on later. For example, if during the Balloons Experiment a student reports some anxiety about "going too far in blowing up my balloon," the leader might say, "Repeat the phrase, 'going too far,' and see what picture or thought comes to mind," or, "What happened when you went 'too far' as a child? See if a specific memory occurs to you." The leader does not wait for any responses to these suggestions. Rather, he moves from member to member, getting their initial reactions and throwing out similar inquiries for each of them to consider. Only after all initial responses have been expressed does he invite members to report what, if anything, has occurred to them in relation to the questions that he raised earlier.

When an unanticipated event occurs, for example, several members ganging up on a fellow member, the leader can raise a variety of eliciting questions: "What was your first reaction when she started criticizing you?" "Do you recall what other thoughts you had as you listened?", "How did you feel when you said what you did in reply?" Another eliciting comment might be, "We've just been through something. I noticed that some people got very excited, some got very mad. Close your eyes and see what comes to mind."

In response to films or in the course of discussions generated by other stimulus material, members often give expression to hostility, for example, toward parents, which is part of a network of ambivalent feelings. It is important to bring into the open such guilt feelings as might be thus generated: "You have just discussed your attitudes toward parents, and some of these attitudes have been obviously critical of them. How did you feel about expressing such feelings?"

Exploring the Dynamic Meaning of Workshop Experience

As members become more able to adopt a "see-what-happens" attitude, and become freer in sharing their reactions, the leader gradually encourages an active "figure-it-out" orientation. He becomes increasingly interested in sensitizing the group to the possibility that the manifest and the objective may have dynamic significance not immediately perceived. He stimulates members to note certain patterns of response which repeat themselves and to consider the origins of and motivational factors underlying these response patterns. "I wonder what past experiences may have made it necessary for you to respond in such a way?"

Simply repeating a member's comment or some significant phrase contained in it and stating that this comment or phrase sounds important and is probably worth thinking about in terms of its meaning in the person's life is one way of underscoring and drawing attention to significant, but unwittingly expressed, statements. The leader may also probe for meaning more directly. Almost any experiment or spontaneous classroom event will elicit very contrasting reactions reflecting the diversity of personalities and of experiential background in Workshop members. A very useful intervention is to raise the question of the meaning of these individual differences in perception or opinion, or what background factors could account for them, or what differences in personality might conceivably be related to them.

At promising points the leader may make interpretive sallies into the possible meaning of a member's immediate behavior or comment. The use of such interpretations is not intended to resolve any particular problem, nor is the leader mainly concerned with the accuracy of his interpretation with respect to the particular content. Rather, his objective is to stimulate the group to think more deeply about what they have taken for granted. Though the leader's emphasis is on the process of sensitization, he nonetheless uses his best insights in a responsible way when he offers interpretive suggestions or underscores members' comments. He needs to draw upon his developing insights into the particular members as well as on his general psychodynamic knowledge so that the exploration of possible meanings will not be contaminated by unnecessary irrelevancies and blind alleys.

A leader needs to be thrifty and careful in his use of interpretations. A too zealous pursuit of this technique can instill the member with an overwhelming self-consciousness: "My God, every little thing I do is meaningful and revealing." We would also suggest that when interpretive comments are offered, they be tentatively expressed: "This could be, I really don't know," "This is just a guess," "It is something to think about if you wish." It would be very good if the leader were dead wrong from time to time in his interpretation. Nothing could be more fatal than for him to be right at every point.

The leader should generally be alert to the possibilities of making use of the immediate Workshop experiences of any one individual in order to highlight something of value to the group as a whole, provided that the individual is not himself sacrificed in any way. On occasion, for example, it is a useful procedure for the leader to pick on one person in the group who seems willing and ready, and to explore with him some of the implications of his classroom reactions, particularly in terms of their historical roots. Such miniature interviews carried on within the group can be useful to the extent that other members identify with this member, projecting themselves into the situation and drawing personal inferences which might lead to some meaningful generalization about the relationship between past and present.

In helping to develop the group's capacity to interpret and analyze, we do not wish to spawn dangerous psychological pests who would go about irresponsibly interrogating and analyzing people. The leader needs to reiterate the idea that the Workshop purpose is to promote self-insight and the management of self, not of others, in interpersonal relations.

The leader should remember that he has at his finger tips a store of knowledge about personality which he can draw upon to give information at appropriate points. Such information can serve the purpose of stimulating further communication of thoughts and feelings on the part of members. A didactic communication can confirm the views that have developed spontaneously among members. Where discussion has led to a point of incompletion, a bit of information, perhaps as a counterpoint to the group's thinking up to this level, may bring the discussion to a more satisfactory point of closure or provocative suspense. Lecturettes on such topics as first memories and dreams have been useful sensitizing and provocative devices in setting up a frame of reference or intimating the significance of an impending experiment, or of an experience just passed.

Exploring Transference Attitudes

The rich array of student-leader relationships which develops in the course of every Workshop offers an exceedingly important area for exploration of the effects which members' experiences with authority figures, including parents, have had on their personality development. Transference relationships are inevitably involved in every session inviting exploitation by the leader as his alertness and sense of timeliness allow. He can, on suitable occasions, deliberately call attention to covert tranference operations which would normally remain beyond the members' awareness. The Seat-Changing Experiment is an example of a planned situation in which transference attitudes can be deliberately activated and elicited for exploration.

In a clinical setting, the Workshop member who is a prospective patient can be usefully alerted to the significance of transference attitudes which will inevitably develop in later therapy situations. One might object that the more progress the leader makes in analyzing and correcting the members' attitudes toward the leader himself, the more their future therapists might be deprived of the opportunity to work through transference relationships in all of their unattenuated intensity. In mulling this possibility over, we concluded that this was hardly a real danger since no more than the merest beginning of a corrective process takes place in the Workshop. It seems to us quite as likely that sensitization, developed in the course of preliminary experience with transference phenomena, may facilitate the development of a capacity for greater appreciation of the validity of transference interpretations intrinsic to successful participation in subsequent therapy.

The Leader's Sharing of His Personal Reactions

As in any creative endeavor, the leader's personality becomes inevitably very much involved in Workshop transactions. He cannot expect to be a thoroughly integrated, all-knowing person himself, and his deviations from perfect integration are bound to make themselves felt in his leadership as they must in all of his behavior. At one time or another conflicts may be stirred up in him around his needs for a "successful" Workshop, for love from the members, or for a safe detachment from the group. He can expect to undergo a variety of feelings including anxiety, surprise, irritation, sadness, perplexity, and elation. It is often useful for the leader to share with the group these personal reactions, even related past experiences. This does not mean that the leader can ever become just another member in the group. He remains a leader, an authority, but one who is ready to acknowledge that he is no less and no more feeling and fallible a human being than any of the other members.

Members generally find it easier to share their thoughts and feelings in response to a leader who does likewise. For many members who have had little or no experience with frank and honest sharing of feelings in their own childhood families, the leader can represent a living example of such sharing. He offers himself as a person with whom they can practice unaccustomed equalitarian, frank, and direct ways of relating. At some appropriate point, however, the leader may need to caution the group against adopting patterns of sharing intimate feelings which may be as extreme and indiscriminate as were their former patterns of inhibition.

By letting members in on his inner workings, the leader can highlight for them the discrepancy between their stereotyped assumptions about authorities in general and the reality of at least this one authority person, the leader himself, towards whom their stereotyped perceptions stubbornly persist. In presenting himself as a human being who has his own mixed feelings and conflicts right in the group situation, the leader is in effect encouraging the group to generalize from this experience with him and to consider the possibility that all the people onto whom they had projected cut-and-dried authoritarian attitudes were also human beings.

Some participants may question cynically the leader's intentions when he takes an equalitarian initiative and feel manipulated by him in his efforts to elicit freer communications. Such cynical reactions, however, need not detract from the potential value of the leader's efforts. In fact, confrontation and discussion of such cynicism may be very beneficial in highlighting the intensity and rigidity of the members' transference attitudes. (At the same time, the leader needs to be secure in the honesty of his own feelings and motivations if a potentially destructive note of paternalism is to be avoided.) Similarly, members who are upset by the leader's expressions of fallibility, out of their need for an authority with a capital "A," may be encouraged to explore their implicit self-perceptions as utterly dependent, immature persons.

Responding to Students' Questions

In the beginning, Workshop students frequently ask a variety of questions of the leader. This in itself is highly involved behavior which merits attention and inquiry from two interrelated points of view: (a) the process of questioning as such and its general place and significance in the Workshop, and (b) the content of particular questions.

The leader is interested not in cutting off questions, but in influencing the emotional and attitudinal context from which they emerge. At the outset the typical member sees himself as too ignorant to work with the problems implicit in his questions and, therefore, hopes to get answers of an authoritative kind. He assumes that personal problems are resolved through receiving the "right" answer, that there are specific answers to specific questions and that the leader has them. He takes the content and form of his questions for granted and does not question their validity.

The leader aims at a transformation of the quality of questions from the kinds at one extreme that seek definitive authoritative answers that "solve" persons' problems to those at the opposite extreme where questions become formulations of problems for further exploration with the acceptance of emerging answers as tentative and provisional. Such a change in the quality of members' questions implies a reduction in rigidity and in the demand for nice, tight, simple solutions. It reflects progress in the tolerance of ambiguity and tentativeness. The process of training has been successful when a member realizes that discovering the useful question can be more important than getting the "right" answer and, equally important, that the process of seeking and finding answers is itself intrinsic to personality growth and is something that no one can do for anybody else.

A leader should be aware that questions can at times be disguised declarations reflecting a variety of unverbalized assumptions, beliefs, upsurges of anxiety, bids for attention, disagreements, and the like. What the leader will do with questions like these will be conditioned in part by the anxiety level, readiness, and maturity of the group. The leader needs to judge what kinds of response would be most catalytic in the way of encouraging further exploration. At times he may wish to focus attention on what lies behind the member's question, "I wonder what prompts you to raise this question at this time?" "I wonder if the question is telling me something in an indirect way?" "What thoughts and feelings were you experiencing just before this question occurred to you?" Obviously, the leader needs to engage the group's interest in the very process of questioning, but he must do so in a way which would not be experienced as a rebuff and which would leave them with the hopeful feeling that they can continue to work productively on the issue raised.

In the early sessions when members ask such questions as, "What does this experiment mean? What was I supposed to get out of it?," the leader might respond by pointing out how such questions reflect the difficulty most students have in letting themselves simply experience a situation without concern for meeting some goal or standard. He might then add, "Do you suppose that you could bear being without an answer to your question for a while and just see what happens next?"

Later in the course, the leader may wish to address himself to the surface content of a question either by giving his own personal opinion and clearly labeling it as such, or by giving information or the consensus of authoritative judgment. If he does the latter, he indicates the tentativeness of these findings and judgments. Certainly, in response to personal questions that students may have about themselves, he must unmistakably avoid any implication that his opinion or the information offered need have a binding, specific relevance to any particular student. He has to emphasize that under the circumstances he does not have access to all of the relevant factors which are locked up in the history of the particular member, and even if he had them, he could not experience them with the same intimacy and meaning. What the leader needs most of all to avoid is a response which is so definitive and authoritarian that it discourages further investigation. He also needs to keep in mind that whatever his responses to the members' questions, these responses have their own impact on the members, and this impact too can be useful to explore. When he sidesteps a question, for example, he might ask the questioning student for his reaction to the sidestepping.

There are certain persistent questions for which every Workshop leader would do well to be prepared with a clear point of view and with strategies for responding to them. Many of these questions have been dealt with in the particular sessions in which they arose, and the reader will find discussions of them in the pertinent commentary. Among these recurrent questions are the following: "Is it better for me to let out my feelings or hold them in?" "I understand why I am angry, but this doesn't help me to control it. What do I do about that? "How can I overcome (this or that trait)?" "Is it good (or bad) to do (this or that)?" "I don't feel I'm getting anywhere in this course. Why is that?" "What do I do about my child?"

Many people come to the Workshop with unarticulated aims of achieving happiness in the sense of final, once-and-for-all resolution of all conflict through the acquisition of a set of invariant rules. The leader should, therefore, be alert to the possibility that communications coming from the group, no matter how sophisticated they may seem, often arise essentially out of this basic orientation. He needs also to realize that his communications to the group, oriented in his set of values (including the acceptance of conflict and frustration as a part of life) may be transformed by each member to conform with the values implicit in his own orientation.

In general, members tend less and less to direct inquiries toward the leader as they develop skill, acquire experience, and come more and more to accept their own ability to explore their questions. But such progress depends very much on the way the leader has handled the members' questions and on the general authoritarianism of his approach.

Maintaining an Optimal Level of Anxiety

The Workshop's subject matter has very much to do with the established defenses of the students. It it inevitable then that effective learning in the area of self-understanding must constitute a challenge of these defenses which is bound to generate anxiety. In fact, we believe that effective learning about the self cannot really take place unless there is a degree of emotional involvement, and unless some measure of anxiety is produced. The leader needs to avoid such a level of reassurance that the whole Workshop experience becomes simply a set of intellectualistic and detached exercises into matters of interest but of no vital concern. At the same time we recognize that it is possible to generate such an excess of anxiety that confusion and flight may very readily ensue. Consequently, the following procedures which help to prevent an excess of anxiety, and to maintain it at an optimal level, have become an intrinsic part of the Workshop process:

1) Students are forewarned about the confusion, frustration, and resistance they are likely to experience at one time or another in the course. They are also cautioned against jumping to premature conclusions about themselves.

2) The leader communicates a noncondemnatory attitude toward all forms of human experience. He combats the too ready tendency of the clinician to focus on "what's wrong" and on the hidden, murky wellsprings of behavior. He encourages students to view their shortcomings as inevitable outcomes of their life experiences rather than simply as faults to feel guilty about. He makes free use of humor, especially in situations that threaten to become too "heavy."

3) The introduction of films and other stimulus situations is carefully timed to fit the apparent readiness of the group. In fact, the leader constantly tries to appraise the level of anxiety his procedures are likely to generate. Unfortunately, there is no precise measure of what constitutes an optimum level to facilitate learning. Here the leader depends on his own powers of observation and his own feeling about the group's readiness to go forward, its resistances, its stress tolerance, and the like.

4) The student is under no compulsion, indeed has full freedom, in deciding how far, if at all, he wishes to become involved or to explore the application to himself of any topic discussed.

5) In the course of exploring classroom events, students often report relevant personal experiences. Such reports are welcomed, but the leader discourages any extended discussion of an individual's current personal problems by pointing out the obvious limitations of the classroom situation for dealing with them. He centers on the difficulties the group shares in the here-and-now classroom situation rather than on those that individual students have outside of class.

6) The leader sets aside the last ten minutes of each session for the airing of any hitherto unexpressed feelings and thoughts, and

during this period he takes the opportunity when necessary to correct serious misconceptions.

7) The students' weekly letters to the leader help to maintain a supportive personal bond, while enabling the leader to keep his finger on the pulse of individual students' vicissitudes.

We recommend that films dealing with "normals" and their current difficulties (for example, "This Charming Couple") be presented early in the Workshop. Later when members themselves begin to take exploratory excursions into their past histories, case history films (for example, "Feeling of Rejection") which relate present difficulties to childhood experiences can be shown with profit. In suggesting this sequence, we have the following rationale in mind: First, most members find it difficult at the very outset to relate productively to films dealing with the influence of childhood, a period that appears so remote from and unrelated to their current preoccupations. (In the first Workshop we noticed that the premature presentation of a film designed to encourage members to think about possible relationships between their childhood and their current adult personalities succeeded only in reminding a number of parents in the group of the "horrible" things they were doing to their children.) Second, many students secretly fear that they may be seriously abnormal persons, quite different from the rest of the human race. We assume that it would be helpful to them to realize from the first that all human beings have their personal problems. From this point of view a film such as "This Charming Couple" can be extremely effective, for it depicts a relationship between a very personable college instructor and a beautiful and talented young woman, two persons who would ordinarily be regarded as well-adjusted, yet whose relationship runs into serious conflicts leading to divorce.

One of the most important factors related to the level of anxiety in the group is the leader's own feelings of assurance concerning himself, the procedures which he uses, and his relationship to the group. This is not to say that the leader is expected to be entirely free of anxiety, but the way in which he copes with his own anxiety publicly before the group can be a very important factor in determining the response of the members. If he is accepting of his own anxiety and its place in the total Workshop experience and is not defensive about it, then it can be a very salutary influence.

It has been our experience that though anxiety and depression have developed in students, they have simply never reached unmanageable proportions. On occasion students come to recognize a need for therapy and arrange to undertake it after the course ends. But the crystallization of a latent need and of the readiness to meet it are very different from creating it. In Workshops involving prospective therapy patients, the assurance that therapy will be available at the conclusion of the course, or shortly thereafter, is an additional support.

In striving to minimize a group's self-condemnation, the leader needs to guard against an excessive coddling of the group which attenuates the learning potential, which makes something pallid out of the confrontation situation, and which fosters the use of one's life history as the new scapegoat in the externalization of responsibility for current behavior. Thus, on one level members need to sense the inevitability of the traits which make them feel ashamed and guilty as outcomes of a past process in living during which they were relatively helpless. At the same time, this feeling of inevitability is the very thing that needs to be challenged as something that can be reversed with the greater degree of autonomy now available to them and with appropriate hard work, honesty, and commitment. In short, the encouragement of a self-accepting attitude needs to occur without diminishing their essential responsibility for their own lives in the present.

Handling Conflicts between Members

What would be helpful for the leader to keep in mind in dealing with conflicts between two or more members which break out in a session? The following are some considerations that may be useful:

1) He should recognize that such conflicts are not to be avoided. They are opportunities for significant here-and-now learning. In general, the leader needs to be resourceful enough to use such incidents as opportunities for developing significant generalizations of value to the group.

2) The leader should set the example for the group in being

genuinely interested in hearing how each party to the conflict experiences the dispute. He should avoid siding with one or the other disputant.

3) After hearing both sides discussed, the leader can express something along the following lines: He is very glad that this has come out into the open. It seems like a significant occurrence. It would be desirable for the disputants to free themselves from questions of who is right or wrong and to focus rather on the meaning of their behavior. Lying behind the conflict, undoubtedly, are many complex and significant factors which could be usefully explored by each party, especially those compelling needs which drove them into opposition.

4) The leader should keep in mind various possibilities for involving the group as a whole in this situation. For one thing, he might invite other members in the group to give their reactions to the very occurrence of conflict itself, apart from its specific content.

5) A didactic intervention may aid in the management of difficult interpersonal situations whose further pursuit by the group would be traumatic and unproductive. For example, after one session in which many angry exchanges had occurred among members and which had ended on a note of high tension, the leader read to the group excerpts on anger from a text[12] which provided some perspective on the universality of this emotion and its significance as a clue to self-understanding.

Timing and Procedural Flexibility

It goes without saying that a Workshop leader cannot conceive of himself as a teacher who pursues a standard syllabus of experiments in a fixed order. He needs to think of his syllabus more in terms of a repertoire from which he will make selections coordinate with his perception of the group's status at any given point. Just because people differ in terms of relative maturity, degree of psychological sophistication, level of self-acceptance, and the pertinence of particular problems, it is virtually impossible to work out a fixed sequence of experiments which would be suitable for all Workshop groups or for all individuals in any given Workshop group.

It seems obvious that the didactic and provocative value of any given Workshop experiment cannot be appreciated in terms of the objective character of the procedure itself. The best of experiments can fall flat with a given group at a given time. The level of the group's development must be a major, if not altogether decisive, factor. Has the group developed to a level of considerable interaction and of personal involvement? How free are they to express their feelings and reactions? To what extent have they been concerned with the dynamic meanings of their reactions and with the meaning and significance of their relationships to each other and to the leader?

The concept of group readiness for the particular experience which the leader wishes to catalyze at any given time involves, on the one hand, the question of emotional readiness, that is, the extent to which members have been rendered sufficiently secure so that they can confront potentially traumatic aspects of themselves without an obstructive degree of anxiety. The other aspect of readiness is more rationalistic and involves the notion of a graded series of experiences where one builds upon the other with certain experiences necessarily preceding others if later experiences are to prove optimally meaningful. For example, the concept of individual differences would appear logically to precede the notion that one's personal reactions must have meaningful motivational antecedents. It would not seem to make much sense to ask a person to explain something that he takes for granted if he has first had no experience in appreciating that what he has taken for granted was really not inevitable, as witness the existence of quite different reactions to the same stimulus situation by other people.

The leader should come to each session prepared with several experiments and introduce each experiment with an experimental attitude. He is not wedded to an experiment. He does not bull his way through the procedure regardless of the resistances which arise. When he feels that a discussion has been about as productive as it can be, he can intervene and suggest that the group move on to another issue or activity. On the other hand, despite a preconceived syllabus and aims for the session, when he discovers the group developing its own dynamic momentum along fruitful, unforeseen lines, he recedes into the background and allows this to go forward.

The leader needs to feel free from time to time to retreat from a situation either because he may have no immediate idea as to how to make productive use of it or because it makes him or the group too anxious. In such instances he needs to be able to say, "Well, something very important is going on here. I don't know exactly what it is, but I think it might be useful for each of us to think about what might be happening. If any ideas should occur to any of us about what has happened here as we move along in this session, I would be very interested in your letting us know about them." Then the group could move on with the agenda, at the same time leaving the door open to return to the incident should something about it occur to one or another member.

Termination

How does one end a Workshop? One of the best ways is to use the last session or two to review the group's experience in the Workshop to date. One technique for doing so is to review the letters, as was done in Session Fifteen in the second Workshop. Another way is to invite the students to recall their earliest memories of the Workshop itself and then, continuing in the Workshop spirit, to explore the differences among these first memories. Another way is simply to invite the group to reminisce about what has happened in the Workshop. Such sessions often end in a mellow, nostalgic mood in which people feel a renewed sense of having gone through an experience that is rather unique and which surprisingly left more of a residual than they had thought prior to this kind of review.

In the New York University Workshop, termination anxiety is virtually nonexistent, probably because students are free to continue on to advanced Workshops which can be repeated as often as they wish. On the other hand, some anxiety regularly arises in clinic Workshops around impending termination, and the leader needs to be prepared for it in terms of dealing with it in some exploratory, analytical fashion. This is a kind of anxiety which is crucial in each person's life, has very different individual meanings for different people, and emerges in the Workshop at a point where its dynamically oriented examination would be most meaningful. Yet, it has been our experience that Workshop groups find it very difficult to review past traumas of separation. Usually, they do not move beyond expression of feelings of regret or relief. Some procedure or experiment remains to be devised which would help groups to tackle more intensively than has been possible until now the meaning separation has had in their lives.

CHAPTER **6**

~~~~~~

A REPERTOIRE OF GROUP EXPERIMENTS

L EARNING is facilitated when a group can be confronted repeatedly with the same dynamic principle or theme embodied in several different experiments. Some participants may be more responsive to verbal techniques, while others may find motoric experiments more meaningful. Some take easily to exploring their childhood experiences; others respond more readily to here-and-now situations. A sensitive leader, aware of a group's particular needs at a given time, is in a much more fortunate position when he can draw upon a wide diversity of methods in accordance with those sensed needs.

The development of group experiments involves a trial-and-error process. Promising procedures need to be applied repeatedly to a variety of groups before their merits or shortcomings under varying conditions can be ascertained. Below we present a series of the most promising experiments developed thus far, representing the distillate of many more procedures that have been tried out over the last ten years. The ingenious leader will, no doubt, invent variations and procedures of his own to meet the specific, unfolding needs of his group, and, of course, this is as it should be.*

The experiments have been divided into groups according to the following central themes: Formative Influences in Childhood,

---

* The authors would welcome receiving from readers accounts of their tryouts of these experiments, revisions of them, or suggestions for new ones.

Personal Characteristics and Processes, and Interpersonal Relations. These groupings are to a certain extent arbitrary, for any one experiment may clearly fall into more than one grouping.

Most experiments are described in sufficiently explicit detail so that a prospective leader may be alerted to specific occurrences, themes, or values which may be anticipated. Where such specification is absent, the recommended procedure is one which produces such a wide, often unpredictable, diversity of classroom outcomes that no regular repeated patterns can be crystallized out.

Some of the experimental tasks are so ambiguous and so outside the practical, conventional realm of everyday life that they highlight, in addition to whatever other themes they may deal with, individual differences in the readiness for commitment to what is trivial, playful, novel, or uncertain. The prospective leader should keep in mind the possibility of exploring characteristic modes of coping with such situations.

While most of the experiments can produce a plethora of psychologically significant material, a leader needs to guard against milking an experiment dry, the temptation to go off into too many different tangents. It is better to stick, as far as may be strategically advisable, to the major focal points of an experiment, and to shift to a second experiment as soon as there are signs of diminishing group involvement. Students who fail to respond to one experiment will often be stirred by a second introduced in the same session.

The leader may suggest that the students obtain looseleaf notebooks and bring these to every session, so that the responses to each experiment may be recorded for periodic review and study. In those experiments in which the group studies the personal documents of individual members, it is usually desirable to mimeograph these documents so that each member may have his own copy for study. Whenever, as part of a procedure, members' written communications are to be read to the class for comment, discussion, or interpretation, members who wish to preserve their anonymity are first given the opportunity to declare (in writing on the top of their sheets) that their statements are out of bounds for this purpose.

The very earliest sessions call for procedures which enable members to become rapidly acquainted with each other and with the nonjudgmental, investigative orientation of the course, and which are especially intriguing but at the same time relatively simple and nonthreatening. Any of the following experiments can serve these opening purposes: Getting Acquainted, Looking at an Ambiguous Picture, First Names, First Impressions, Devising Sentences with Ambiguous Words, Value Patterns.

The experiments can be used in a variety of sequential patterns and within diverse frames of reference. Some leaders may prefer to structure the course within the framework of a particular theory which would rationalize a certain progession of topics and the selection of particular experiments. Thus, a leader may view the process of extending self-understanding as a process of sensitizing people to Freud's topological model. He might, therefore, select and devise experiments with an eye to introducing students in some orderly fashion to the id, ego, and superego. Another leader, given another theoretical framework, might organize a course around the three interrelated concepts of drive, threat, and defense.

For our part, we have not concerned ourselves with pursuing a finely reasoned out model of personality development. We have rather oriented ourselves towards psychodynamic concepts and phenomena that cut across most theoretical systems as, for example, psychological determinism, unconscious motivation, the significance of early childhood experiences, and the like. The content of any particular experiment is essentially secondary to the dynamisms for which it serves as a vehicle. Our primary interest is always in maintaining contact with the group and in engaging the curiosity and emotional involvement of the students. From this point of view, a swift change of pace from session to session is more appropriate than hewing to some systematic progression.

It is not to be inferred from these remarks that we lack an overall rhythm in our approach. We have already mentioned that we tend to emphasize a simple awareness of experience at first and move gradually to the exploration of the dynamic meanings of Workshop experience.

Formative Influences in Childhood

The experiments in this group direct the student's attention to those childhood experiences, particularly with his parents, which had a shaping influence on his development. Some experiments tend to stir up long forgotten memories. Others focus on patterns of identification within the family. Still others center on discovering relationships between specific current behaviors and childhood events. By placing his own pattern of recalled experiences against the contrasting background of the many different patterns revealed in the classroom, each student has the opportunity to see the significance of his particular experiences from a new perspective.

Birth Order. The leader groups the members according to birth order (oldest children in one group, youngest in another, and so on), with no one group containing more than five students. The subgroups locate themselves in different parts of the classroom and then go on to explore the specific experiences they had by virtue of their birth order. In his instructions the leader needs to emphasize that the focus of the discussions should be on clarifying what each student's birth order position meant to him individually rather than on seeking out common patterns. Such common patterns as may spontaneously emerge in the course of discussion would not, of course, be ignored.

After about twenty minutes the leader halts the discussion and instructs the subgroups to write out completions to the following sentences:

1. When told she would have to do the whole thing by herself, Rose . . . .
2. Whenever they asked Frieda to be in charge, she . . . .
3. Bill sometimes thinks his family . . . .

The small groups then continue their discussions, now exploring in a series of go-arounds how each student's sentence completion might reflect feelings, needs, wishes, or past experiences related to his birth order position.

About fifteen minutes later the leader brings the subgroups together and invites a general discussion of the group's experiences and findings. At some appropriate point the leader may in-

vite the members to explore possible parallels between their be-
havior in the subgroups and their past relationships with siblings.
The showing and discussion of the film, "Sibling Relations and
Personality," then concludes the experiment.

This experiment can be a useful vehicle for examining childhood experiences relating one's position in the family constella-
tion and the current attitudes, values, and coping mechanisms
traceable to these experiences. Two notions may be usefully integrated, namely, that one's position in the family is a structural
element which can precipitate commonly shared problems, and
that individuals differ in how they cope with these problems. The
application of this experiment in Workshops I and II and accompanying commentaries will be found on pages 38ff. and 116ff.

Capsule Autobiography. Each member writes out his life history, using no more than a single page. The leader collects these
life histories and follows a procedure similar to that of the First
Memory Experiment. Each life history is discussed in terms of its
projective implications with particular reference to such questions
as the following: How does the student organize his past history
within a limited compass? Is there a major theme around which
the autobiography is organized? How much space is devoted to
family, school, and other themes? What note does the first sentence strike? What significant persons are mentioned in what
sequence, and in what context?

Family Drawings. Each member draws his whole childhood
family, including himself as a child. The drawings may present
the family in some group activity, in posing positions, or in any
other way the student wishes, and each family member is identified by caption. Students then exchange their anonymous drawings with each other. When a student gets a drawing he studies
it briefly and writes a one sentence reaction or impression on the
other side of the sheet, stating what strikes him about the family
as a whole, any particular person, the location of various members
to each other, facial expressions, or any other features. He initials
his written reaction and then exchanges this drawing for a new
one. Each student picks up his own drawing after all the students

have written their reactions to all of the drawings. Each student then studies by himself the comments written in reaction to his drawing. The floor is next thrown open to discussion. Some students may wish to read off all the interpretive comments written in response to their drawings and comment on each. Others may wish to query specific students about their written impressions.

This experiment often stimulates insights with respect to relationships in the family which unexpectedly get projected into the drawing and which were not noticed by the person himself, although they may have been obvious to others. The leader alerts the group to the possibility of long forgotten memories being recalled, and encourages the sharing of such memories.

Family Photographs. Each student is invited to bring in three to five photographs of himself as a young child, pictures in which he appears with parents or other family figures. A set of photographs, with the owner's consent, is projected one at a time onto a large screen so that the group can study the child's stance, facial expression, physical closeness with others in the photograph, and other physical features. The group, often unaware of the photographed subject's identity, gives its impressions of the child's personality, the problems he may have faced as a child, and how he might have attempted to cope with them. Finally, the individual whose photographs were presented gives his reaction to the group's speculations. This procedure is repeated for as many students as there may be time.

Like the Family Drawings, this experiment is of value in training the student in the observation of details of posture, positional interrelationships, facial expression, and the like, which, ostensibly trivial, incidental, and taken for granted, may nevertheless have pervasive psychological significance.

Family Sayings. The leader informs the group that every family has its own favorite expressions, proverbs, slogans, advices, admonitions, or warnings. For example, "What will people think?" "Do you think money grows on trees?" "Your mother is your best friend." "You have to learn in this world how to swallow stones." As practice, the students may watch the family scene from the film, "Angry Boy," and write down statements from the movie dialogue which in their opinion were probably habitual and repetitive in that family. Then the leader instructs, "Close your eyes and see what repetitive sayings from your own family pop into mind. Note these down as they occur to you, together with the source of each statement."

After members have complied with these instructions, each student in turn reads off his list of family sayings. Students are encouraged to question each other about the circumstances surrounding one or another saying, and to remain alert to the differences in the value orientations and "atmospheres" of different sets of sayings. Some students may be struck by the marked preponderance of sayings recalled from one parent over the other. Some may notice that father's and mother's sayings conflicted. Without the leader having to say so explicitly, the members become more aware that these repeated sayings expressed core values and attitudes which, in permeating the psychological atmosphere of the parental home, entered significantly into the development of their own personalities.

First Memory. The leader asks each member to write out his very first memory. He then introduces the notion that first memories may reflect both shaping past experiences and significant current attitudes towards ourselves and others. He presents some sample childhood memories and discusses with the group various clues contained in them and possible inferences to which they might point. The group is encouraged to speculate freely about what these memories might imply with the understanding that their speculations are possible hypotheses only. He then asks the members to examine their own recollections and to write interpretations of them on the other side of their sheets.

The leader collects the papers and invites the group to analyze and discuss in turn a number of memories selected from among those submitted. (The selection of memories is of course limited to those voluntarily offered.) In each instance the leader reads to the group a member's memory without revealing the identity of the author. He asks for the group's reaction. After the members give their interpretation, the author's interpretation is read, and he is invited to give his reactions to the group's speculations. This procedure is repeated with the memories of as many other students as possible. Applications of this experiment in Workshops I and II are described on pages 54ff. and 110ff., respectively. The dynamics of this experiment are discussed on pages 57ff. and 112ff.

A wide variety of modifications is possible. Instead of simply requesting the very first memory, the leader may ask for a series of early memories, for example, the three earliest memories, or the first five memories of mother. The group can then search for significant trends, sequences of events, or repeated patterns in the memory series.

Paper-Pencil Conversation. The group is separated into pairs. One student in each pair is assigned the role of parent. The second student is assigned the role of an 18 year old who returns home at 4 A.M. from a Saturday night date. Each pair engages in a written "conversation" on a sheet of paper which they pass back and forth between them. The "parent" in each pair "speaks" first by writing the angry statement, "This is a fine time for you to be coming home!" The "teenager" writes his reply on the sheet and passes the sheet back to the "parent" for the "parent's" written response. The "parent" answers in writing and passes the sheet back to the "teenager." After fifteen to twenty minutes these written conversations are brought to a halt. A pair volunteers to read their exchange aloud with appropriate dramatization. After the group discusses the exchange, the procedure is repeated with as many other pairs as there is time for.

This experiment provides the group with a training exercise in interpreting the give and take of an actual interpersonal exchange, one in which anger is experienced, expressed, and coped with in a variety of ways. For example, in one exchange, the "adolescent" was defiantly belligerent and the "parent" apologetic, while in another, the "parent" succeeded in inducing guilty responses in the "adolescent" by adopting a martyr's role. Students may become curious about the dynamic origins of such differences, and are encouraged to recall relevant experiences with their own parents. (Writing out a conversation has the advantage of permitting a whole class to participate simultaneously and allows quick "re-plays" of any exchange without requiring a tape recorder.)

Following is a useful variation: The group sits in a circle. Each person engages in two written conversations simultaneously, play-ing the part of parent to the student on his right and the part of adolescent to the student on his left. Thus, each student has the opportunity to compare the similarities and differences in the way he played both roles and whether playing both roles simultane-ously led to some interactive influence between them. (One student noticed, for example, that the anger he could not express towards his "parent" was directed against his "daughter.")

Endless variations of this experiment are possible, with pairs playing the parts of husbands and wives, employers and em-ployees, and the like, and with dialogues created around a variety of opening lines. A student may even be paired off with himself by instructing him to write out a talking-to-himself dialogue in which "I" converses with "Me."

Patterns of Familial Identification. The leader presents sets of three items (such as those listed below) one at a time and asks the members to write down with which item in each set they would most associate themselves and why. These multiple choice sets can be extended and modified in various ways, limited only by the imagination of the leader.

> yellow, red, blue
> food, clothing, shelter
> circle, square, triangle
> plant, animal, mineral

The leader next requests each member to repeat the above pro-cedure, first selecting with which item in each set he would most associate mother, and then father. Upon completion of this task, members are invited to review and compare the associations which they have selected for themselves and their parents. At appropriate points the leader may raise such questions as the fol-lowing: In what way are you most like and unlike your mother? Your father? Can you speculate on how these similarities and dif-ferences arose? What has been the effect on your life of these similarities and differences?

Sentence Completion Autobiography. Students fill out a set of incomplete autobiographical sentences. Examples of sentence stems which have been found useful are listed below. The leader can review with the group all the completions of any one student, noting patterns and trends and inferring underlying dynamics, or else individual items (selected either at the discretion of the leader or suggested by the students).

My childhood . . . .

Father was the kind of man who . . . .

He usually . . . .

My mother can be best described as . . . .

She usually . . . .

Mother and I . . . .

Father and I . . . .

I was happiest when . . . .

I was angry when . . .

I was afraid when . . . .

I felt blue when . . .

Family meals were times when . . .

On Sundays . . . .

On my birthday . . . .

When I was ill . . . .

I used to look . . . .

In school . . . .

With other children my age . . . .

When I had my first wet dream . . . .

When I first menstruated . . . .

When I first heard how babies were made . . . .

I was told that playing with myself would . . . .

I used to daydream that . . . .

I never realized that . . . .

I was surprised to learn that . . . .

At night I . . . .

In the bathroom . . . .

When I did something wrong . . . .

I had a friend who . . . .

When I was between 3 and 6 years old . . . .

When I was between 6 and 10 years old . . . .

When I was between 10 and 15 years old . . . .

In my spare time I liked best to . . . .

At home my favorite room was . . . .

Structuring the autobiography along sentence completion lines permits inclusion of items, such as those dealing with sex, which ordinarily fail to be included spontaneously, either in the first memories or in the capsule autobiographies.

Talking with Parents. The leader asks the group to close its eyes and to live out in its imagination an actual childhood verbal exchange with mother. Members are encouraged to notice specifically who starts the talk, the specific statements mother and child make to each other, how they feel during the talk, the room in which the talk occurs, where parent and child sit in relation to each other, the time of day, and how the talk ends. After five minutes the leader asks the group to open its eyes and share with each other what they experienced.

Each student next prepares a written list of as many different topics as he can recall about which he had some kind of verbal exchange with mother in childhood. The various topics are orally reported and listed on the blackboard. For each topic on his list the student then indicates, by means of a suitable notation, whether the exchange was usually initiated by mother, as well as the average duration of each exchange. Each student now records the number of topics on his list, the percentage initiated by mother, and the average duration per exchange. The frequency distributions for each of these variables is noted on the blackboard.

In the discussion which follows the leader may raise such questions as "To what extent did your talks with mother meet your needs for affection, care, guidance, and recognition?" Why were some topics easier to talk about with mother than others?" "Can you think of ways in which your behavior today in relating to people may be a derivative of your pattern of talking experiences with mother?" The above procedure can be repeated usefully in relation to father.

The intimacy and amount of verbal communication between parent and child is a fairly manifest process in people's experience, yet it is often taken for granted and rarely examined in the specific ways suggested above. This experiment underscores the importance of communication in its own right as a vehicle for feelings of self-acceptance, belonging, and enrichment, and for the process of identification.

The Leader Interviews a Student. The leader asks for a volunteer to be interviewed in front of the class for about ten minutes. Before the interview begins, the leader divides the class into two groups, one whose task is to observe and take notes on the interviewee, and the other whose task is to do the same for the leader.

The subgroups are alerted to pay particular attention to evidences of heightened tension in either the leader or the interviewee. The leader may begin interviewing the volunteer in any number of ways, for example, by asking him what he would feel most comfortable in being interviewed about, or to tell something about his current hobby, or to report how it feels to be in front of the group. Whatever the starting point, the leader gradually steers the interview from some contemporaneous point to related childhood experiences. After the interview, the group shares its observations and reactions. The procedure is then repeated with as many other volunteers as time permits.

This experiment can demonstrate in simple, rapid, sometimes dramatic fashion possible dynamic relationships between some significant current experience and patterns of past childhood experience. It is also an exercise in observing people in communicative interaction, an exercise designed to expand one's sensitivity to what goes on between people in interaction and to sharpen one's awareness of those personal sets which play a selective influence in what is noticed or overlooked.

What did your Mother Say? The PALS Test by Williams[33] was developed to enable a child to rate his parents as sources of guidance and affection. This projective test includes a series of eight cartoons showing a mother and a child in a problem situation which requires that the mother respond in some way. Four typical answers that a mother might make are shown below each cartoon. The child being tested is asked to circle the answer he thinks the parent would give.

For Workshop use, each cartoon is projected onto a screen and is used in an open-ended way without the accompanying multiple choice answers. For example, one cartoon shows the child and his mother at the dinner table, and the child is saying, within a balloon, "But, Mommy, I don't like that. Do I have to eat it?" Above the mother's head there appears an empty balloon. The Workshop members are invited to record the response that they would be inclined to make if they were the child's mother. When each cartoon has been responded to in this way, the test is repeated, but this time each member is instructed to write a response that he recalls his own mother actually having made in a similar situation or one that he imagines she might have made. The group now discusses its responses, scene by scene.

Through examining their responses under the two given conditions, Workshop members can come to a sharper picture of their perceived relationship with their parents, and the extent to which they have identified with them or have leaned over backwards to do just the reverse of what they did.

What Makes Mothers Tick. The leader presents a brief, dramatic description of an overprotective mother. Students are invited to jot down as many different causal factors as they can think of which might underlie her overprotective behavior. These lists are reported in a go-around and then discussed. If necessary, the leader can draw the students' attention to specific differences in the content and sequence of their lists. Students vary in their readiness to see different dynamics. For example, some find it easier to see the overprotective mother as someone whose child is sickly and needs extra care, while another may more readily see the mother as someone who is fundamentally rejecting. Thus, various conceptions of mothers emerge, contributing to an understanding of mothers as people with their own varying and complex dynamics, and these conceptions can, in turn, be related to the students' experiences with their own mothers. This experiment can be repeated with reference to oversubmissive mothers, rejecting, or other kinds of mothers, as well as to different kinds of fathers.

This experiment can draw students' attention to the multiple causal possibilities underlying the same surface behavior. The discussion which this experiment stimulates also often highlights the dynamic principles that a simple major factor may be a consistent feature of different behaviors in the same person, and that a given attitude or behavior may be the resultant of converging multiple factors. In addition, this procedure offers an experience in "brainstorming." The latter's free-wheeling spirit often has a salutary, loosening effect on some rigid students who habitually confine themselves within a narrow frame of reference in contemplating any phenomenon. It is for them an exhilarating, if sometimes mildly threatening, experience to glimpse the rich, potential yield of relaxed inhibition.

Who Wrote Which Stories? The leader asks the class to invent and write out three stories (no longer than five sentences each), one about a boy and a gun, a second about a teenage girl and a teacher, and a third about a young man and his employer. After these stories are written the leader collects all the papers. He invites two students to volunteer to have their stories read anonymously to the group. After reading the two sets of stories, the leader announces to the class, "I would like you to judge which set of stories was written by which one of these two volunteers. Before making your decision, it will help you to interview each volunteer in turn about his childhood. Ask him questions which you feel will be relevant and helpful to your judging the authorship of these stories." The group then questions each volunteer in turn. After each volunteer has been questioned separately, the leader suggests that members put single questions to both volunteers at the same time and that they notice how the volunteers' answers to the same question compare.

Students tend to ask questions which focus on background facts, rather than on feelings or on the quality of the parent-child relationship, and which elicit relatively uninformative "yes" and "no" answers. The leader influences the group's questioning by himself asking questions of the volunteers which illustrate those lines of inquiry which can be most usefully pursued in trying to understand someone else. He also at times directly suggests revisions of questions formulated by students. For example, when a student asked, "Did you like your teachers?", the leader suggested that the question could be a more informative one if formulated as follows: "How did you feel about different teachers that you had?" When another student asked, "Were you a fearful child?" the leader intervened, "Why not assume that he had his fears as all children do and put the question more sharply, 'What do you remember frightening you when you were a child?'" In the course of "teaching" members how to question each other more effectively, the leader indirectly communicates concepts and areas of content relevant to the understanding of human beings and their development.

After the group has interviewed the volunteers, they make their judgments as to the authorship of each set. The leader then announces who the actual authors are. Members give their reactions to the announcement and discuss how they arrived at their true or false judgments. The above procedure can be repeated with as many pairs of volunteers as time permits.

Toward the end of the session the leader may inquire as to how volunteers felt about being questioned (they are sometimes defensive) and how students felt about asking personal questions (they are sometimes reluctant to invade another's privacy or to risk "hurting someone's feelings"). Exploring the defensive attitudes of both the volunteer and the probing student helps to lay the groundwork for future mutual exploration of childhood experience among the students.

This experiment can be a convincing exercise in searching out relationships between early formative experiences and contemporary patterns of behavior. Groups usually find that they can guess the authorship of different sets of stories correctly, and this helps to bolster their confidence in their own powers of interpreting and assessing. At the same time there are usually enough "misses" to make the group aware of the complexities inherent in the process of understanding another.

Personal Characteristics and Processes

Under this heading we have grouped those experiments which, most directly and cogently, invite the student to confront himself as an individual. They ask him to focus on his traits and capacities, his attitudes and values, his feelings and fantasies. For convenience in locating experiments concerned with a given general topic, we have subdivided this group of experiments into those concerned with the self as a person, those focusing on inner feelings, those stressing undirected thought, and those which direct attention to bodily experiences.

The Self

This group of experiments focuses on the student's self, the "I" that sets goals, plans, initiates, persists, or defends itself in the face of challenges and threats, and struggles to meet its needs and to live up to certain values—all with an accompanying sense of high or low competence, self-esteem, and inner conflict.

Death. The leader asks the class to close its eyes and to imagine as vividly and realistically as possible the following: "You are in the doctor's office. He looks very serious. He tells you that you have an incurable illness and can expect to live only a few more months. Imagine yourself in his office. You can see the doctor sitting at his desk. His instrument cabinet is to his left. Dark drapes shut out the light from the window at his right. You are really there, and the doctor is really telling you this. What do you feel? What do you say to him as you leave the office? Now you are in the street. What thoughts cross your mind? Watch yourself as you walk. Where are you going? Do you feel like telling anybody what has just happened? If so, whom? What plans flit across your mind? Watch yourself. Keep your eyes closed and see what happens next." These instructions are spoken slowly and somberly. When the leader finishes, he waits for a few minutes in silence while the class immerses itself in the fantasy. Then he asks them to open their eyes and to report and discuss what happened.

Explorations of attitudes toward death can shed light on the way one deals with life, with people, and with challenges and threats. In the course of discussing this experiment, students often become sharply aware of the preciousness of life and of how much they have been taking it for granted, of their hitherto secret illusions that they will live forever, a feeling which has permitted them to continually postpone facing what they want to do with their lives, and of how their attitude toward death, whether articulated for themselves or not, has been a more potent factor than they realized in the way they have organized their living.

Devising Sentences With Ambiguous Words. Students are instructed to make up a sentence which will include three given words (for example, steal, watch, bear) selected for their ambiguity of meaning. This procedure is repeated with additional sets of ambiguous words such as the following which were obtained from a study by Riggs.[25]

cut, plot, land	fall, strain, can
miss, pet, hand	mail, dream, march
see, end, fly	mine, wish, right

After the group has written its sentences for all the sets, the leader initiates a series of go-arounds in which members read off their sentences for a given set and then compare and discuss the individual differences noted. If necessary, the leader may draw the group's attention to variations in the sentences' themes, the different ways in which specific words were interpreted, whether sentences are in the imperative, declarative, or interrogative mode, and the degree to which sentences are subjective-personal-feeling versus objective-impersonal-intellectual. When all sets have been explored, the leader invites each member to review all his sentences for evidence of any trends or repetitive patterns reflecting current needs or past experiences.

Drawing Dots. This experiment was inspired by a procedure described by McClelland.[*1] The leader instructs the class, "Put down as many or as few dots as you wish on a piece of paper and then try to connect these dots with a line that does not cross itself." As students engage in this task, the leader looks over their drawings, shakes his head with feigned, but obvious, displeasure and then gravely announces that he will give the group one more trial. (Obviously, it is impossible to do poorly in this task.) The discussion which follows the second trial may center on any of the following topics:

1) The factors determining the number of dots each member put down in the first trial. For example, some students load their sheets with dots, sometimes with the aim of insuring "success." Others may put down the absolute minimum of two dots, sometimes on the assumption that this is most "efficient."

2) What the leader's request for a second trial meant to the students. Some feel anxious or guilty at seeing the leader's disapproval. Others, feeling satisfied with their performance, experience anger at his dissatisfaction.

3) How and why the second trial resembles or differs from the first. Some students start off with the conviction that they will be inadequate to doing the task, and this is only reinforced by the

---

*References to sources of procedures are intended simply to acknowledge the origin of the ideas involved, and there is no necessary implication that the procedures as used here duplicate their use or purpose as described in the original reference.

leader's asking them to repeat the drawing, so that they strain for a more complicated performance the second time. Others simply repeat their first performance, sometimes defiantly. Still other students take pleasure in seeing what new designs they can create.

This experiment calls the student's attention to the prominent role played by attitudes toward authority and toward accomplishment, aspiration, and competition as organizing principles in his style of life.

Drifting. Students are instructed to drift and wander around the classroom as aimlessly as possible without talking to each other. There is usually considerable giggling among the members as they begin moving around the room. Gradually the group falls into an eery silence as some members wander by themselves, and others move together through the room as if in a herd. Many members begin to find the whole situation quite discomforting. Almost invariably, one or two students, unable to continue, return to their seats. Gradually others join them. Soon only the leader and a few diehards continue to wander, while the rest of the class looks on nonplused as to what to make of all this. The leader finally halts the wandering.

Though the situation is manifestly contrived, this experiment can nonetheless be effective in stimulating emotionally involved discussion of such themes as conformity, independence, compulsivity of goal orientation, and the dynamics of self-consciousness.

First Names. Each person in turn, including the leader, announces his first name and tells the group about a favorite something from childhood—a person, an object, an activity, or whatever. Following this go-around, the leader asks the members what they observed as they listened to each other. Parents are rarely mentioned as favorites, and this is brought to the group's attention for its comments. He then asks the members to write down as many of the first names in the group as they can recall. Students vary markedly in the number of names recalled, and factors other than sheer memory capacity are discussed which might account for this range of differences. In a second go-around members read off the first three names that came to mind, and then consider whether these first recalled names might have had some special significance for them. The leader draws the members' attention to the fact that some members included him among the first three names, and others did not. He wonders what might be involved in this difference. He then asks each member to close his eyes and to repeat his own name over and over to himself until some image, feeling, thought, or memory pops into mind. These name associations are then reported aloud to the group. Finally, the leader invites members to point out those persons in the group whose names they still could not remember and to ask for their names.

This experiment is a useful icebreaker. It is a rapid means of acquainting members with each other, and in helping them to identify each other by name. It is also an intriguing introduction to psychological dynamics. Applications of this experiment in Workshops I and II together with commentaries will be found on pages 26ff. and 108ff.

Getting Acquainted. Any one or combination of the following go-arounds can give each student an opportunity to reveal himself, to observe the self-revelations of others, and to note his reactions to both experiences:

1) Each member answers a specific projective question such as, "What great person, living or dead, do you admire most and why?" or, "If you had to be an animal, what kind of animal would you most like to be?"

2) Each member picks out some personally meaningful object in his possession, displays it to the group, and reports its history and his feelings about it.

3) A set of TAT cards, or other pictures, is lined up against the wall. Each member is asked to review all the cards and pick one card which interests him most. Then in a go-around, each person presents his chosen card, his reactions to it, and an invented title for the picture.

After each go-around the leader invites the members to share their observations and to relate them, where pertinent, to such reactions of pleasure and displeasure, of relaxation and tension as they may have experienced. The projective character of the personal revelations which these experiments involve tends to foster a feeling of sharing, of communality, and of intimacy which the identification of self through the communication of vital statistics is far less likely to accomplish.

Looking at an Ambiguous Picture. An ambiguous picture, for example, a picture of a woman who can be perceived as young and pretty or as old and haggard,*is projected onto a screen. Members are asked to simply describe what they see. They are astonished to hear the sharply different perceptions that are reported. Gradually, it begins to dawn on the group that the slide can be seen in two ways. The leader then states, "It is possible to see the slide in either way, yet some of you saw it one way, and others saw it quite differently. What is your reaction to having gone through this experience?" Some students are interested in the fact that there are these different perceptions and in the factors which might underlie such differences, be it past experiences or current needs. On the other hand, there is always a number of students who react by evaluating their performance: "Which perception is the right one?" "Which picture is it better to see first?" "What's the matter with me if I can see only one picture but not the other?" The leader can point up for exploration these individually different reactions to the very fact of individual differences.

Mirror Image. Each student brings in a pocket mirror. The mirror is kept face down until after the following questions have been discussed: What comes to mind about looking at yourself in a mirror? Have you ever seen an unfamiliar side of yourself in a three-way mirror? What was the experience like? Have you ever passed by your mirror image without realizing that you were looking at yourself in the mirror? If so, what was your first reaction to the "stranger?" Have you ever looked in a mirror and seen something in your image which reminded you of one of

---

*A slide of this "Young Lady-Old Lady" picture was obtained from Arthur D. Little, Inc., Acorn Park, Cambridge 40, Mass.

your parents? What was your reaction? What recollections come to mind about the wall mirror in your childhood home?

The student is then invited to look at himself in the pocket mirror, but only at the left half of his face, covering the right half with his hand. He jots down the various features, traits or expressions that he sees in the left side. After the members have shared their reactions to this experience, the leader instructs them to follow a similar procedure, this time looking at the right facial half, and suggests that quite different features, traits, or expressions may now be evident (this usually does occur). In the discussion which follows, the students may pursue such questions as whether the two sets of perceptions might reflect some important inner conflicts, and whether either set reminds them of one of their parents.

This experiment can be useful in bringing into focus the self-concept, conflicting attitudes toward the self, and possible relationships between the self-concept and one's relationships with parents. The leader may wish to caution the group against assuming that the anatomical differences between the left and right facial half do actually contain the significances attributed to them.

Money. The leader asks the group, "Suppose you could have as much money as you wished for, in one lump sum, how much would you want?" In a go-around the members report the amounts of money wished for and their reasons for these chosen sums. Some students are extremely modest in the sums they wish for, while others wish for millions of dollars. The reasons underlying the chosen sums reflect a wide variety of personally significant factors. For example: "Enough to support my family for twenty years." "I'd never have to work again." "I could give to charity."

The leader next invites students to guess how much money they have on their person. Students share their estimates and how they arrived at them. Each student then checks his estimate against the facts. Some students find that they knew exactly how much money they had on their person, others that they un-

derestimated or overestimated. Their reactions to these findings
are then discussed. Now the procedure is repeated, but this time
students make estimates as to how much money the leader has on
his person. They give their reasons for their estimates. The
leader then divulges his actual amount of money.

This experiment elicits an array of attitudes towards money,
both as an end in itself and as an instrumental value in relation
to one's style of life and life goals. Students can become more
aware of the variety of feelings, attitudes, and symbolic values
which become attached to money in our culture.

Seat-Changing. The leader observes aloud that some members
tend to take certain fixed seats each week while others tend to sit
in different seats from session to session: "What might underlie
these different patterns?" He then suggests that each member
pick a seating place as different as possible from his present one.
He asks for the members' reaction to this suggestion. Then at his
signal, the members get up and change their seats. The leader
too changes his seat.

When the group has finished the seat-changing, the leader asks
what they observed and experienced as they went about the
task. The discussion which follows may touch on such aspects of
the experience as the following: the resistance to or eagerness for
change, the wish to sit or not to sit next to a specific member,
indecisiveness about where to sit, competitiveness for particular
places, how the classroom looks from the new position, the reaction to the leader's new seating position. The leader may raise
such questions as the following: How radically different is your
new seat from your old one? Which shifts were largest, which
smallest; from what points of view? Who thought of sitting in the
leader's chair? On the arm of the chair, on the table, on the floor?
Interesting, isn't it, that these seating places didn't occur to you.
I wonder why? Would you have sat in these places if you had
thought of them? Why not?

After discussion of these questions, the leader requests the
group to return to their old seats, and once they have done this,
he asks them for their reactions to this new change. Some students usually prefer to stay in the new seats but comply with the

leader's instructions to return to the old seat. He draws this to their attention and inquires into the reasons for their compliance.

The application of this experiment in Workshop II is described on page 143ff. A discussion of the dynamics of this experiment will be found on page 146ff.

Ten Commandments. Members are invited to write out as many of the Ten Commandments as they can recall. Distortions of recall, omissions, and the order in which the Commandments are recalled can be discussed from the point of view of their personal significance. The leader next instructs the members to write out ten personal, self-directed commandments which they would like to be able to follow in the future. The leader collects the papers and reads aloud one commandment after another. The leader now steps out of his usual role, for as he reads each item he gives his reaction to it, either expressing his agreement, or challenging any specific commandments which strike him as excessively arbitrary, absolutistic, or unrealistic. For example:

Commandment	Leader's Response
"Don't be sorry for yourself."	"Sometimes a self-respecting sorrow may be appropriate."
"Avoid arguments."	"Some arguments may be useful or necessary."
"Look for the best in everyone."	"Are there not times when this may be self-defeating?"
"Quit trying to be perfect all the time."	"That makes good sense, although this is easier to tell oneself than to do."
"Don't let obstacles stop you. Overcome them."	"A good general knows when to retreat."

While the leader is very direct in expressing his felt disagreements, he encourages students to argue with him, "This is what I think. What do you think?" He also takes care to acknowledge that a particular commandment with which he disagrees may have relevance and value for the person who formulated it, but that he is questioning it as a prescription for mankind in general.

This experiment draws the students' attention to their tendency to impose upon themselves coercive, absolutistic values. Conventional myths, cliches, and shiboleths in our culture are brought into view for critical examination. The extent to which these beliefs and values have been taken over uncritically from one's parents may be explored.

✳ *Value Patterns.* The leader reads off a set of three statements. Each member decides which one of these statements he considers most important and which one least important. The group is then divided into subgroups according to their patterns of choices. An illustrative set of items might be: "To be generous toward other people." "To be my own boss." "To have understanding friends."✶ All those who chose, "To be generous toward other people," as most important and, "To be my own boss," as least important gather together in the same subgroup to discuss the reasons for their choices. Similar subgroups are formed for every combination of choices. After five minutes of discussion the subgroups gather together to respond to another set of items. Below are examples of other such sets:

> To be well liked.
> To be free from having to obey rules.
> To be in a position to tell others what to do.
>
> To do what is morally right.
> To go out of my way to help others.
> To have people willing to offer me a helping hand.

After several sets of values have been responded to, the subgroups reassemble to discuss the total experience. Such discussion may center on the content of the subgroup discussions, the factors which underlie different value patterns and the origins of such differences, or on the nature of the interaction among the members of each subgroup.

This experiment, in forcing the student to make choices, can help him to become more aware of those values which guide his efforts and give them meaning. Also, students within the same

---

*Items were taken from the *Survey of Interpersonal Values* by Gordon[9] and are reproduced with permission of Science Research Associates.

subgroup usually become aware of the fact that significantly different antecedents, motivations, and meanings may underlie their common sets of choices. Another useful outcome stems from the experience of finding one's self in different groups depending on the set of values from which the choices had been selected. On observing the fluctuating composition of subgroup membership, the student comes face-to-face with the diversity and complexity of the value pattern interrelationships which define individual personality. Finally, this experiment is an excellent one for bringing people together and introducing them to each other in a rather novel context.

Volunteering for an Unknown Experiment. The leader informs the group, "Each of you will be required to participate briefly in an experiment. I will tell you about the experiment after we decide the order in which each of you will participate. Who volunteers to be first, who second, etc.?" As each person volunteers, the leader lists the person's name on the blackboard. When the whole group has volunteered, the leader invites them to guess at the nature of the experiment. After the variety of guesses have been discussed, the leader divides the members into three subgroups: those who were the first to volunteer, those who were last, and the group of in-between volunteers. Each subgroup is instructed to discuss amongst themselves what subjectively experienced factors were involved in its particular order of commitment. After fifteen minutes the whole class convenes to discuss its reactions.

The leader may be alert to a wide variety of possibilities in the discussion which follows. He may, for example, focus on the issue of how different people relate to the unknown, what anxieties, competitive strivings, or eager anticipations are experienced, and how these are handled either by volunteering early, late, or in-between. He may be interested in drawing the group's attention to the diverse dynamic origins which can underlie similar commitments.

Who Am I? The leader asks the members to close their eyes and to see what first comes to mind when they put the following question to themselves: "Who am I?" The group reports and discusses its responses, and then repeats this procedure with the following two questions, each in turn: "Who did my parents want me to be?" Who do I want my child to be?" This experiment can be useful in calling attention to self-identity, ego ideal, and parental influences on the development of both.

Word Suppression. The leader instructs the group, "Select some one word. Select a word which stands for something in your life that you would like to control, overcome, or eliminate. Now close your eyes, and for the next two minutes do all you can, using whatever procedure you wish *not* to think of the word you selected." After the two minutes are up, the group is asked to discuss its experiences. Most students fail to shut their chosen words out of consciousness, though a wide variety of ingenious methods are used, for example, humming a tune, counting to 100, and repeating the Lord's Prayer. For some, the selected word seems to exert a compulsive hold by virtue of its intense appetitive appeal or symbolic value. For others, it is experienced as a conflict between complying with and rebelling against an authority's prohibition.

Discussion may pursue such questions as the following: What determined your choice of words? Does the mode of suppression which you adopted reflect a characteristic pattern in your life? What experiences of inner conflict in everyday life does this experiment remind you of? Does the inability to suppress the word reflect a "weakness" of will power? At some point during the discussion, the leader may say, "You notice that a part of you tried to avoid thinking of the word, while still another part of you kept intruding with the word, and still another part of you was engaged in observing this conflict. What does this remind you of in your everyday life?"

In general, this experiment draws the group's attention to the role of conflicts in people's lives, in particular those conflicts which involve efforts at suppressing some insistent drive and at defending one's self against the return of the suppressed.

Emotions

The major intention in the following experiments is to draw the students' attention to the role of emotion in their lives, and of certain key emotions (for example, anger) in particular. They sensitize students to the central importance of noticing their feeling reactions as clues to self-understanding.

Anger. The leader asks the group to complete sentences relating to the experience of anger, for example:

I become irritated when . . . .
When I get very angry, I . . . .
When you are hot under the collar, it is best to . . . .
I used to get angry at my mother when . . . .
I could get angry with the teacher of this class if . . . .

Each of these sentences can be the subject for a go-around and discussion. Then each student writes down an estimate of the number of times he becomes irritated or annoyed during an average week. The frequency distribution of these estimates is placed on the blackboard and discussed. Students are next asked to explore with the group as many specific instances as they can in which they experienced some degree of annoyance, even if only fleetingly, with one or another member of the class or the leader. It helps if the leader starts the ball rolling by sharing his experiences of annoyance with the group or specific members.

Students find it easy to intellectualize about anger in general. The aim of this experiment is to encourage the dissipation of guilt or other factors which inhibit the sharing of intimate experiences and feelings about anger. This experiment can be useful in focusing students' attention on the degree to which they are aware of their anger, the meaning and function of anger in their lives, and the ease, extent, and manner in which it is expressed. Similar procedures may be organized around other emotions such as fear and affection.

Hurt Sentences. Members write twenty sentences in which the word "hurt" is used. They then review their sentences in search of trends, for example, the relative frequency with which "hurt" was used in an emotional or physical sense, the circumstances under which "hurt" occurs, the frequency of reference to "hurt" in oneself or in others, and the use of the verb "hurt" in a passive as against an active-transitive sense.

This experiment draws attention to the ease or difficulty of recognizing or acknowledging personal feelings versus events in the physical realm. It may also stimulate some students to become aware of particular areas of emotional vulnerability.

Listing Emotions. Members write down as many emotions as they can think of within one minute's time. They then report what happened while they engaged in the task. The leader asks members to add up the number of emotions listed. He writes the frequency distribution of these totals on the blackboard. The group considers what might be reflected in the fact that some students' lists of emotions are much longer than others. Members next compare the number of positive emotions on their lists with those that are negative and consider what a preponderance in one direction or the other might reflect. A count is then taken of the most frequently occurring emotions in the group's lists. (These "populars" usually include love, hate, anger, and fear.) The leader emphasizes that these feelings are key affective reactions which all humans need to come to grips with in their lives. He asks such questions as, "Which of these feelings do you feel comfortable feeling?" "Which make you feel uncomfortable?" In what different ways do you express these feelings?" Members are asked to notice the order in which the three most popular emotions appear in their own lists: "Does the sequence reflect some actual priority of one emotion over another in your life?" Those who omitted any of the "popular" emotions are invited to consider the question, "Is it possible that the omission of this particular feeling might point to its special significance in your life?"

What are You Feeling Right Now? The leader asks the students to close their eyes and to imagine themselves in the following situation: "You are in class now, and suddenly a violent thunderstorm breaks out. The rain is coming down in buckets. Listen to that crash of thunder! It's really pouring outside." After portraying this event verbally, the leader tells the members to open their eyes. He promptly asks, "What are you feeling now? Right this minute!" Students will usually report their thoughts rather than their feeling reactions. For example, one student replied, "I should have brought my umbrella." In response the leader needs to actively draw this oversight or omission to the student's attention. Thus, in this instance, the leader responded, "You are telling us what you think you should have done, but you haven't said how you actually feel." The student answered, "Well, I don't feel afraid or anything like that." The leader pointed out, "Now you are telling us how you *don't* feel, but I still want to know how you *do* feel." The student then exclaimed, "Well, I guess I feel disgusted with myself for not having listened to the weather report." Sometimes a student claims that he did not feel anything. The leader may then comment, "Only dead people don't feel anything. When you say you don't feel anything, this probably means that, for some reason, you are not letting yourself be aware of what you *are* feeling."

The above procedure can be repeated several times with the leader inviting the group to imagine themselves in a number of different situations likely to stir up feelings. After a number of such exercises and rapid fire exchanges between leader and members in which he repeatedly confronts them with their failure to report feelings, the group gradually begins to catch on to the kinds of data that are called for in response to the question, "What are you feeling now?"

This experiment can sensitize students to the difference between affective and cognitive reactions, and to the use of cognitive reactions as a defense against coming to terms with one's feelings.

Free Association, Fantasy, and Dreams

These experiments enter a realm of thinking and imagination characterized by varying degrees of freedom from considerations of reality, logic, and goal directedness. Through studying their free associational processes, fantasy productions, and dreams, students are introduced to new avenues into their private worlds which can reveal the personal meaning of events in their lives. These experiments may also be viewed as an introduction to symbolic processes, to the notion that things can be more than they seem to be. They are exercises in examining ideas and acts in imaginative and intuitive ways essential to the exploration of their dynamic significance.

Associations to Numbers. The leader gives the following instructions: "When I give you the signal, pick out any two digit number at random. Now say this two digit number to yourself repeatedly until some image, word, or feeling occurs to you. Now concentrate on this associated image, word, or feeling and see what new image, word, or feeling it, in turn, brings to mind. Continue in this same way, seeing what association arises in reaction to each preceding one. At each point write down whatever association occurs to you, starting with the two digit number that you first thought of. Ready? Go!" After about five minutes the leader calls a halt and invites the members to share their series of associations and their reactions to the experience.

Students are often surprised at the associations which occur to them in response to an apparently random, meaningless number. The frequent emergence of significant associations invites the student to consider the possibility that unconscious psychological determinants may affect the course of the associative process. Some students recall long forgotten memories. Students who experience blocking may be encouraged to explore what such blocking might reflect. The leader, at some appropriate point, can inform the group that this free associative procedure can be engaged in during any class experiment, that students can use their responses to an experiment as a stimulus in the same way that the two digit number was used.

Doodles. Students are instructed, "Put down as many or as few dots as you wish on a piece of paper and then connect them with a line that does not cross itself." At the group's completion of this task, the leader says, "Look at your drawing. What could it symbolize, if it were a symbol, about your childhood family? Might it symbolize some important relationship you had with one of your parents, or some significant family event, or some emotional atmosphere that characterized life at home?" Most students find this task strange at first, but as some members report their symbolic associations, others begin to catch on and do the same.

Some examples: "The design brings to mind the locked doors I hid behind whenever I was hurt at home." "This triangle reminds me of being an only child and both parents wanting me on their side." Students are frequently impressed to find that the associative elaboration of an apparently trivial design viewed arbitrarily as a symbol can lead to meaningful associations.

In the second part of this experiment, the leader instructs, "Close your eyes and think of your relationship with your mother, how things were between you, how you felt toward each other. What was the essence of your relationship with her? Now, put down some lines on paper in doodle fashion to suggest what your relationship with your mother was fundamentally like." When the group has completed this task, the leader invites them to repeat the procedure, but this time in relation to father. Volunteers, one at a time, display their drawings to the class for its associations and interpretations and then give their reactions to the group's comments.

In addition to stimulating members to think about their relationships with their parents and to jog their recall of what transpired in these relationships, the experiment brings home the point that formal characteristics of movement in drawings and the patterns of content which they produce can have expressive and symbolic properties.

Dreaming About the Class. The leader gives the following instructions: "Place a pencil and paper next to your bed tonight. Before falling asleep, think about this class, any aspect of this class at all, and make up your mind to dream about it. As soon as you wake up in the morning, jot down your dream, even if it seems to have nothing to do with the class. If you don't recall any dreams at all, try again the following night. If, during this next week, you cannot recall any dreams, then make up a dream about the class, and clearly label it as such."

In the next session, the leader opens the experiment by presenting one at a time to the group a few samples, selected from his repertoire of paradigmatic dreams, as a practice exercise in interpretation. He selects dreams which are simple, relatively easy to interpret, but susceptible to interpretation on more than one level. He asks the members to consider what each dream suggests about the kind of person the dreamer is, and the kind of problems with which he might be trying to cope. He urges members to be as open as possible to the thoughts and feelings which occur to them as they listen to a dream, disregarding whether these thoughts and feelings seem logical, sensible, or relevant. At the same time he reminds the group that its speculations must be considered at best only guesses. After the group gives its reactions, the leader conveys some pertinent facts about the dreamer which lead to a deeper clarification of the dream's meaning.

Following this preparation, the leader invites each participant to write out his interpretation of his own dream. After all papers have been collected, the leader presents a number of anonymous dreams inviting the group to offer its interpretations of each in turn. In each case, the leader concludes the discussion by reading the interpretation offered by the dreamer himself. The procedure followed here is similar to that outlined for the First Memory Experiment.

This experiment introduces members to still another source of data for self-exploration, namely, the symbolic significance of dream content. It can also be useful in helping members to become more aware of the implicit attitudes and roles they enact in the Workshop, and especially of their perceptions of the leader and of what the Workshop is all about. Applications of this experiment in Workshops I and II, together with commentaries, will be found on pages 79ff. and 141ff.

Inventing a Dream. The leader describes dreaming as a kind of thinking in concrete, pictorial terms which expresses, most often in symbolic terms, our needs, wishes, feelings, conflicts, problems, or possible solutions to these problems. He then instructs the group to invent a "dream" around some specific theme, for example, envy. He emphasizes that the "dreams" they devise should be both revealing and concealing simultaneously. In a go-around the members relate their "dreams," and the group has a first-hand experience of noting how the same theme may be symbolized in different ways by different persons. In later discussion the group's speculations about one or another "dream" may be checked against the "dreamer's" intentions.

This experiment is an exercise in the use of concrete images as symbols. It represents an effort consciously and deliberately to accustom the group to think in a language which is customary to the artist and available to most people as a relatively unconscious process in sleep. This experiment is effective in helping skeptical students make a transition to an acceptance of the meaningfulness of dreams, and thus lays the groundwork for the Dreaming About the Class Experiment. In addition to being useful, as a relatively brief training experience in the exploration of dreams, the procedure can also be used as a means of investigating any particular topic such as sex or sibling rivalry.

Inventing a Story. The leader asks the class to invent and write out a story (no more than five to eight sentences in length) about a boy and a violin. After these stories are written, the leader collects all the papers. He reads each story aloud without identifying the author. After reading a story he speculates about what might be reflected in it in terms of the author's attitudes, values, and past experiences. He free associates to different elements of the story. He points out various features that differentiate it from other stories on the same theme. In short, the leader illustrates in action how one might go about responding interpretatively and intuitively to a fantasy production. As students catch on to the process, they are invited to speculate along with the leader about each story. After a story is responded to in these ways, the author is invited to give his reactions to the leader's and the group's comments.

This experiment, in addition to helping students to become more sharply aware of the self-revealing value of their fantasies and daydreams, can also be a useful introductory exercise to the process of interpretation in general and to the First Memory and Dreaming About the Class Experiments specifically.

Bodily Experiences

This group of experiments can be effective in opening up ordinarily taboo areas (for example, sex) for exploration. They aim at eliciting general attitudes toward bodily functions and instinctual indulgence, with particular reference to the possibility that the degree of acceptance of such bodily functions may be an indicator of general self-acceptance. They also focus the students' attention on the range of psychological contexts within which a physical act can derive meaning.

Attitudes Toward One's Body. This experiment follows the same procedure described in the Value Patterns Experiment, except that the following sets of items are used:

To take a bath
To have my hair cut (or done)
To brush my teeth

To suck a sourball
To chew an almond
To swallow ice cream

To take a bath
To take a shower
To have a massage

To stretch
To yawn
To breathe deeply before an open window

To scratch an itch
To evacuate bowels
To void a full bladder

To kiss
To be kissed
To hug

To have a good meal with a friend
To get a good night's sleep
To have a good orgasm

Balloons. Members are requested to bring in balloons. The leader inquires how they went about obtaining their balloons, whether some members forgot to bring balloons or brought more than one, and how the group feels about playing with balloons.

The leader asks the members to blow up their balloons as far as they wish, to tie a knot at the end, and to observe what they experience as they do this. He requests members to rub their blown-up balloons gently against their cheeks, keeping eyes closed as they do so, and allowing some image to pop into mind. Next members make noises with their balloons in any way they wish (slapping, rubbing, tweaking) and notice what these noises bring to mind. The leader asks the group to look at the shapes of their balloons and to see what these shapes remind them of. Students will usually refer to various objects or animals, but tend to be very reticent about mentioning penises, breasts, or nipples. This reticence is brought to the group's attention for discussion. As a final task, the leader invites the group to break their balloons in any way they wish and to observe themselves as they do so.

A detailed description of the application of this experiment in the two Workshops will be found on pages 66ff. and 124ff. The properties of this experiment and the opportunities it can present to a group for dramatic self-confrontation are discussed on pages 71ff. and 128ff.

Feces. The leader gives the following instructions, "Write out your earliest memory involving your feces, stools, or what is commonly referred to as 'shit.' After you have written these memories, I shall collect them and read them to the group anonymously. Before you begin, I should be interested in hearing your immediate reaction to this task." As one might expect, there is an intense emotional reaction on the part of many members, some to the leader's use of the word "shit," others to the "silliness" of the task, and a few to the fact that no memories at all come to mind. After the group has written its memories, the leader collects them and reads them aloud, one at a time, discussing each before moving on to the next. After all memories have been read, the leader invites the group to report any new recollections that may have occurred to them as they listened.

Holding Hands. The leader asks the group to stand in a circle. All members clasp hands and close their eyes. The leader moves around the circle silently and firmly squeezes each pair of clasped hands for a few moments. The group then returns to its seats and shares its reactions to what transpired. The discussion usually centers around various positive or negative reactions to physical contact, both with one's classmates and with the leader. For example, some students enjoy being part of a group in this physically linked manner, while others feel anxious or constricted. Some interpret the leader's squeeze as friendly while others experience it as a form of criticism.

This experiment can be valuable in stimulating exploration of attitudes toward physical contact, intimacy, belonging to a group, and closeness to authority.

Yawning. The leader instructs the members to close their eyes and yawn once. The class then discusses its reactions. Some members are usually so embarrassed at the prospect of yawning in public that they cannot even start one. Some may feel rebellious about having to yawn "upon command." Still others may simply enjoy the experience. Sometimes a few find to their dismay that once having started they cannot stop yawning.

The leader next raises questions about the different motivations for yawning, past yawning experiences, both embarrassing and pleasurable, and what students were told about yawning as children. At one point the leader asks if they can see any possibility of their attitudes towards yawning bearing some relationship to their attitudes towards eating, sex, and other bodily functions.

The leader then asks the members to estimate how many times, on the average, they yawn in a week. (Some people are intrigued by the question. Many feel that it is ridiculous: "How should I know how many times I yawn in a week? Who pays attention?" The leader may counter, "Isn't it interesting that most of us don't pay attention?") A number of people estimate they yawn 100 or more times a week while at the opposite extreme there are some who claim they rarely or never yawn. The leader invites the group to give its reactions to this range of differences.

In the final part of the experiment, the leader declares, "From now on, anyone who feels like yawning during the session should feel free to do so as openly and as unrestrainedly as he wishes.

How do you feel about this rule?" Some students are enthusiastically for it. Some see the rule as unnecessary since they yawn when they please anyway. A few students are vehemently against the rule: "It's rude to yawn." "People might be hurt if you yawn while they talk." "If you let the bars down around yawning, where will one stop? There would be chaos, and we would all be like animals." These individual differences are brought into focus for discussion.

Interpersonal Processes

In this section are grouped those experiments in which modes of relating to other people (as a general social group, as individuals, and as authority) help to reveal characteristic psychodynamic dispositions of the individual. These exercises have much in common with those which focus on formative influences in childhood. Both sets of experiments are concerned with essentially similar psychodynamic data viewed, however, from different vantage points in the cycle of development. As such, they complement each other in affirming the continuity of psychological development from origins through enduring dispositions, to contemporary attitudes and behavior. In the series of experiments which follow, the stress on contemporaneity is achieved largely through situations which require the student to commit himself in one or another form of action. The experiments are grouped as they concern interaction with the social environment in general, with fellow students in the immediate Workshop situation, and with the leader as an authority image.

Relating to the Social Environment

The following experiments focus on one or another aspect of an individual's relation to his social environment. In these exercises, the social environment is construed as a nonspecific group entity. The emphasis is on the largely implicit role of the group as an anonymous generality in helping define the individual's self-image, in eliciting characteristic defenses, in organizing conventions which affect his behavior, and in evoking varying degrees of dependence.

Misleading the Group. Five volunteers are instructed to report a set of three childhood incidents, either a set in which all three incidents are true or all three are fictional, or a set in which two incidents actually occurred and one is invented, or a set in which two incidents are invented and the third is true. The volunteers are told to report these incidents in whatever manner or sequence they believe will most mislead the group as to which incidents are true and which invented. Thus, the true event should be told in such a way as to make most members feel it is a fiction, and the fantasy events should be conveyed with such an air of authenticity as to persuade most of the class that it actually occurred.

The group listens carefully to the first volunteer's three episodes and then writes down its judgments as to the truth or falsity of each. The volunteer then identifies which incidents, if any, are true. Each student notes the number of times he was misled, and a frequency distribution of these "scores" is recorded on the blackboard. The foregoing procedure is repeated for the next volunteer.

After the last volunteer, each student makes a count of the total number of times he was misled by all five volunteers. The frequency distribution of these "total scores" is then recorded on the blackboard. The group then gives its reactions to the findings noted on the blackboard and discusses such questions as the following: How did volunteers experience the conflict between the disposition to tell the truth and the tendency to deal in fantasy. How did they feel about being required to deceive and mislead? How did they consciously set about to deceive the group, what strategy did they adopt, and what assumptions about the group was this strategy based on? How did members feel about being in a situation fraught with the possibility of being deceived? Why were some volunteers more successful misleaders than others? Why might some members have been more often misled than others? What recollections come to mind about being misled by one's parents or, contrariwise, misleading them? What might the volunteer's specific choices of real or invented incidents reflect about him?

In a variation of this experiment, the leader may ask all members to write out a set of three childhood incidents in whatever combination of true and invented episodes they choose. These recorded incidents may then be exchanged among the members with each member judging the authenticity of every other member's set of events.

This experiment focuses attention on trust and distrust, and on honesty and deception as defensive mediators of interpersonal relations. Exploration of the origins and dynamics of these attitudes as systematic expressive and defensive dispositions opens up the possibility of their more flexible and, hence, more adaptive operation.

New Year's Eve. In the session immediately preceding New Year's Eve, the leader raises for discussion such questions as the following: What do you typically do on New Year's Eve? How do you usually feel? Is being part of a large, gay crowd important to you on that night? What are your thoughts and feelings as midnight approaches? Exactly at midnight? What are your thoughts and feelings on New Year's Day? What have your experiences been in relation to making New Year's resolutions? After discussing these questions the group is given the assignment of observing themselves and others on New Year's Eve. Their observations are then reported and discussed in the session immediately following the holiday. A similar procedure may be followed with respect to Christmas, Mother's Day, or a typical Sunday. Each of these special days has its own conventions about what one is supposed to do and feel on the given day. To what extent have students taken these conventions for granted? To what extent have they questioned them?

This experiment can highlight the discrepancies between socially dictated, institutionalized attitudes and feelings and the realities of one's own subjective experiences, and how individual modes of coping with this conflict vary. Some students may be stimulated to explore possible changes in behavior which has hitherto been taken for granted and which has persisted because of uncritical, passive compliance. Problems of widespread alienation and self-dissatisfaction in our culture may also be focused on. For example, behavior on New Year's Eve may be seen as an effort to overcome depression through exaggerated gaiety, alienated aloneness through being part of a large group, and self-dissatisfaction through making resolutions to improve.

Planning a Party. Five students volunteer to role-play a "class committee" meeting at a member's home to plan a party for the Workshop group. They are instructed to make the party plans as realistic or as fantastic as they wish. The volunteers form a small circle in the middle of the room while the rest of the class sits in a circle around them. The surrounding spectator group is divided into a convenient number of subgroups with each instructed to focus its observations on one of the committee members.

The "committee" discussions often turn out to be quite humorous. Nonetheless, real conflicts almost invariably develop among members around one or another issue. For example, one student protested against his committee's "prosaic" plans and pressed for a party aboard an airliner! After the class has eavesdropped on the "meeting" for about twenty minutes, the leader halts the "meeting," and throws the floor open to discussion. Each subgroup gives its particular impressions of the committee member to whom it paid special attention. Group phenomena such as rivalry for leadership and the development of alliances are brought up for exploration. Members are also encouraged to give their reactions to the different committee participants. At some appropriate point, committee members are invited to share with the group their covert, subjective reactions to what transpired. If there is time, another group of five volunteers can repeat the experiment.

This experiment is a training exercise in observing a group in action in which the observers have an opportunity to check their reactions against the reactions of others and the private experiences of the group participants themselves. It introduces the students to the phenomena of group dynamics. Observations of individual roles in the context of group experience often leads to significant self-insight.

Second-hand Impressions. This experiment was inspired by Dinnerstein.[8] The leader tells the group, "Imagine that a new family, the Joneses, has moved next door to you. You have not met them, but you are curious to know what they are like. You try to develop some impressions from things that you overhear neighbors saying in conversation as to the kind of people they are.

The first neighbor's remark you happen to overhear about the Joneses is, 'Don't the Joneses have a nice looking bunch of kids?' Now on the basis of this single remark, would you write a brief statement of your impression of the Joneses at this point?" After a minute or so, the leader continues, "The next day you overhear another neighbor remark, 'I had an interesting conversation with Jones today.' Now on the basis of the *two* remarks write your impression of the Jones family." The leader continues in a similar fashion with each of the following "overheard" remarks: "I hear the Joneses are very friendly people." "Don't the Joneses have an awful looking bunch of kids?" "I had a boring conversation with Jones today." "I hear the Joneses are snobs."

After writing out their sixth impression, as many members as there is time for read aloud their series of responses and report what happened to them during this experience. Some students' impressions shift in line with the shifting neighbors' judgments. Others persist in seeing the Joneses in positive terms throughout and discredit or discount the neighbors who made negative judgments. A few students may insist on postponing forming any impression until they have seen the Joneses for themselves.

This experiment is intended to bring into focus students' varying degrees of dependence on the social field and their pessimistic or optimistic orientations toward people.

Shouting Names. The leader asks several students to volunteer to hear their names shouted. At a signal from the leader, the group in unison shouts a volunteer's name three times, each time more loudly than before. When all of the names have been shouted, the group discusses the experience. Volunteers vary in their reactions to hearing their names shouted. For example, one student winced, as if he were being scolded, but another glowed with pleasure at being "the center of the stage." The shouting students also vary in their reactions. For example, while some may be embarrassed about shouting in a classroom, others may enjoy the freedom and tension release of the experience.

This experiment often brings into the open feelings of inadequacy and self-consciousness, castration anxieties, ambitious strivings, exhibitionistic needs, and the like. The critical role of

early authority relationships in the genesis of these feelings and
needs, and the implicit vesting of authority in the group frequently emerge in the discussion.

Silence. The leader instructs the members to maintain silence.
After five minutes the leader breaks the silence and invites the
members to give their reactions to the experience. The procedure
is then repeated, but this time silence is maintained with eyes
closed.

This experiment alters the conventional anchorages and supports which are habitual and taken for granted in social situations.
Silence with eyes open removes a certain amount of social feedback, and when eyes are closed, even the visual opportunities for
feedback are cut off. What happens when students are deprived
in these ways of normal orientating data? How do they handle
this situation? As might be expected, students react in sharply
different ways. While some students, for example, withdraw comfortably into themselves, others feel anxious and vulnerable when
they are cut off from the social field. A member's thoughts may
turn to past events or future plans, or may revolve fixedly about
the immediate present situation. The discussion in this experiment may take a wide variety of turns with attention being paid
to one or another aspect of the relation between self and social
environment.

Relations among Workshop Students

These experiments confront Workshop participants with patterns of attraction and repulsion existing in the group, their specific images of each other, and their emotional reactions to these
images. Students are stimulated to become aware of their fears or
hopes with respect to how others see them, the actual impressions
they make on others, and to reassess their self-concepts in the
light of such impressions. Also focused on are the intensity or
special character of the needs which govern the kind of perception one has of others, and what needs and behavior may underlie
the kind of image one tends to project.

Exercises in which there is student-to-student confrontation
contain some risk of hurt. It will be noted, however, that modi-

fying factors are built into each of the interpersonal exercises in order to limit possible traumatic impact. In fact, it is our experience that these experiments tend to influence the group in the direction of making the membership more warmly cohesive. They build a backlog of mutual understanding in the group which facilitates a more rapid and perceptive appreciation of those subjective factors which underlie interpersonal conflicts that break out from time to time among Workshop members.

Choosing a Family. The leader states, "Let us imagine that you could create a family of your own. Choose from among the other students present whom you would like to be your mother, father, younger sibling, older sibling, spouse, son and daughter." Members write down their choices for each category. In a go-around each member reports his choices together with some explanation of each. Members then share their observations and reactions, and focus on such questions as the following: How were you seen by others? What does your pattern of choices suggest about what is important in your life and what you may have missed in your own family? Who was most frequently and least frequently chosen for which role? What were your reactions to having or not having been chosen for this or that family role by this or that member or number of members?

First Impressions. If it seems appropriate, the leader may devote a part of the first (or even the second session) to eliciting members' first impressions of each other. He asks if there are any people in the group who would be interested in learning what other students' first impressions of them were. He can point out that this is a one-time opportunity in the course, and that while other people's first impressions may or may not be valid, it may still be of interest to note what they are. There are usually several students who invite such impressions and several members willing to give them. After members have given their frank impressions of a student, the leader invites the student and the group to give their reactions to the experience.

Giving and Taking Coins. Each student puts all the coins in his possession on his desk. The leader does likewise. The leader states, "In this experiment you will give away as little or as much of your change as you wish to as few or as many people in this group as you choose. What you give away will be for keeps. Take your time in deciding just what you want to do. You can begin passing out money whenever you are ready." Leader and members soon begin moving around the room distributing varying amounts of change to others in the group. When this distribution has been completed, the group shares its reactions and observations with particular emphasis on their choice of recipients, the amounts distributed, how they themselves felt about being recipients, and their response to the leader, either in terms of giving or not giving him money, or in terms of receiving or not receiving coins from him.

This procedure usually elicits a wide range of dramatic and significant behaviors. For example, one student paid much more attention to who was putting money on his desk than to his own giving. Another student was chagrined to find that she gave so much money away and got so little in return: "This is so much like the way I feel about doing things for people and always being disappointed at how little appreciation I get back." One student was moved by the unexpectedly large "gifts" of money she received. One member was so preoccupied with not hurting anybody's feelings that she compulsively gave an equal sum to each person in the group.

In the second part of the experiment, the leader tells the students, "Keep all the coins that are now in your possession out on your desk. This time, however, you are free to take as little or as much money as you wish from as few or as many persons in the group as you choose. In other words, you are now free to help yourself for keeps to as much money as you wish from whomever you wish in the group." Again the students move around the room, this time picking up change.

This phase of the experiment is usually fraught with considerable drama and conflict. For example, one student despite an intense wish for "a lot of money" was painfully inhibited about taking any coins. Another student concentrated solely on "making a profit." One member was interested only in taking money from the leader: "I was mad at you because you hadn't given me any money the first time, and I felt you owed me something."

In addition to focusing on members' relations to each other, this experiment highlights the critical role of giving and receiving in the dynamics of interpersonal relations, and in symbolizing personal worth, affectional need, and the ability to love and to receive love. It also brings into focus a variety of personal and cultural attitudes toward money.

Patterns of Interpersonal Association. The members list in writing the first names of three same sex friends, of three opposite sex friends, and then of spouse, mother, father, self, three best liked Workshop members, and the Workshop leader. Next to each name they list as many adjectives descriptive of the person as may apply. At the completion of this task the leader asks the members to examine their sets of traits for whatever relationships or trends they can discover. For example, one student noticed how similarly she perceived all her boy friends. Another student noticed that the adjectives used to describe her husband were very similar to those used to describe her father. Still another student noticed that he used more adjectives for his mother than for any other person. One member, noticing how often he used the trait "smart," began to realize how much emphasis he placed on intelligence.

The purpose of this experiment is to stimulate reflection on selective interpersonal association as an outcome of active choice subject to psychodynamic influence rather than of passive acceptance of fortuitous circumstance.

Personal Constructs in Classifying People. This experiment was inspired by Kelly's[15] "Role Construct Repertory Test." The leader requests three students who are interested in learning what impression the group has of them to volunteer to be subjects. He then asks the group to judge in what ways any two of the three volunteers are alike and different from the third. The members write down as many different sortings as occur to them about the trio in question. Members then give their impressions orally, some noting a resemblance in one pair of the trio, others in another pair. For example, "Bert and Lenny are like volcanoes that explode, whereas Irving is like a volcano that just rumbles underneath." After the group has given its impressions to a particular trio, the group's categorizations are discussed, and the trio is invited to give their reactions to what they have heard about themselves. Then the group turns to another trio. After repeating this procedure with several volunteer trios, the leader asks the students to review all of their sortings and to consider whether the categories they used in their pairings may reflect aspects of themselves.

Predicting the Group's Impression of Oneself. The leader asks each student to write two personality sketches, one describing how he sees himself, the other conjecturing the consensus of the group's impressions of him. The leader collects these papers and reads unidentified self-descriptions to the class one at a time. The group is invited to guess the author of each self-description. Once a person is identified, his second sketch, his judgment of the group's impression of him, is read to the members for their point-by-point confirmation or correction.

Many students expect the group to see them in exaggeratedly negative ways, and it is a relieving, corrective experience for these students to find their fears unconfirmed. Even if a person is correctly in touch with a group's negative impression, the student's very insightfulness of this often stimulates the group to confirm his judgment in a gentle and accepting way. The structure of the experiment has a built-in safeguard against the stimulation of excessive anxiety since the procedure centers on what each person is ready to bring up in his prediction of the group's opinion of him.

Who Resembles Me Most? The leader invites each member to consider which three classmates resemble him most in one or another attitude, characteristic, or behavior pattern. Each student's selections and his bases for comparison are revealed in a go-around. (The experiencing of negative judgments of one's self by another student is usually softened by virtue of the evaluator's acknowledgment that he possesses the same negative trait.) In the discussion which follows, questions such as these may be considered: How authentically did members perceive themselves and each other? To what extent were the points of resemblance valid and to what extent were they projected assumptions? Did the three persons chosen have some special importance, perhaps related to past family relationships, above and beyond the particular similarities pointed to? Which persons in the group were chosen most often and which least often, and what might these different frequencies of choice reflect? How did individual students feel in being chosen by this or that person for this or that point of similarity?

Who Talks How Much? The leader instructs: "Assume that all the words uttered by all of us in this course thus far could be put into a bag. Now estimate what percentage of these words were uttered by each person in our group including the leader and yourself. List each member's name in the group (don't forget your name and the leader's) and next to each name note your estimated percentage. Remember that all your percentages should add up to 100." When the group has completed this task, the leader records each student's estimate for every other person in the group on the blackboard, and the findings are then explored.

Estimates which are markedly out of line with the group consensus can point up students' exaggerated images of their own degree of verbal participation or the exaggerated reactions of one student to another. Variations in the number of words ascribed to the leader are especially noteworthy and may be explored in relation to varying kinds and intensities of needs on the part of students for the leader's active verbalization.

Unlike previously described experiments concerned with projective factors in the formation of impressions of others, this experiment involves subjective estimates of a homogeneous sample of objectively observable behavior. The revelation of projective factors in the formation of such estimates can be particularly effective in underscoring some of the dynamics of interpersonal relationships.

Student-Leader Relations

The following experiments confront the student with the extent to which his characteristic orientation to authority, as reflected in his reactions to the leader, contains elements of excessive dependency, submission, rebellion, gullibility, distrust, competitiveness, identification, exhibitionism, and the like. In addition to pointing up his need-oriented perception of authority, these experiments as a group represent a challenge to the student to enter, within realistic limits, into more nearly equalitarian relationships to authority, and to examine those inner factors which interfere with the establishment of such relationships.

Arguing with the Leader. Three volunteers leave the room. In their absence the leader tells the class that he will debate some issue with each volunteer, and he invites the members to note what happens. Then one student at a time is called in, and the leader debates with him for a few minutes about some mutually agreed issue, but does so as unfairly as he can. With an air of authority he interrupts repeatedly, introduces irrelevancies, contradicts himself, becomes overexcited, invents facts, and points out fallacies that do not exist. Some volunteers try to deal as rationally as they can with the leader's "craziness;" others are paralyzed and stopped cold; still others become equally heated and irrational in their arguments. After each debate, both the volunteer and the group give their reactions and observations. At some appropriate point, the leader may inquire as to whether their clashes bring to mind any family conflicts experienced in childhood.

This experiment can elicit a wide range of transference reactions, bring to awareness a variety of techniques for coping with irrational authority, and evoke early identifications and alliances in familial power struggles.

Correcting a Correct Sentence. This experiment was inspired by a "trick" described by Rice.[24] The leader asks the class to write the following instructions so that they may refer back to them as often as they wish: "Look over each of the words in the sentence on the blackboard carefully. Can you find just one word in the sentence which, if you crossed it out, might correct the sentence?" The leader then writes the following sentence on the blackboard, "The words in this sentence do not add up to ten." He cautions the members not to talk to their neighbors during the experiment.

There are usually a few students who do not tamper with the sentence because they recognize that it is already correct as it stands. Most people in the group, however, cross out the word "not" in their efforts to comply with the instruction's apparent directive. The leader raises the question as to why some students were misled and others not. What usually emerges from the ensuing discussion is that a number of students recognized that the sentence was correct, but mistrusted their own judgment and submitted to the authority of the instructions. As one student put it, "I thought the sentence was all right, but since you had instructed us to correct it, I assumed that there must be something wrong with it that I hadn't been able to see." If, as sometimes happens, a student protests, "I don't see that this experiment means much except that you deliberately set up a trap, and we fell for it," the leader can acknowledge that he did, indeed, set up a trap, but he may add, "Still what was it in you that made you vulnerable to falling into my trap, and how come some students didn't fall for the trap?" The leader also inquires of the minority who did not tamper with the sentence what factors governed their behavior. Such an inquiry may elicit that some of these students were chiefly influenced by intense suspiciousness of what the leader was up to.

This experiment is intended to draw members' attention to uncritical attitudes toward authority and to the anxiety which countering authority, even on the basis of their own immediate experience, tends to generate. Even if one accepts a certain reasonableness in the majority's taking the leader's honesty of instructions for granted, it is still interesting to note how the students' submissive orientation to authority can be so powerful as to lead them to mistrust the evidence of their own senses. This experiment may also point up the excessive suspiciousness and distrustfulness toward authority existing in some students and the origins and meaning of such distrust in their lives.

Guessing the Leader's Behavior in Real Life Situations. The leader presents several actual situations from his own life, one at a time, to the group. He invites students to postdict how he reacted, what he felt and did in that situation. After the group has given its conjectures for an incident, the leader confides how he actually did react, often much to some members' surprise. Below are examples of incidents in one leader's life which have been found useful.

1. A policeman stops the leader for driving too fast.
2. He is told by a doctor that he needs an operation.
3. His three-year-old son disobeys him and runs across the street.

The individual differences in the postdictions that students make and the discrepancies that are revealed between these post-dictions and the leader's actual reactions point up their varying need-oriented perceptions of authority. This experiment may also bring to the fore the extent to which the students' defensive stereotyping of the leader-as-authority may interfere with their authentic relating to him.

Guessing the Leader's Thoughts. This experiment was inspired by a study by Bass.[2] The leader gives the following instructions: "In this experiment we shall see if you can guess what I am think-ing of. I shall ask you to make twelve guesses. Write your guesses on a blank sheet of paper." He then asks the following questions:

1. Am I thinking of yes or no?
2. Am I thinking of approve or disapprove?
3. Am I thinking of agree or disagree?
4. Am I thinking of accept or reject?
5. Am I thinking of like or dislike?
6. Am I thinking of true or false?

The above series is repeated to constitute items 7 through 12. After the group has recorded its guesses, the leader invites the members to explore their reactions during the experiment itself and the nature, sequence, and determinants of their guesses. At some appropriate point the leader may reveal that his thoughts actually followed no particular pattern.

Life is full of irrational demands, and this experiment repre-sents one of them. How do different students cope with such ir-rational demands, particularly when imposed by authority? Some take the assigned task seriously and study the leader's face and voice closely for clues as to what he might be thinking. Still others are preoccupied with outwitting the leader. Other students refuse to become involved and simply make blind guesses. Some students consistently make positive guesses, while others make guesses which are consistently negative. A review of such pattern consistencies often brings to light tendencies toward magical idealization of authority, hostile and cynical anticipations of rejection, as well as basic orientations to life in general.

Interviewing the Leader. The leader offers to be interviewed "along any lines whatever" by three volunteers, one at a time. However, he does not guarantee to answer all questions. He invites the group's immediate reactions to this prospect. Some members are extremely interested in learning about the leader's personal life; others feel that it is not right to invade the leader's privacy; some fear they will learn about his weaknesses. When faced by a student interviewer, the leader answers any and all questions as frankly as he comfortably can. He exercises his right not to answer any questions which he regards as too personal. The group shares its reactions and observations after each interview.

There are wide variations in the students' styles of interviewing and the topics they cover. For example, one student scrupulously avoided any personal inquiries and dealt in a somewhat challenging manner with the leader's academic qualifications, while another student focused with friendly interest on the leader's early family life. The implications and possible origins of such variations in warmth and intimacy of relationship to an authority figure are discussed. In addition, this experiment constitutes still another practice exercise in observing an actual instance of interpersonal communication and in analyzing what dynamics underlie the process.

On Being Chosen. The leader invites two students who have shown themselves to be sensitive observers to take notes on the session and to write up at home a "thoughtful analysis" of the session's events for presentation in the following meeting. The two chosen students are asked for their reactions to having been selected by the leader. These usually vary from feeling "honored" to feeling "unworthy." The remaining members are also asked for their reactions, especially to not having been chosen. Their reactions include feelings of rejection, jealous rivalry, or relief.

Quizzing the Leader. Each member is invited to formulate a single question which he would like to put to the leader. The leader emphasizes that these questions may be along any lines whatsoever. There then follows a go-around in which each person asks his question of the leader, and the leader responds to it in the best way he can. When questions are too unclear for the leader to answer, or if he does not know the answer, he simply states this to be the case and then moves on to the next questioner. Questions vary widely and include inquiries about the leader's personal life ("Are you married"), the facts of psychology ("What is the meaning of repression?"), the personality of the questioner ("What is your impression of me?"). After the completion of the go-around, the group gives its reactions to what has happened.

The discussion may center on such topics as the differences in the kinds of questions asked, how questions might reflect unstated or unconscious concerns or themes on the part of the questioner, how each person felt about the opportunity to ask a question, and how members reacted to the leader's answering. Members may explore their disappointment in discovering that the leader did not know all the answers or that some of his answers were necessarily stated in general terms or with qualifications. They may explore the difficulties they found in formulating a useful or productive question. At some appropriate point the leader may stimulate the members to recall and discuss what questions and answers they exchanged with their parents.

This experiment is useful in exposing and combating students' tendencies to transfer residues of infantile anticipation of parental omniscience onto the leader. At the same time, students are helped toward a tolerant appreciation of the magical thinking which wishfully oversimplifies their problems and their solutions.

The Leader Commands. Without preliminaries the leader begins the session by asking the class to stand up. After they have complied, he directs them to sit down. He then gives a succession of rapid-fire commands to sit and to stand, shifting in the direction of these commands from the group as a whole to specific individuals to clusters of individuals. For example: "The whole class, stand up." "Bill, Jack, Mary, sit down." "Now, everybody sit but Arlene." "Everybody stand." "Everybody sit." "Helen, stand." These orders, spoken in a dominating, arrogant, imperative tone of voice, continue until more and more students begin to disobey. In the discussion which follows, a variety of issues may be explored in the area of relationship to authority, for example, the factors underlying compulsive obedience, the discomfort or exhilaration of defying authority, and the pleasure or embarrassment at being singled out. At some point the leader may inquire as to what childhood experiences resembled the situation in this experiment.

The Leader is Delayed. The leader enters the class and, without preliminaries, role-plays the part of John Smith: "My name is John Smith. I am a member of the administrative staff. We just got a call from the office from your instructor. He told us that he has been unavoidably detained and asked me to take attendance and to tell you that he expects to arrive in about a half hour. He would like you to carry on the class by yourselves until he arrives." The students readily enter into the leader's role-playing game responding, nonetheless, with the authenticity of participation in a real experience. If any members begin to direct specific questions to "John Smith," he answers then as briefly and as disinterestedly as possible. Usually experiencing the situation as a challenge to being on their own, the class soon becomes involved in deciding what to do without the leader, at times quickly settling upon some procedure and carrying on, while on other occasions becoming ensnarled in frustrating bickering. At some point, John Smith may step out of the room for five minutes, literally leaving the group on its own.

Later the group and the leader reunite, and they discuss what happened, considering such questions as, "How did you feel at first when you learned that the leader would not be present?" "What took place in the group as you observed it, and how did you feel about it?" "What did you notice happening in yourself and in others when John Smith left the room, and when the leader returned?"

This experiment stimulates exploration of the nature and extent of members' dependency on the leader. Often there is confrontation of obstacles which interfere with more autonomous functioning as well as consideration of latent capacities for independence and creativity.

The Leader Scolds. Without warning, the leader suddenly interrupts an ongoing discussion and, without looking at anyone in particular, he exclaims angrily, "You students back there have been talking ever since this class started. I think that's terribly rude, and I wish you would stop. I'm getting sick and tired of your whispering and buzzing to each other while the class is going on. If you can't keep quiet, you can get out!" Not realizing that the leader was play-acting, most members react with shock, and a tense hush usually falls on the class. Then, suddenly relaxing, the leader lets the class know that he has been play-acting. He inquires, "How did you feel when I scolded those imaginary students?" Some members report that they sided with the leader and felt that his scolding must have been justified, others empathized with the "scolded students" and experienced the leader as very "mean," and still others were badly frightened and even guiltily felt as if they had been the ones talking out of turn. The possible origins of these varied reactions are then explored.

CHAPTER 7

~~~~~~

IS THE WORKSHOP A FORM OF THERAPY?

MANY people have raised this question. Workshop members themselves, as they are introduced to this experience, have wondered about it. A number of our colleagues have been very ready to say, "The Workshop is nothing but therapy. Why don't you not only call it that, but make it even more so by extending the number of sessions?" Involved in the Workshop may be found devices or processes that bear an evocative likeness to things that good teachers use, and others will find methods and processes which have a suggestive resemblance to things that go on in therapy, but neither of these findings makes the Workshop precisely conventional education nor conventional therapy.*

Although the classification of the Workshop, whether as education or as psychotherapy, seems to us of no great import, a number of distinctions between the Workshop and psychotherapy may be noted:

1) The Workshop is clearly set apart from most self-styled psychotherapy procedures in its structure. The size of the Workshop group, from thirty to sixty students, is far in excess of that considered optimal or even maximal in almost all current concep-

---

*We believe it is likely that just as the Workshop has borrowed much in its evolution from the techniques of individual and group psychotherapy, so too it may have something to contribute to group psychotherapy and possibly even individual psychotherapy. Many of the Workshop techniques of stimulating self-confrontation seem readily adaptable for use in psychotherapy to initiate or highlight lines of inquiry which have been evaded or otherwise overlooked.

tions of group psychotherapy. The Workshop has a definite time
dimension; it ends after fifteen weeks.

2) Workshop aims overlap therapy aims, but they are far from
identical. The therapeutic process is presumably oriented toward
a therapeutic outcome. Self-understanding and movement toward responsible autonomy are, when pertinent, instrumental. In
the Workshop, therapeutic outcomes are secondary and incidental. The initiation of processes of self-understanding and movement toward responsible autonomy are essentially ends in themselves.

3) The Workshop depends on personal involvement to achieve
generalizations. In psychotherapy, generalizations have little
place except as background guides to the therapist in his effort to
help the patient resolve personal involvements.

4) In the Workshop, inter-student and student-leader transferences rarely develop the intensity often characteristic of therapy. Psychotherapy is often concerned with the resolution of
transference. The Workshop is concerned only with directing the
student's attention to its existence.

5) The Workshop follows a syllabus, albeit a flexible one, em-
ploying a repertoire of more or less controlled procedures, including game-like ones, in order to elicit preconceived effects. In
most psychotherapy the "syllabus," if present at all, is more in the
background of the therapist's mind as a kind of loosely structured
pattern of expectations with regard to the development of the
therapeutic process. Special procedures, such as role-playing,
are sometimes used in some therapies. But most often they are
less structured, less controlled, and certainly they are far less
varied.

For those who regard "psychotherapy" a misnomer for what is,
in essence, a structured relationship designed to facilitate personal growth, the problem of drawing distinctions between the
Workshop and psychotherapy disappears. The difficulty, we
think, lies in the inappropriateness of the concepts mental health
and therapy, both borrowed from medicine and implying that
what the therapist does is to treat in order to eliminate an illness.
The "illness," however, is to be defined in terms of entrenched
attitudes, covert values, and reaction patterns which militate

against effective functioning. Is the task of the mental health educator any different in essence? Is he not also concerned with the modification of intrapsychic obstacles which inhibit the individual from moving on to more autonomous and richly rewarding modes of self-affirmation and expression?

In practice, it would seem that the distinction between the treatment for mental ill health and education for positive mental health rests on whether the client is below or merely at the level of the social reaction average in overall adaptation. If the client is below the social reaction average in overall adaptation, he is said to suffer from an illness and to be in need of treatment. If he is at the social reaction average or above, he is regarded as already well and in a position to profit from further education. The distinction between treatment and education would thus seem to be less a matter of intrinsic essence and more a matter of secondary extrinsic variables. From this point of view, both psychotherapy and mental health education, including the Workshop, are educational procedures, differing one from the other in the logistics called for by the particular situation, the characteristics, and the unit size of the population served, and the like.

CHAPTER 8

~~~~~~

RELATED APPROACHES

The search for novel and effective approaches to the problems of mental health and illness, responsive to the same social needs which stimulated the Workshop, has produced many varied and imaginative methods. Perhaps most similar to the Workshop, at least in its emphasis on participant-observer exercises, is the course in self-development described by Perls, Hefferline, and Goodman[23] as part of their exposition of gestalt therapy. The course is a self-administered one in which the reader engages in a series of graded tasks and notices what inner factors interfere with the accomplishment of these assignments. For example, he may be instructed to concentrate on his breathing, or to visualize specific fantasies, or to imagine the reversals of specific everyday situations. The reasoning underlying each task is discussed in detail by the authors, and various possible responses and difficulties are presented. Bearing a considerable resemblance to the approach by Perls et al, though written in a popular, inspirational vein, Huxley[11] presents a manual of self-administering exercises ("recipes") designed to aid the reader in reliving significant past events and sharpening his self-awareness. Both of the above works, being self-administering programs, possess the advantage over the conventional didactic texts of enlisting the reader's active participation, but lack the Workshop's provision for group interaction and for "supervision" of the process of learning.

The training or T-group movement,[4] to a large extent inspired by the National Training Laboratory in Group Development in

264

Bethel, Maine, aims at improving the functioning of small groups, with particular emphasis on the processes of communication, problem solving, and decision making. Miles[20] describes in detail a large number of specific group training procedures, many of which could be adapted to Workshop purposes. The typical T-group resembles the Workshop in its emphasis on the immediate here-and-now, on members' analyzing their feeling reactions to each other, and on learning through one's own experiences. Unlike the Workshop, however, in the usual T-group there is more focus on the social than on the personal self, sessions tend to be unstructured, the group decides its own agenda, and there is little emphasis on relating the here-and-now to each individual's life history or on the use of free associations, fantasies, or projective techniques. In Sensitivity Training,[28, 31] a recent variation of the T-group approach, there is a shift in focus from the development of group interpersonal skills to a greater concern with the individual's self-understanding and central life values. Weschler and Reisel[31] present a vivid session-by-session account of one training group, including excerpts from trainees' diaries, the trainees' personal reactions, and the commentary of a clinical observer. Rothaus, Morton, Johnson, and Cleveland[27] describe another variation of the T-group, a four-week training laboratory in which autonomous groups of psychiatric patients learned to use self-rating scales as the chief means of heightening their awareness of personal and group dynamics and of motivating them to experiment with new ways of behaving.

Numerous educational programs are directed at parents or teachers,[5, 6, 7, 10, 30] not as target groups in their own right, but mainly in terms of their being in a strategic position to further the mental health of children in their care. Classes in personal adjustment and human relations are offered in a number of colleges as practical aids to living.[21] Many of these programs and courses use group discussion as a basic method, with content either stemming directly from the participants' own immediate concerns or being introduced through lectures, case studies, films, plays, study outlines, role-playing, and the like. Outstanding among the college courses is the Self-Knowledge Workshop reported by Jones.[14] Psychoanalytic in its orientation, it combined discussion meetings involving here-and-now transactions and lectures on technical subjects. Also worthy of special note is Lehner's[16] introductory psychology course in which basic psychological concepts are taught through the use of students' responses to a detailed and carefully structured antobiographical questionnaire.

The efforts of those whose work has been reviewed here briefly, as well as our own Workshop, point to the likelihood that a growing recognition of social priorities will lead to an increasing shift in emphasis in the field of mental health from the function of psychotherapy to that of mental health education. We anticipate that, as the field of mental health education develops, more attention will be given than has been true in the past to the clarity with which goals are defined, to creative experimentation in methodology, to the articulation of theoretical models of man implicit in varied approaches, and to rigorous evaluation of results.

REFERENCES

1. Atkinson, J. W. (Ed.): *Motives in Fantasy, Action and Society*, Chapter 21, McClelland, D. C.: Risk taking in children with high and low need for achievement, pp. 306-321. Princeton, N. J., Van Nostrand, 1958.
2. Bass, B. M.: Undiscriminated operant acquiescence. *Educ. psychol. Measmt.*, 17:83-85, 1957.
3. Bettis, M. C., Malamud, D. I., and Malamud, Rachel F.: Deepening a group's insight into human relations: A compilation of aids. *J. Clin. Psychol.*, 5:114-122, 1949.
4. Bradford, L. P., Gibb, J. R., and Benne, K. D. (Eds.): *T-Group Theory and Laboratory Method*. New York, John Wiley, 1964.
5. Brim, O. G., Jr.: Recent research on effects of education in human development. In R. H. Ojemann (Ed.) *Four Basic Aspects of Preventive Psychiatry*. Iowa City, State University of Iowa, 1957.
6. Brim, O. G., Jr.: *Education for Child Rearing*. New York, Russell Sage Foundation, 1959.
7. Committee of Pennsylvania Mental Health, Inc.: *Mental Health Education: A Critique*. Philadelphia, Author, 1960.
8. Dinnerstein, Dorothy: The source dimension of second-hand evidence. *J. Soc. Psychol.*, 45:41-59, 1957.
9. Gordon, L. V.: *Manual for Survey of Interpersonal Values*. Chicago, Science Research Associates, 1960.
10. Harvard Medical School and Psychiatric Service, Massachusetts General Hospital: *Community Mental Health and Social Psychiatry: A Reference Guide*. Cambridge, Harvard University Press, 1962.
11. Huxley, Laura A.: *You Are Not the Target*. New York, Farrar, Straus, 1963.
12. Jersild, A. T.: *When Teachers Face Themselves*. New York, Bureau of Publications, Teachers College, Columbia University, 1955.

13. Joint Commission on Mental Illness and Health. *Action for Mental Health*. New York, Basic Books, 1961.
14. Jones, R. M.: *An Application of Psychoanalysis to Education*. Springfield, Ill., Charles C Thomas, Publisher, 1960.
15. Kelly, G. A.: *The Psychology of Personal Constructs*. Vol. 2, *Clinical Diagnosis and Therapy*. New York, W. W. Norton, 1955.
16. Lehner, G. F. J.: *Explorations in Personal Adjustment*. New York, Prentice-Hall, 1949.
17. Malamud, D. I.: *A Participant-Observer Approach to the Teaching of Human Relations*. Chicago, Center for the Study of Liberal Education for Adults, 1955.
18. Malamud, D. I.: A workshop in self-understanding designed to prepare patients for psychotherapy. *Amer. J. Psychother.*, 12: 771-786, 1958.
19. Malamud, D. I.: Educating adults in self-understanding. *Ment. Hyg., N.Y.*, 44:115-124, 1960.
20. Miles, M. B.: *Learning to Work in Groups*. New York, Bureau of Publications, Teachers College, Columbia University, 1959.
21. Morse, H. T., and Dressel, P. L. (Eds.): *General Education for Personal Maturity*. Dubuque, William C. Brown, 1960.
22. Murphy, G., and Kuhlen, R.: *Psychological Needs of Adults*. Chicago, Center for the Study of Liberal Education for Adults, 1955.
23. Perls, F. S., Hefferline, R. F., and Goodman, P.: *Gestalt Therapy*. New York, Julian Press, 1951.
24. Rice, D. D. (Ed.): *What Makes You Tick?* New York, Harper and Bros., 1958.
25. Riggs, Margaret: An investigation of the nature and generality of three new personality variables. *J. Pers.*, 20:322-344, 1952.
26. Rogers, C. R.: *On Becoming a Person*. Boston, Houghton Mifflin, 1961.
27. Rothaus, P., Morton, R. B., Johnson, D. L., and Cleveland, S. E.: Human relations training for psychiatric patients. *Arch. Gen. Psychiat.*, 8:572-581, 1963.
28. Tannenbaum, R. J., Weschler, I. R., and Massarik, F.: *Leadership and Organization: A Behavioral Science Approach*. New York, McGraw-Hill, 1961.
29. Travis, L. E., and Baruch, Dorothy W.: *Personal Problems of Everyday Life*. New York, Appleton-Century, Crofts, 1941.

30. U. S. Department of Health, Education and Welfare, National Institute of Mental Health: *Evaluation in Mental Health.* Washington, U. S. Government Printing Office, 1955.

31. Weschler, I. R., and Reisel, J.: *Inside a Sensitivity Training Group.* Los Angeles, Institute of Industrial Relations, 1959.

32. Whipple, J. D.: *Especially for Adults.* Chicago, Center for the Study of Liberal Education for Adults, 1957.

33. Williams, W. C.: The PALS test: A technique for children to evaluate both parents. *J. Consult. Psychol., 22:*487-495, 1958.